The Hills of Hawkstone and Attingham

Portrait of Sir Rowland Hill, attributed to Sampson (in the manner of Holbein), 16th century, oil on panel. (Mercers' Company Picture Collection Catalogue Number 019.)

The Hills of Hawkstone and Attingham

THE RISE, SHINE AND DECLINE OF
A SHROPSHIRE FAMILY

JOANNA HILL

Joanna Hill

PHILLIMORE

2005

Published by
PHILLIMORE & CO. LTD
Shopwyke Manor Barn, Chichester, West Sussex, England

© Joanna Hill, 2005

ISBN 1 86077 322 2

Printed and bound in Great Britain by
CAMBRIDGE PRINTING

Contents

List of Illustrations		vii
Introduction and Acknowledgements		ix
Preface by Richard Hayes		xi
1.	The Earliest Hills · Court of Hulle · Sir Rowland Hill, Kt	1
2.	The 'Great' Hill	11
3.	The Evangelist Brothers: Sir Richard Hill, Bt, MP and the Reverend Rowland Hill, Renowned Preacher	40
4.	General Rowland, 1st Viscount Hill, Part 1	63
5.	General Rowland, 1st Viscount Hill, Part 2	84
6.	The Final Generations after Waterloo	120
7.	Hills in Shropshire Politics: The Election Scandal	131
8.	Hawkstone Hall · The Park · The Citadel	142
9.	The Noel-Hills (Berwicks) of Attingham Park	163
10.	The Bankruptcy · The Dispersal Sale · The Lawsuits	178
Epilogue		189
Pedigree of the Hill Family		191
Notes		200
Bibliography		205
Index		207

List of Illustrations

Frontispiece: Portrait of Sir Rowland Hill

1.	The 'Great' Hill	36
2.	Samuel Barbour Hill (1691-1758)	37
3.	The Rev. Rowland Hill	57
4.	Rowland, 1st Viscount Hill	72
5.	Miniature of Rowland, 1st Viscount Hill	89
6.	Rowland, 2nd Viscount Hill	109
7.	Robert Chambré Hill	112
8.	Clement Delves Hill	118
9.	3rd Viscount Hill	122
10.	HMS *Bacchante*, 1879	124
11.	Sir Clement Lloyd Hill (1845-1913)	126
12.	Sir Clement Lloyd Hill with Ugandan natives, 1890	128
13.	Election jugs for John Hill, 1796	135
14.	Election jugs, 1835, 1841	139
15.	George Hill with otter hounds	143
16.	Pleasure gardens, Hawkstone	144
17.	A pond in the restored gardens, Hawkstone	145
18.	Plan of Hawkstone Park	147
19.	Hawkstone Hall	147
20.	'Old Jones' at the Grotto, Hawkstone	151
21.	View from Red Castle	152
22.	Grotto Hill, Hawkstone	154
23.	Aquatints of Hawkstone Park	156/7
24.	Faux arch, Hawkstone	158
25.	Grotto, Hawkstone	158
26.	The 'Obelisk', Hawkstone	159
27.	The Citadel, Hawkstone	161
28.	The Noel-Hill family tree	162
29.	Attingham Park	169
30.	Picture Gallery, Attingham Park	177
31.	Cronkhill, Attingham	177
32.	Various pieces from the original Hill Collection	186

*For
Alexander, Nicholas and their children—
a little family history*

Introduction

I do not pretend that this is a scholar's book, but I hope that it will be of interest, not only to descendants of the Hills who created and lived at the great houses of Hawkstone and Attingham, but also to more general readers. After all, there are not many families in England who can boast as many as six entries in the *Dictionary of National Biography*.

With a few notable exceptions, Hill family members were not in a position to help me with my research, largely owing to the bankruptcy sales that scattered the contents of Hawkstone, accumulated over 350 years. I found moreover that recent articles on Hawkstone contained both factual errors and what can best be described as family myths. I was fortunate in that my grandfather, the last but one of the Hills to be born in the Citadel, purchased a number of paintings at the dispersal sale in 1895. My father, Clement Hill, lived at the Ranger's Lodge at Hawkstone from 1965 to 1971, and the time that I spent there led to my fascination with the Park. Crawling through the thick clumps of a botanical thug known as *rhododendron ponticum*, scrabbling up the broken paths and steps, scaring myself in the sombre depths of the Grotto and climbing the Obelisk with its view, it is said, of 12 counties on a clear day, I gradually came to understand what an extraordinary place the romantic Park had been. Lately restored, it can once again be enjoyed by visitors as it was in the late 18th and 19th centuries.

Hawkstone Hall itself is now owned by the Order of the Redemptorists and is seldom open to the public. Fortunately the gift of Attingham to the National Trust in 1947, following the death of the 8th Lord Berwick, has preserved both that house and its contents: the Attingham archives have been deposited with the Shropshire Records Office. Both the Shropshire Records Office and the National Archive were, naturally, excellent sources of material during my research.

I would particularly like to thank Richard Hayes of Shrewsbury, an authority on both of the houses and the Hill family in general. He read and commented on each chapter, added snippets and gave me endless encouragement. The illustrations have come from many different sources and I am grateful to Pamela Jane Bruce for excavating her attic and finding some of the amusing early 19th-century photographs. I would also like to thank Simon Walford, of Walford

Associates Landscape Architects, who drew my attention to some photographs of the Park taken in 1900. I was fortunate in having the help of an excellent local photographer, Francis Diaz of Montsempron-Libos in south-west France, who scanned almost all the illustrations to disk and vastly improved the aged and faded photographs.

I am especially grateful to the Worshipful Company of Mercers, the senior livery company of the City of London, which gave me a generous grant towards publication. A big thank you, too, to my niece Louisa Bury, who designed the leaflet which was circulated to Hills all over the world and led to some generous pre-publication contributions. I hope that the book may now arouse some interest in restoring the important family monuments in St Luke's Church, Hodnet, Shropshire. Any proceeds from the sale of this book will go towards the restoration.

Finally, my sincere thanks to Noel Osborne, Managing Director of Phillimore, for undertaking publication of the book, to Nicola Willmot, Production Director, and to Simon Thraves, who took on the unenviable task of editing.

Illustration Acknowledgements

Frontispiece reproduced courtesy of the Mercers' Company. The National Trust have supplied the following images: NTPL/Matthew Antrobus, 28, 29; NTPL/Mark Fiennes, 30. No. 1 is reproduced courtesy of Shrewsbury Museums Service; no. 31 is reproduced courtesy of Alex Ramsay/Country Life Picture Library; no. 4 is from a private collection. No. 6 is reproduced courtesy John Noott. Jacket illustration from Christie's, Private Collection.

Subscribers

THE WORSHIPFUL COMPANY OF MERCERS
NIGEL HILL
ALEXANDER AND CHRISTINA BASTIN
R. TANNER
RICHARD HAYES
NOEL HILL
PROFESSOR AND MRS CRAIG HUGH SMYTH
B. AND S. GRIFFITHS
JILL JACKSON HILL
S. HILL/A. CAMPBELL
NICHOLAS AND MAIRI BASTIN
T. MORLEY
R.S. HILL
R.K. HILL
R. EDMUNDSON
I.R. AND C.M. HILL
R. LOCKWOOD
GERALD HILL

GEORGINA POLE-CAREW
BRIAN HILL
P.J. BRUCE
PETER HILL
ANNETTE HILL
B.D. CONEY
H.R. HILL
R. MORLEY
JAMES HILL
MARY LANGFORD
D.M.M. REITH
C. POULSON
DAVID HILL
JUDY HARRIS
R. LEES
A. JUHRE
K. BURRELL
PHILIP HUGHES

Preface
by Richard Hayes

Shropshire is a hidden county with hill country of outstanding beauty in the south and prosperous flat plains in the north, all with secret villages, ancient churches and solid brick farmhouses. Out of this remote land arose a family aptly named Hill, whose fascinating story Joanna Hill tells in vivid fashion in these pages. In its heyday this family owned a vast acreage in north Shropshire, the junior branch presiding in neoclassical splendour at Attingham and the senior in more homely grandeur at Hawkstone. Joanna Hill has done a great service for all who love Shropshire and who relish the doings of our forebears who played their part in the history of our country.

Nineteenth-century extravagance led to a painful demise of the house of Hawkstone, and for a century a veil of regret lay over the place and the name. Joanna Hill, at the right moment, reveals to us the glories of earlier years, not least the little-known exploits of the 'Great Hill' three hundred years ago in Turin. General Rowland, Lord Hill's loyal support of Wellington is described in fresh detail. Both these men lie in Shropshire soil, soil which provides perhaps the most lasting memorial to this creative family: the early romantic park set amongst the sandstone hills of Hawkstone.

The glory of the Hills has lain hidden, but Joanna Hill has lifted the veil and the light of their charity and their exploits once more gilds the story of Shropshire and of England.

'MAY THE HILLS OF SHROPSHIRE LAST AS LONG
AS THE SHROPSHIRE HILLS'

CHAPTER ONE

The Earliest Hills
Court of Hulle · Sir Rowland Hill, Kt

THE HILLS were a Norman family, as demonstrated by the original name, de la Hulle, coupled with the motto 'Avancez'. Hills were first recorded in the county of Shropshire in 1202 during the reign of King John (1199-1216). A Robert de la Hull had a piece of land, being part of a 'knights fee', at Hull near Burford, not far from Ludlow in the south of the county. A descendant is recorded as William de la Hulle[1] of Court of Hull in the reign of Edward I (1272-1307), followed by Hugh Hull, also referred to as 'de la Hulle' (married to a daughter of Hugh de Wlonkeslow, also known as 'Longslow') in the time of Edward II (1307-27). Another William de la Hulle, who died in 1421, added the estates of Buntingsdale through his marriage. The spelling seems to have varied and is found with and without an 'e'. By the time of William de la Hulle's son, Griffith de Hille in the period of Henry IV (1399-1413), the 'u' has been changed to an 'i'. Griffith married Margaret Warren who was descended from Hamlet Plantagenet, an illegitimate son of Henry II (1154-89), which gives an interesting bit of blue blood in the early pedigree! The family appears to have been adept at marrying heiresses—an art sadly long lost.

We can put more flesh on the bones by the time that their son, Humphrey Hill of Buntingsdale (reign of Henry V, 1413-22), had his three sons. His wife was Agnes Birde, who brought the estates of Malpas in Cheshire into the family.

The eldest son, William, inherited the properties of Buntingsdale and 'Hill Court' or, as it became known, 'Court of Hull' and finally Court of Hill. The second son, Ralph, had two sons in his turn: the elder another William, 'of Bletchley', and the younger Humphrey. The third son, Thomas 'of Malpas', also had two sons: the elder another Thomas and the younger, the Rowland who was knighted in 1542 and became first Protestant Lord Mayor of London in 1549.

It was through Sir Rowland and his great wealth that his cousins William 'of Bletchley' and Humphrey respectively inherited Soulton, near Wem and Hawkstone, which remained in the family for over 350 years. Humphrey had several children, his heir being the first Rowland Hill (Rowland 2) to reside at Hawkstone. A number of other Rowlands followed, and this does tend to make their history a little confusing but, perhaps fortunately, it seems that none of them did anything very significant until the late 17th century. (See Pedigree 1.)

A genealogical account of the Hills of Court of Hill and of Alcaston, Shropshire, compiled by a family member, the Rev. T. Leonard Hill in 1854, and found in the Shropshire Records Office, does not give much information of any interest.[2] It merely serves to underline the astonishing number of parsons spawned by this family! The Alcaston link is of little interest: one Leonard Hill, born in 1567, had 13 children. His eldest son, Thomas, married an heiress to the manor of Alcaston, and the family estates at Court of Hill were therefore left to his son, Andrew. Alcaston had been a fine Elizabethan mansion which fell into ruin in the 19th century and was eventually pulled down.

The third successive Rowland (Rowland 3) at Hawkstone was the incumbent at the time of the Civil War, when the family apparently had a difficult time, although it is hard now to differentiate between hard historical fact and more romantic family fantasy. Since there was a significant battle at Shrewsbury, it is certainly conceivable that the legend which has him imprisoned in the Red Castle in the park is true. Certainly Sir Richard Hill (2nd Baronet), who was responsible for at least half of the great landscape park in the last quarter of the 18th century, commemorated the event in a long inscription on an urn.

It is thus apparent that by the 17th century the family was spread over the county and between its various branches owned a very significant amount of land. The principal early successes who made their mark in the world were, first, the Lord Mayor in the 16th century and, secondly, Richard Hill, the 'Great' Hill who was born in 1654 (frequently quoted as 1655) and who amassed the fortune which he was to leave principally between his three nephews, Rowland (5) (of Hawkstone), Thomas (of Tern Hall/Attingham) and Samuel (Shenstone), on his death in 1727. It was this fortune which helped to raise the Hill family to the status of gentry and obtained a baronetcy for Rowland of Hawkstone in 1727.

Court of Hill, home of the senior branch of the family

The most recent building on the site is a handsome house largely rebuilt in 1683 which appears little changed today. The owner at the time was Andrew Hill, who served as one of the Barons of Exchequer in 1695, but on the whole the Court of Hill line does not seem to have made much of a mark in the world. The house stands on Clee Hill near Burford, Shropshire and has magnificent and far-reaching views over eight counties. Of no great size, it is very much 'all of a piece', although there is evidence of the earlier houses on the site and the eastern end is built of rubble masonry dating possibly to the late 16th century. It is likely that the earlier house was built in a Tudor 'H'. The house the earliest Hills lived in has vanished, but descriptions of the present house and the way of life enjoyed there in the 18th century have been left to us by the diarist, Mrs Lybbe Powys, who visited in 1771. She was related to the Hills by marriage and wrote:

> Court of Hill is an ancient building, spacious, not uncomfortably so, situation particularly fine. The house stands on a steep knoll which is laid into paddock, from three sides of which 'tis impossible to conceive a prospect more beautiful, except for want of water. You look from a vast eminence down on valleys so sweetly diversified, then the county rising, mountain above mountain, almost reaching to the clouds ... Behind the house is a fine grove bounded by a vast mountain called Clee Hill; dreadfully steep to ascend but dismally so to descend, tho' they make nothing of it in their coach or on horseback. At the top indeed one is rewarded for all the frights and trouble in the view around you.

The owner at the time of Mrs Lybbe Powys' visit was her husband, Philip's cousin, Thomas Hill, the grandson of the builder, Andrew Hill. This Thomas was Member of Parliament for Leominster for a few years but is not recorded as having spoken. His fortune seems to have been derived from lime workings and quarries on Clee Hill. Mrs Powys describes the elegant house party that August:

> [The Hills'] manner of living is always in the superb style of ancient hospitality, only their winters are spent in London. You see hospitality blended with every elegance of fashionable taste; but they have a vast fortune and only two children, both girls, one ten and the other five. Their house, Mrs Hill says, is ever full of company, as at present. Our party sixteen in all, relations; but they have nine good spare chambers ... The Miss Hills each have a servant. I've already seen eight maids; how many more there be I know not.

Alas, this prosperity did not last. The elder daughter succeeded to the property on the death of her father in 1776. She married a Thomas Lowe and their descendant, A.N.V. Hill-Lowe, finally sold the estate in 1926.

Sir Rowland Hill, Kt (1492-1561)

The first really significant Hill was Rowland, second son of Thomas of Malpas and Hodnet. Thomas was a younger son of Humphrey of Court of Hulle, Wlonkeslowe and Buntingsdale. Rowland is sometimes referred to as having been born at Hawkstone but this is certainly inaccurate since he is known to have bought Hawkstone and other land in the parishes of Hodnet and Weston in 1556. In his Will, amongst many other bequests, he left money to the church 'in Hodnet where I was born', which seems conclusive.

Rowland was to live the greater part of his life in the religious tumult of the Reformation although he was born in 1492 during the reign of Henry VII, who was too preoccupied with sorting out his new kingdom to worry much about religion. Henry VII's extraordinary younger son, Henry VIII, who succeeded his father in 1509, was a very different man. His desire to discard his first wife, Katherine of Aragon, who was unable to bear a living child after the birth of Princess Mary, touched off the rift with the Vatican. Initially the Pope, Clement VII, seemed inclined to grant an annulment,[3] but with the sack of Rome in 1527 by the Emperor Charles V, the Papacy came directly under his influence. Charles was not going to permit Clement to divorce Henry from the Spanish-born wife who was his aunt!

Having failed to get the annulment, Henry declared himself Supreme Governor of the Church in England by passing the Act of Supremacy in 1534. What Rowland Hill thought of these developments we do not know, but he appears to have been quite adept at either sitting on the fence or changing his coat to suit the different regimes. It soon became apparent that Henry needed money. Thomas Cromwell, a sharp and brilliant lawyer, hit on the notion of closing the monasteries and removing from them the extensive lands, buildings and the vast store of ecclesiastical treasures that these institutions had been building up through centuries. In the short space of four years the monasteries, abbeys, and chantries had virtually disappeared and approximately 7,000 monks found themselves out in the world. The lands were sold off or given to those enjoying the King's patronage. This had the effect of making the new owners 'protestant', at least outwardly changing the religious balance in England. By the time of Henry's death in 1547 the ratio of Catholic to Protestant was about 50:50.

The short reign of Henry's son, Edward VI, saw one important event that made the Protestant Reformation more acceptable to many: Cranmer's new prayer book, the first edition of which appeared in 1549. It managed to harmonise the ancient language of the Catholic Latin and the new English, and its acceptance brought about a change that Catholic Queen Mary was unable to reverse. But it was not until the accession of the 'officially' moderate Protestant, Queen Elizabeth I, that stability was achieved.

This was the period of radical religious change that Rowland Hill lived through. The young man, born in the depths of rural England, was apprenticed to one Thomas Kitson (Kytson), a London mercer, rapidly demonstrated a good head for business and in 1519 was made a Freeman of the Mercers' Company, one of the largest of the City guilds.[4] His place of business was 'over against the church' of St Stephen Walbrook, which was destroyed during the Great Fire of 1666, though the monument to him survived. He prospered at a time when wool was being exported to the continent and exotic silks were coming the other way. In 1536 he seems to have been a Member of Parliament, being one of a number of commoners appointed by the Court of Aldermen on 27 January 1536 before the final session of the Parliament of 1529 to 'discuss such matters as shall be profitable for the Commonwealth of this city'. By this time he was a highly successful merchant. State Papers of King Henry VIII record that he was one of the King's creditors 'which was content to forbear until a longer day'.[5] It would be true to say that he probably did not have much choice, and it may also have put him in a good position to purchase property such as monastic holdings during the Dissolution. He certainly acquired a great deal of property at this time, including the former Abbey of Haughmond in Shropshire, which was suppressed in 1539 when it was 'acquired' by Sir Edward Littleton, who sold it on to Sir Rowland in 1542.

Haughmond is first mentioned in Domesday Book in 1086; the name eventually became Hadenhale and then Hadnall. Gilbert de Hadenhale surrendered a part of the village of Hadenhale and the whole of Hardwicke (many years later to be the home of 'the General' Rowland Hill) into King Henry II's hands on his visit to Shrewsbury in 1158, and Henry promptly gave it to the Canons of Haughmond. Haughmond had been established with a grant from Eleanor of Aquitaine in c.1110 as an Augustinian abbey. Rowland gave this holding to his nephew James Barker on his marriage. In the State Papers Domestic of Henry VIII, we read that William Hyll (cousin of Sir Rowland), rector of Stoke upon Tern, had a mortmain licence to 'alienate the rectory and certain lands of the rectory in Netherstoke and Stoke upon Tern to the value of 20s a year to Roland Hyll, mercer of London and his heirs'. These lands were then regranted along with others to the said William and his successors 'for ever'. Also in 1540 the lands of the monasteries of Betton and Combermere were obtained by Sir Rowland, and in 1541 he obtained grants of property formerly owned by the Abbey of Vale Royal near Chester. In 1542, at the considerable cost of £962 11s. 8d., he had a grant in Fee (a Fee was land held—in England always heritable—on condition of homage and service to a superior lord who retained the actual ownership) of various lordships of the manor and several advowsons (advowsons gave the right of presentation of an individual to a benefice or living, the 'patronage' of an ecclesiastical office or living), as well as the former monastery of Shrewsbury and the lands of Lilleshall and Wombridge monastery. He purchased Hawkstone in 1556 together with the Soulton estate for £700 from a lawyer called Adderley. He must have acquired the greater part of his land in the Shropshire region during this time. It appears that people held no scruples about profiting from the Dissolution of the Monasteries.

During the reign of Edward VI, Sir Rowland is listed as having provided 'two great horses' and on 5 June of 1547 he appears on a list of those who were to remain at home in the event of a threatened invasion by the Scots and the French who were supporting the claim of Mary Queen of Scots to the English throne.[6] In July he was nominated under Middlesex as a member of the Privy Chamber or Council at Large and was taxed for two lighthorses and two 'demilances', which refers to the two 'half lances' or lightly armed men he was required to provide. In the following year he again appears as liable to contribute two horses and one 'demilance' and was taxed £1,500, which was a very high figure. By May 1555, he was a Justice of the Peace for Shropshire.

In addition to his purchase of property, Sir Rowland was a builder: he was responsible for four bridges in 1550 alone. Two were constructed in stone and had 18 arches each, one being over the Severn at Atcham (Attingham) and the other at Terne. The other two were built of wood.

Rowland Hill was Warden of the Mercers' Company in 1536 and Master in 1543, 1550, 1555 and 1561. There are three known portraits of him. One, by Sampson, a Dutch artist painting very much in the style of Holbein, is in the Mercers' Hall in London. There is a lengthy inscription in Latin at the bottom of the panel, hard to decipher. Above, written in French, is inscribed: *'Adieu Monde puisque tu descois tout, Infamis tout, chastes tout, a la fin oblive tout'* ('Farewell world, for you deceive all, you dishonour all, you punish all, in the end you put all into oblivion', translation by the archivist/curator of the Mercers' Company, Ursula Carlyle). Other paintings are at Attingham and the Museum of London.

Sir Rowland was a Sheriff of London in 1541, which is when he received his knighthood, and on Michaelmas Day 1549 he was elected Lord Mayor.[7] According to S. Bindoff's *House of Commons*, a few days after his election came the fall from power of Protector Somerset.[8] On 7 October two letters were read to the Common Council of London; one was to the retiring mayor, Sir Henry Amcotes, and the second was directed to Amcotes and Hill purporting to come from the King (Edward VI). In fact it probably came from Somerset. The letter asked for 1,000 men to defend the King. This could not be complied with because Sir Rowland and the Aldermen had already spoken to the Earl of Warwick, whom Hill probably supported. Warwick led an opposition that quietly took over the government and the Duke of Somerset was eventually executed. It was hard to back the right horse! Warwick was created Duke of Northumberland but was executed by Queen Mary despite his vehement protestations that he was a true Catholic. The same source refers to Rowland having been married, although other accounts of his life say that he was unmarried. It tells us that the usual mayoral procession to St Paul's on Candlemas (2 February) was cancelled by reason 'of the late departure of my lady mayoress to the mercy of almighty God'.[9]

At the end of young King Edward's short life writs were issued summoning a Parliament for 18 September 1553, and Hill was one of the four members elected by London. Thanks to Edward's death this Parliament never met, but the same four men were re-elected to Queen Mary's first Parliament. Sir Rowland does not appear to have opposed the re-introduction of Catholicism by Mary but, all the same, was dropped as a Commissioner for Middlesex and Shropshire in 1554. He subsequently sat for Surrey in 1557 when the incumbent Lord Mayor of London invoked an ancient right permitting all previous lord mayors to sit as Justices of the Peace. Sir Rowland was evidently a busy and successful man.

Sharpe and Wriothesley both record an interesting incident concerning Rowland during his term as Sheriff in 1542.[10] Their accounts differ slightly but the essence seems to have been that Sir Rowland and the other Sheriff, Henry Suckley, prevented the Sergeant 'at Mace' (Sergeant at Arms) from removing a Member of Parliament called Ferris from prison in the City of London. Ferris, who is described as a 'burgess of Plymouth' according to the narratives of Hall and Holinshed, was arrested at the 'suit' of a man called White for a debt although he had merely stood surety. Ferris was also a page in King Henry's household. In the fracas the Sergeant's mace bearing the Royal Crown was broken, which was the equivalent of a direct insult to the person of the King, and relations between the City of London and the Parliament were often strained. Despite the fact that Sir Rowland thought better of his action and did release the prisoner, he and Suckley were arrested and brought before the Bar of the House by the Speaker. They were sent to the Tower, the King wishing to demonstrate that the highest court (Parliament) being in a sense 'his court' should not be blocked by a lower court, i.e. the Sheriff of London:

> Wherefore the Mayor (Sir Michael Dormer) and certain of the Alderman shewed to the Lords of the Parliament and to the Commons house, also the 29th of March desiring them to be good lords and masters to the said sheriffs and the 30th March they were released again by the assent of the Parliament House and ... without paying any fyne saving tax and other charges which stood them 20 pounds.

Despite this event, Rowland was knighted by the King shortly afterwards.

Sir Rowland built churches at Hodnet, where many Hills are buried, and at nearby Stoke, where his cousin William was the parson. His enormous holdings by the end of his life gave him, it is said, 1,181 tenants. In 1560 he divided up his properties for 'the avoidinge of contencon and varyens as otherwyse hereafter might arise amonge them for the division and particon thereof'.[11] He obviously had a good understanding of human nature! He left bequests in London to St Bartholomew's, Christ's Hospital, and churches such as St Lawrence Jewry. He established a school in Drayton (Market Drayton in Shropshire), leaving minutely detailed instructions in his Will for its maintenance.

His numerous nephews, nieces and cousins did very well. He seems to have been determined to establish the Hills in comfortable circumstances. He gave his niece, Alice Barker, Stoneleigh Abbey. The Abbey had been given to Charles Brandon, Duke of Suffolk by his brother-in-law, King Henry VIII, but the supposed curse of owning lands seized from the Church was blamed for the death of the Duke's two sons and the property passed to William Cavendish of Trimeley. Cavendish sold it to Rowland Hill. Alice's husband was Sir Thomas Leigh, Sir Rowland's former apprentice and business partner. (The Leighs still live at Stoneleigh, which is now run as a Trust and has been extensively restored with funds provided by the Heritage Lottery Fund and the European Regional Development Fund.) Alice's brother, James, who had already received Haughmond, was also given property at Walcot. Another niece called Alice married Sir Reginald Corbett and the couple appear to have done exceptionally well out of Sir Rowland. They inherited Stoke on Tern, the Malpas property (which came to Rowland through his mother), together with land at Childs Ercall, Drayton and Darnell Grange in Shropshire. Perhaps the two most interesting bequests were Soulton to his cousin William Hill and Hawkstone—the biggest plum of all—to his cousin Humphrey. In fact, Humphrey pre-deceased his benefactor, so that Hawkstone was inherited by his son Rowland, the first to reside there and establish the dynasty.

Sir Rowland died on 28 October 1561 of the 'strangwylyans'—an affliction so far not identified![12] His funeral took place on 5 November in St Stephen's, Walbrook. Machyns gives an account of the funeral, mentioning:

> a standard and five pennons of arms, and a coat of armour and a helmet, a crest, sword and mantle and eleven dozens of escutcheons of arms and he gave 100 gowns and coats to men and women and there were two heralds of arms, Master Clarencieux and Master Somerset, and my lord mayor, the chief mourner Sir Richard Lee [Leigh?] Master Corbett etc. etc ... and 50 poor men in good black gowns, besides women, and the Dean of Pauls made the sermon.

This was followed by a great dinner in the Mercers' Hall and 'a great moan made for his death'.[13]

That he was a public benefactor seems evident. He was 'the unwearied friend of the widow and the fatherless. He clothed annually 300 poor in his own neighbourhood and although childless he constantly kept up a great family household where he maintained good hospitality'.[14] At a period when education was seriously neglected largely due to the closure of the monasteries, he supported students at both universities, giving money to Jesus College, a former nunnery, and funding students at the Inns of Court. In all he appears to have been a genuine philanthropist!

Somehow, despite being a professed Protestant under Henry VIII and Edward VI, he maintained his position under Catholic Mary and even served as a commissioner against heresies and seditious books. Under Elizabeth I, Rowland Hill helped to execute the Act of Uniformity and Supremacy requiring the use of the Book of Common Prayer. He died in 1561, the start of the Anglican Church as we know it today.

His tombstone on the south side of St Stephen's Walbrook bore the following inscription:

> A friend of virtue, a lover of learning,
> A foe to Vice, and vehement corrector,
> A prudent person, all truth supporting,
> A citizen sage, and worthy Counsellor,
> A lover of wisdom, of Justice and...
> Loe, here his corps lyeth, Sir Rowland Hill by name,
> Of London late Lord Mayor and Alderman of fame.

The Soulton Branch

H. Forrester's 'Some Old Shropshire Houses and their Owners', published in 1924, records that there was a Roger Corbet living at Soulton in the 13th century, and there are remains of a moated house in the grounds. The manor of Soulton together with that of Hawkstone was purchased in 1556 by Sir Rowland Hill for the sum of £700. The present Soulton Hall was built in 1668 by Thomas Hill. (There were many Thomases at Court of Hill and at Soulton but almost none in the Hawkstone line.)

Soulton Hall, Wem still stands. Today it appears as a handsome Carolingian house in rose-red Tudor brick. It has lost its original gables. The house consists of three floors, with stone-dressed mullioned windows. An imposing entrance door with Roman Doric columns is surmounted by the coat of arms of the builder, Thomas Hill. This Thomas served as Sheriff of the county in 1681. His second wife was Elizabeth, daughter of Sir Richard Corbet of Shawbury, and this accounts for the inscription on a barn 'Andrew Corbet, 1783'. After Thomas's death in 1711 his son, also Thomas, did not live at Soulton, presumably preferring the other family house at Bletchley, and the house seems to have been let. In 1799 it is recorded as having a Mr Barnett as tenant and was offered for sale. It was bought by kinsmen, the Hills of Hawkstone, and added to their huge estate. The Corbet family appears constantly in the Hill pedigrees, not always happily! Today Soulton belongs to a family called Ashton.

1. The 'Great' Hill. Painting by Charles d'Agar (1669-1721).

CHAPTER 2

The 'Great' Hill (1654-1727)

SIR ROWLAND, the 'Lord Mayor', died in 1561 and the next Hill to make his mark was not born for another hundred years. In the interim the separate branches, Court of Hill, Soulton and Hawkstone, began to establish their own 'dynasties'. Of these, it is only the Hawkstone line and its later offshoot, that of Attingham, that are of significance.

England was in a great state of upheaval—the like of which had not been seen since Henry VII defeated Richard III at Bosworth Field in 1485—when Richard Hill was born in 1654. The Civil War had recently ended with the execution of Charles I in 1649 and the establishment of a 'Lord Protector' in Oliver Cromwell. The Hills of Hawkstone had declared for the King during the Civil War. Anecdotally, Rowland (grandfather of Richard), and also perhaps his son, yet another Rowland, is said to have been imprisoned in the Red Castle following the Battle of Shrewsbury and to have escaped and hidden in one of the many caves that riddle the cliffs in the Park, but how much of this is true is now impossible to know. It was, however, enough to inspire a later Hill, Sir Richard, the whimsical 2nd Baronet, to place an urn commemorating the fact when he was undertaking the landscaping of the Park in the last quarter of the 18th century.

The first Sir Rowland (the Lord Mayor, Rowland I) had settled Hawkstone on his cousin Humphrey but, as noted in Chapter One, this man died before the Lord Mayor and it was *his* son, Rowland II, who succeeded to the property. A confusing succession of Rowlands followed: Rowland III (1594-1644), and his son, Rowland IV (1624-1700), who married Margaret Whitehall and had a number of children. Their marriage settlements list the Hawkstone property as consisting of 150 acres of pasture, 10 acres of woodland and six 'messuages' or hearths, which means dwellings of some sort. The only one of any consequence was the manor house itself and that was of no great size. The estate was apparently still much the same as it had been when settled on Humphrey in 1560. Rowland IV and Margaret's eldest son, yet another Rowland, died young and thus their second son, Richard, came eventually to inherit in 1700. This was the man who was to exceed the acquisitions even of the first Sir Rowland and to establish the family among the leading landowning gentry in the county of Shropshire. He can probably be safely regarded as both the cleverest and the most successful of the whole family from its earliest days to the present. It is in Owen and Blakeway's *Sheriffs of Shropshire* that we find this man described as the 'Great' Hill. It is safe to assume from this and other sources that he was, indeed, a person of some influence and consequence in his time.

In order to understand and appreciate Richard Hill's career it will be helpful to consider some of the historical background to the events in which he played a part. Rowlands II and III lived through a time of religious struggle in Europe. In France the wars of religion between Catholics and Huguenots continued throughout the early life of Henri IV (1557-1610). Henry signed the Edict of Nantes in 1598, giving the Protestants freedom of worship, but under Cardinal Richelieu this freedom was steadily eroded in the first half of the 17th century, and it is during this period that frequent references occur to the plight of Protestants, particularly in France and Piedmont. Cromwell, staunchly religious, supported Protestant groups throughout Europe—not least the exiled French Vaudois with whom the Great Hill was to become so involved during his diplomatic career in Turin some fifty years later. His intervention on their behalf secured them 25 years of religious liberty, ended only by the Revocation of the Edict of Nantes by Louis XIV in 1685. At the time of the Great Hill's birth—March 1654—the great Protestant sea-faring nations of England and the Netherlands were themselves engaged in intermittent naval warfare which ended temporarily in 1667 with the Treaty of Breda, in which Holland ceded Nieuw Amsterdam (New York) to the English.

Rowland IV and Margaret spent their days at Hawkstone during these great events, grieving at the death of their eldest son Rowland and attending to the education of Richard. His boyhood witnessed the Restoration of Charles II and the Great Fire of London. Details of Richard Hill's education are a little confused. He is almost invariably listed as having gone to Shrewsbury School but it appears that he was there for only a short time before moving to Eton, where he was a King's Scholar. He then went to St John's, Cambridge where he graduated in 1675, becoming a Fellow. He subsequently took Deacon's orders. In 1714 he was elected a Fellow of Eton.[1] Harwood, in his *Alumni Etonenses* (1797), wrote, 'he was a person of gaiety and expence early in life, but afterwards enjoyed places of great trust and emolument ... he was a very useful servant to the Crown and a person of great address and general knowledge'. He served first as tutor to Earl Burlington's sons and then to Lord Hyde (who came to be known as 'the Satyr'), son of the 1st Earl of Rochester. Hill's activities in the following ten years are otherwise unrecorded, but he apparently caught the eye of Richard, Earl of

Ranelagh. Ranelagh was serving as Paymaster to the Forces and he appointed Hill as Assistant Paymaster to the army in Flanders in the 1690s. He was to hold this undoubtedly lucrative post for nine years.

Louis XIV's persecution of the Protestants in France—the Camisards, the Cevennois etc.—was so harsh that many fled the country taking with them skills that could not easily be replaced. It is estimated that more than 200,000 left France and this number included artisans such as silk weavers and silversmiths. Army officers also sought refuge abroad. Richard Hill was to have a very long connection with these communities both within France, in Savoy, and also in Switzerland and Germany, where Protestant refugees relied heavily on the financing of their humble needs by England and, to a lesser degree, Holland. Long after Hill had retired from diplomatic life in 1708, he was still connected with these people, to whom pensions continued to be paid by King George I following the death of Queen Anne in 1714.

In 1689 war had been declared on France by the uneasy alliance of England and Holland, who now shared the same ruler in William of Orange. France seemed all-powerful in the 1690s and an 8,000-strong contingent of English soldiers was sent to Flanders under the command of John Churchill to try to counteract the French king's pretensions. From 1692 Louis XIV concentrated on fighting his enemies on land after British victories and the loss of many French ships at Cap La Hogue and Cherbourg in that year. A big problem for the English army in Flanders was desertion: Jesuits persuaded soldiers to serve the exiled Catholic King James and in 1693 a large-scale desertion occurred at the camp at Louvain, largely orchestrated by a Scottish Jacobite called Father Clark.

It was thanks to the Whig government, to the City of London as the centre of world trade, and to the incorporation of the Bank of England in 1694 that England was able to maintain a war chest deeper than that of King Louis despite the fact that France had a population some three times greater than that of her enemy. During these years Richard Hill began to make the fortune which would raise his family from minor squires to the ranks of the landowning aristocracy. A few years later his father was quoted in Blakeway's *Sheriffs of Shropshire* as saying, 'My son Dick makes money so fast; God send he gets it honestly.'[2] It would have been completely normal practice at this period to indulge in a certain amount of 'lucrative arithmetick'. Money voted by Parliament for the Army could be invested by the Deputy Paymaster and any profit on the investment counted as a perquisite. Hill, unlike Lord Ranelagh, seems to have acted honestly in carrying out his financial responsibilities. He 'bore a fair name in his day' and was 'much esteemed by King William', according to Bishop Burnet.[3] Hill was a man of great abilities together with considerable charm and presence. His portraits, which may be seen in Shrewsbury Museum and Art Gallery and at Attingham,

Shropshire and Tatton Park, Cheshire, show a handsome fellow dressed in the first style of fashion.

His account books demonstrate that this 'accountant' Hill was a scrupulous official who frequently picked up overcharges.[4] We are fortunate in having access to many of his documents. These were discovered at Attingham in 1844 by the Reverend Blackley, domestic chaplain to the 2nd Viscount Hill, and many of his letters were published in two volumes by that gentleman in 1845. Apart from his official correspondence the letters contain references to more frivolous items, such as the bay trees he ordered to be shipped to Holland, or his complaints when the Customs service seized his new lace cravats. He was certainly a man of address and intellect but also of a practical bent. In 1694 Ranelagh complained to London that 'the Bank' was slow to supply Hill with the value of the bills, grumbling that it was hard to besiege towns with no subsistence and money and adding that there were also difficulties in paying in 'forraigne' bills and perplexity over our 'coyne'. Apparently the newly incorporated Bank of England sometimes refused to accept Treasury securities against letters of credit—demonstrating its independence even in its infancy—so, when pushed, Amsterdam lent the King three million florins. The year 1694 also saw the creation of the National Debt, which was 'invented' by William Paterson and the Whig Chancellor of the Exchequer, Charles Montagu. England became virtual paymaster to the Grand Alliance thanks to her prosperity, while in 1695 Louis XIV had to impose a highly unpopular poll tax to finance the war.

The Duke of Savoy, with whom Richard Hill was to become intimately involved in the course of the War of the Spanish Succession, was already proving a 'dodgy' ally to England, the Dutch and the Holy Roman Empire, requiring frequent and enormous injections of money to retain his loyalty. He began a persecution of Protestants that would have continued had he not, after much backsliding, eventually decided to break his alliance with Louis XIV. He had thrown in his lot with the French after promised money had failed to arrive from England. (In February 2002, an American company, Odyssey, working with the Royal Naval Museum at Portsmouth, announced the discovery of the wreck of a treasure ship at a depth of half a mile in the Straits of Gibraltar.[5] It seems likely to be the *Sussex*, an 80-gun British warship and part of a fleet which sailed to the Mediterranean in 1693. The loss of this ship, with its cargo of gold and silver coins of unknown value, may have been the cause of the Duke's defection to the French.)

With John Churchill temporarily dismissed from command of the Army things went badly in Flanders, but in 1695 King William achieved his own personal victory at Namur. A painting recording this still forms part of the decoration of the Saloon (*c*.1740) at Hawkstone and shows King William, the Elector of Bavaria and Richard Hill surveying Namur. Hill greatly admired the King and found him intelligent and hard working, although certainly lacking any obvious charm. He purchased full-length portraits of William and Queen Mary, both of which still hang at Hawkstone. These paintings presumably hung first at Richard Hill's house in Richmond or at Cleveland Court, St James, and would have been moved to Hawkstone after his death in 1727.[6]

Hill's duties were wide-ranging and in 1696 he was described as both Paymaster General and also Envoy Extraordinary to the Elector of Bavaria. (The Elector was to prove very troublesome to the allies in the War of the Spanish Succession when he sided with Louis XIV—a choice he lived to regret.) The year 1697 saw the signing of the Treaty of Ryswick, which brought a very temporary and uneasy peace lasting for four years and merely allowed all the participants to recover and re-equip themselves.

State Papers Domestic for 1696 contain letters to Hill from James Vernon, Secretary of State for the Northern Department, written during Hill's sojourn as Envoy to Brussels and the Hague.[7] Many of these concern requests from Catholics in exile for permission to return home to England. Licences were signed personally by King William and were granted sparingly and with care since there were many 'enemy' Jacobites trying to return. In a letter dated 1 April 1698 Vernon wrote, 'I know not what countrymen they are that flock to you (in Brussels) from France. If they are Irishmen, there is little hope they will ever be good for anything.' In May Vernon wrote of worries over the suspiciously large numbers of English Roman Catholic priests finding a means of returning home by serving as chaplains to foreign ambassadors holding diplomatic immunity. It was also a period of anxiety owing to the frequent attempts on William's life. A letter dated 10 May tells Hill of one licence that the King has signed and hopes that more applicants for licences will approach Hill, noting that 'there is such a resort of the St Germains tribe [the exiled King James lived at the Château de St Germain] into those parts [i.e. the Low Countries]. Since it is not very easy to remove them, it would be worth while to know what they are doing. Methinks some of those, who shew such an impatience for returning into their country, should be willing to do something for the service of it; and they will see we are not hard hearted when they will give any proofs that they are friends to the Government.' Vernon adds that he has heard a rumour as to another assassination plot and says that some 'cut-throats' are planning to come by Dunkirk and some by Ostend. He asks Hill to try and infiltrate these groups with his people (presumably spies) to learn what is really happening. A ship expected at Gravesend with returning exiles was to be searched thoroughly and anybody on board who did not have the requisite signed permit would be sent back to the Continent or imprisoned.

This was also the time when Charles Talbot, 12th Earl—and 1st and only Duke—of Shrewsbury, was in power. He had become Secretary of State in March

1694. He was a very intelligent and interesting man and in the two published volumes of Richard Hill's letters there are many from Talbot written when he was out of office and living in Rome during Hill's stay in Turin.[8] He had a 'wild' mother who was a 'pensioner of France' and who certainly took an active part in Jacobite intrigues, which meant that the Duke was himself suspected of being pro-Jacobite. He was born Roman Catholic but became a 'token' Protestant in 1679. With some of the great Whig families, such as the Devonshires, and Thomas Osborne, 1st Duke of Leeds, he was deeply involved in the overthrow of James II and served as Secretary of State in 1689 and 1694. Ill health—he was frequently spitting blood—led him to leave office in 1700 and go to Rome, where he spent three years. A comment of his to the King in July 1696 shows how slippery and double-dealing an ally the Duke of Savoy was considered to be. Victor Amadeus was evidently in close secret talks with France at that time, just as he was to be again when Richard Hill was at his Court a few years later.

Hill was sent on two delicate diplomatic missions to Turin. A third journey planned for 1708 never came to pass, probably because of his poor health. The first was in 1699 and it is from this date onwards that much of his correspondence survives. The incomplete collection of his papers is now in the Shropshire County Records Office, courtesy of the National Trust, which today owns Attingham, and the late Lady Berwick.[9] It includes one of the ciphers he used, with a translation by his secretary, John Chetwynd, including an example of one of the keys.[10] Chetwynd was with Richard Hill through many trials, and was a very able deputy. He later succeeded his father as the 2nd Viscount Chetwynd of Ingestre, in Staffordshire. Some of the correspondence is damaged, some of it consists of copies made by Chetwynd, often with Hill's handwritten notes, and there are original autograph letters.

Richard Hill's correspondence reveals the diplomacy, spying and intrigue involved in the political manoeuvering taking place to prevent Louis XIV dominating the continent of Europe, and also to give aid to the persecuted Protestants. Letters in English, Latin, French, Dutch and German provide a fascinating account of Hill's service at the Court of Savoy under both King William and then for a much longer period under Queen Anne, when he spent more than three years abroad mainly in Turin but also in Genoa, Leghorn and Nice. He was given 'extraordinary' powers to treat, to dispense large sums of money, and to send orders to the Mediterranean fleet, Sir George Rooke and Sir Cloudesley Shovel being the senior admirals. He was closely in touch with the Court at Vienna where England's representative, Stepney, had a difficult job trying to urge the Emperor into some sort of action on behalf of the Alliance. He was a member but was more interested in suppressing a Hungarian rebellion in his own territories.

On his second mission Hill communicated almost daily with Marlborough (John Churchill) who was busy rolling up the French at the battles of Blenheim and Ramillies. Hill and Marlborough appear to have been on excellent terms, enjoying a high degree of mutual respect. The rest of Hill's correspondence was to and from the Lords Treasurer and Secretaries of State in London which included over the years the Earl of Nottingham, the Duke of Shrewsbury, Lord Godolphin, Sir Charles Hedges and Robert Harley, later Earl of Oxford. There are also letters from the Archbishop of Canterbury, Prince Eugene of Savoy (a very able soldier in the service of the Emperor and, incidentally, cousin to Victor Amadeus of Savoy), the Duke of Savoy himself, Sir George Rooke, 'King Charles III' of Spain (the allies' candidate King of Spain, opposing Louis XIV's protégé and grandson, Philip V, the successful contender), various bankers and money lenders in Frankfurt and Amsterdam and long, importunate and wordy letters from exiled Vaudois pastors pleading for more help.

(It is interesting to note that Mr Blackley appears to have started work on the correspondence in 1842 when the Vaudois were once again begging the British, whose Foreign Secretary was then the Earl of Aberdeen, for help in persuading the King of Sardinia to cease their persecution. Their grievances and distress were almost exactly the same then as they had been at the end of the 17th century, and the behaviour of the reactionary King Charles Albert, who was the direct descendant of Victor Amadeus [created 1st King of Sardinia in 1718], paralleled that of his wily ancestor.)

In Hill's letters frequent use of both the Gregorian and Julian calendars is made in dating the same letter. Most of Europe employed the more accurate, and 'modern', Gregorian calendar by this date, but England continued to use the old-fashioned Julian calendar until 1752. Pope Gregory III introduced the modern calendar in 1582 and it was gradually adopted throughout the continent—Hanover commenced its use in 1700. Both 'Old Style' (OS) and 'New Style (NS) dates were used in diplomatic communications, presumably to avoid misunderstandings, and Hill certainly used both when corresponding with allies who had changed to the New Style. Between the two calendars there was a difference of ten days prior to 1700 and eleven after that, which meant that between January and 25 March two different years could appear in the date.

The first mission to Savoy undertaken by Richard Hill in 1699 was officially designed to convey King William's compliments to the Duke on the birth of a son and heir. The real purpose was, of course, to stiffen the resolve of the Duke to commit himself to the Grand Alliance in the next war with France that could already be seen on the horizon. The Duchess of Savoy was a Princesse de France, the daughter of Henrietta Maria (the beloved 'Minette', sister to Charles II) who had been married to the debauched Duc d'Orléans, brother of Louis XIV. The royal ramifications made the Duchess cousin to William III's wife, Queen Mary (died 1694), and the future Queen Anne, and niece to Louis XIV.

Hill received his instructions and official credentials from King William on 31 May 1699.[11] He appears to have been already at the Hague, where he served as Ambassador in succession to Sir Joseph Williamson. In a letter dated 21 June 1699, which it seems probable he received at the Hague, some Vaudois begged Hill to try and achieve the release of eight of their brethren who had been prisoners in the French galleys since 1688 despite the signing of the Treaty of Ryswick in 1697. Hill certainly had many meetings with the Dutch Grand Pensionary, Anthony Heinsius, since the Protestant Dutch were also anxious to keep Savoy in the Alliance and to give aid to the victims of religious persecution. He then set out for Turin and has left an excellent account of his travels there, the time he spent in Savoy and his relations with those in power. From other correspondence addressed to him in London in November of 1699, it seems that he had returned to England by that date.

Hill travelled via Brussels, through Champagne and Burgundy, to Lyons.[12] He remarked on the abject poverty of the French countryside but noted that the towns and cities appeared to be very prosperous—the result, he thought, of an 'absolute government'. At Rheims, Dijon and Bonne [sic] he learned 'what a prodigious quantity of wines was sent every year into Flanders, Holland and Germany,' and commented, 'I am persuaded that the buying of wines and brandies from France and selling horses to them during the whole course of the war, was one of the greatest faults which the allies did commit.' He found Lyons to be a great and beautiful town, helped by its situation between two great rivers and its proximity to Italy and Switzerland. He commented, however, that its manufacturers, especially in the silk industry, were feeling the loss of many of their Protestant workers who had fled from the religious persecution. He gives an amusing description of the 'Bank' of Lyons: 'which is so famous, is purely imaginary not built upon any real funds ... the use of the bank is this, all payments are made at Lyon four times in the year, i.e. every three months. At those times all traders meet, debtors and creditors. Every one brings an abstract of the balance of their accounts; and so they transfer from one to another and pay their debts by "rencountering", which is due to every (one) and this is what they call *il giro di banco* ....' There was also a system for lending at three per cent per quarter or 12 per cent per annum which Hill describes as being unusually high due to poor trade and scarcity of money. He was always looking at things with his accountant's eye.

On reaching Savoy, Hill noted that the people did not seem to care much for their Duke, and would be quite content to return to French rule. Occupation by the French forces had brought prosperity and now they were suffering from the swingeing taxation imposed by the Duke. The success of Hill's missions to the Duke of Savoy was all the more laudable in that he did manage to keep Savoy in the Grand Alliance despite the pro-French feeling of the people—other, of course, than the persecuted Vaudois.

The Duke being away taking the waters at St Maurice on his arrival in Turin, Hill took the opportunity to deliver his formal messages of congratulation to both the Dowager Duchess and the young Duchess, and in return was warmly invited to attend their courts held each day. He pronounced the young baby Prince to be as 'lusty, prosperous and thriving child that ever was seen'. After a week in Turin with the Duke still away, Hill travelled to Milan to visit the Prince de Vaudemont, who had recently been a General serving in Flanders and for whom Hill 'always had a mighty veneration'. He was apparently received with great warmth and lodged in the royal palace.

Back in Turin, Hill was received by the Duke, Victor Amadeus, and apparently treated with every courtesy. The Duke expressed his respect and veneration of King William and his wish to do everything to meet his obligations as a member of the Alliance and, of course, his gratitude for the protection and help he had received. The Alliance was important to both parties; the Duke benefited in that France was prevented from overrunning his country once again, and the English and Dutch in that the French were forced to maintain an army on their south-eastern flank, thus weakening their power to fight in the Low Countries. Savoy's participation in the Alliance also provided a means of protecting the Duke's Vaudois subjects despite his tendency to harass them.

The Duke was an absolute ruler who confided in very few senior ministers. During the course of his conversations with the Great Hill he spoke freely of his hopes of being offered the Spanish throne. Poor mad Charles II of Spain was expected to die at any moment and France and Austria were already manoeuvering to fill the 'vacancy'. Victor Amadeus felt that although his position in the line of succession was more remote than that of the French and Austrian claimants, his candidature for the Spanish throne, being less contentious, might well prove more acceptable to everyone. Hill understood from this that the Duke had already been trying to rally support in Spain but he felt the need of King William's backing and was putting out a 'feeler' to Hill in the hope of receiving encouragement from London. Victor Amadeus also feared that if Louis of France or the Emperor of Austria acceded to the Spanish throne, he would have one or the other on his eastern frontier, since Milan was then a Spanish possession. His own accession to the Spanish throne would give him control of the Spanish territories in North Italy. For his part, Hill was making sure that the Duke kept to the full letter of the treaties he had signed with the other members of the Alliance, both with respect to free trade (the Duke's barques had seized several

English merchant ships off Villa Franca [Villefranche] although he had been forced to relinquish them eventually) and also with regard to the Vaudois.

In 1701 war broke out again with France once more playing the aggressor. Louis XIV, confident that England would not support Holland actively so soon after the last war, set out to carve up the Spanish 'overseas' territories, including part of the Netherlands. The Governor-General of the Spanish Netherlands was none other than the Elector of Bavaria, who had by this time entered into an alliance with France.

All participants in the struggle had been awaiting the death of Charles II of Spain. This wretched man had been born mentally subnormal and deformed, with an exaggerated 'Habsburg' jaw which made it hard for him even to eat. His death had long been expected but he hung on to life, such as it was, dying only in 1700. Since he had not been able to produce an heir, the succession to the Spanish throne was to be disputed by Louis XIV and the Emperor, as well as the Emperor's grandson, with the Duke of Savoy a more distant candidate. Louis finally managed to obtain the crown for his grandson, Philip, Duc d'Anjou, with Charles II actually naming the boy as heir in his Will, which was signed virtually on his death bed. This was naturally infuriating to the Emperor and worrying to England since while the country was terrified by the idea of Louis XIV wielding control over an empire as vast as that composed of Spain and France. The Emperor Leopold had first tried to obtain the Spanish throne for his second son by his second wife (the Archduke Charles), and the ensuing struggle between the Holy Roman Empire and France launched the long new war. The Archduke Charles was supported by the English/Dutch/Empire Alliance when war broke out and was considered to be King Charles III of Spain. Richard Hill was heavily involved in supporting the Archduke's cause in the war and in sending supplies to his army in Spain and to the fleet under Sir George Rooke. Many copies of letters to Hill survive from the years 1703-4.

Charles' pretensions to the Spanish throne were finally abandoned with his accession to that of the Holy Roman Empire on the death of his brother, the Emperor Joseph, but this was not until 1711. Another candidate, and one destined to make 'family feeling' run very high, was the Emperor Leopold's grandson (through his first wife), the Elector of Bavaria, Joseph Ferdinand, but he died in 1700. Hill had been special envoy to this gentleman in Brussels in 1696 and then succeeded Sir Joseph Williamson as Ambassador at the Hague in 1699. Spain was not very enthusiastic over its new King Philip V, and nobody thought for a single moment that the country could be truly independent of its bellicose neighbour while France was ruled by his grandfather.

When King William's horse Sorrel put his hoof into a molehill in the park at Hampton Court in 1702, throwing his royal rider, it was an accident that would not have been fatal to most people, but William, already constitutionally not very strong, died two weeks later.

Richard Hill now found himself in the service of the last Stuart ruler, Queen Anne, younger daughter of James II. In May 1702 Hill was appointed to the Council of Prince George, the Queen having married Prince George of Denmark in 1683. The new reign—short though it was—was to prove a magnificent period in English history and Richard Hill was right at the centre of state events and diplomacy, involved in great decisions, friend and colleague to all the great personalities of the day. Religion in England remained unswervingly Protestant.

Marlborough made haste to reassure the Great Pensionary of the Netherlands of his country's continued support. The role of Stadholder was temporarily vacant following the death of William, who had no immediate heir.

The defection to France of Hill's former friend, the Elector of Bavaria, was two-fold in its effects: it enabled Louis XIV to enter the Spanish Netherlands and, with Bavaria lying adjacent to Austria, a route was laid open from France to the heart of the Habsburg Empire.

Richard Hill's appointment as Envoy Extraordinaire to the Court of Savoy was gazetted in London in July 1703.[13] He was then told to remain at the Hague and assist in negotiations with the States General prior to leaving for Turin. In Turin, Victor Amadeus was, once again, bitterly torn. Should he withdraw from his alliance with the French and throw in his lot with the allies? The latter were promising him so much in terms of money and support but had they the power to protect him in the event of a French invasion of his country, which would surely follow if he joined the allies? The Envoy of the Emperor, the Count d'Aversberg, travelled to Turin in great secrecy and was shut away in a villa belonging to the Duke, who visited him 'incognito' late at night. The Duke was demanding more and more concessions from the allies, which usually amounted to more money. Letters streamed into London to Sir Charles Hedges, a Secretary of State, and to Hill waiting at the Hague; these were principally from Mr Stepney, English Envoy to the Court at Vienna (he was also a well known poet and is buried in Westminster Abbey).[14] Stepney was in a difficult position while the Emperor continued to vacillate, taking more interest in affairs in Hungary than in the west. War had almost bankrupted the Empire and Leopold resisted any efforts to extract more money from him for the Alliance. This meant that Queen Anne had to promise to pick up his share of the cost of maintaining the war effort. Hill was told to wait at the Hague while the delicate negotiations were under way. As long as the Duke of Savoy wavered over his allegiance it was feared that he might refuse to receive Hill on his arrival in Turin, for fear of angering France, and this would be tantamount to a refusal to meet the Queen, whose personal representative Hill was.

Hill was still working hard on the share of costs with the Great Pensionary, trying to persuade Holland to pay more than one third of the cost of the subsidy to Savoy. Under their previous alliance in the War of the Treaty of Augsburg, Holland and England had paid two-thirds and Spain the other portion. Now they had to readjust. Desperate to save the negotiations from failure, England finally undertook to pay two-thirds if Holland would pay the rest. Without this sum, Victor Amadeus refused to 'turn his coat'; he drove a very hard bargain. The sum involved was 80,000 crowns a month with a 'sweetener' up front of 100,000 crowns. This payment was very secret and Hill worked on the negotiations over the payment with no official accreditation to the Hague. The Emperor was contributing nothing but troops; he could not afford to. Another secret part of the deal involved the Duke revoking all previous edicts against the Vaudois and other Protestant groups living in Savoy-Piedmont.[15]

Hill was, at the same time, still negotiating with the States General over their commitment in both ships and money to the Archduke Charles' journey to Portugal and then into Spain. The Dutch were refusing to contribute more than 12 ships and eventually Hedges told Hill not to press this point too hard but to try to ensure that the ships they were providing would be ready together with their troops when the Archduke was ready to sail.[16] The Grand Pensionary may have been at the head of the States General but his powers were limited and he could not commit to anything without all 17 States of Holland being in agreement.

Stepney wrote to Hill on 5 September 1703, referring to 'our new King (the Archduke or "Charles III") ... I reckon he will be declared [King of Spain] on the 10th inst'. He added that he had finally managed to obtain permission for him to take leave in England; it would not turn out so! At the end of September Hill received a letter from a minister of the Duke, Count de la Tour ('the little man'), written at Chambéry and indicating that Hill should not proceed yet to Turin. At the same time Hill heard from William Aglionby, English Envoy to the Swiss Cantons, that he had heard de la Tour was going to meet someone from France on the border and 'there conclude the bargain with old friends'![17] De la Tour was considered to be 'more a Frenchman than a Savoyard'. Was he about to throw his lot and perhaps that of Savoy in with France after all?

In early October Nottingham wrote to Hill assuring him of his imminent departure for Turin and adding that should he not be welcome on his arrival there he could travel on to the Republic of Venice as the Alliance was anxious to try to bring her and also the Duke of Tuscany on board in order to bolster strength on the Italian side. He was directed to try to prevent money being sent from officially neutral Genoa to the French army in Italy and, if the practice continued, to treat Genoa as an enemy. Nottingham also told him that he was to endeavour to persuade Victor Amadeus to abolish or at the very least reduce customs tariffs imposed by Savoy at the port of Villa Franca (Villefranche). He pointed out that it would be mutually beneficial for the Duke and the British merchants if he could buy the goods carried by the English ships for his army more cheaply.

Hill was also being strongly encouraged to press the Grand Pensionary to contribute money to Monsieur Arnaud, a Protestant leader, for an undertaking to which Queen Anne was highly committed. The plan was for Arnaud to raise a regiment of refugee Protestants from the Vaudois. This regiment would then take on the French in the Cevennes to aid their 'brothers' still there. In addition to bringing help to these persecuted people, it would also serve to keep a French army well occupied on that flank. The refugee officers living in exile in England following the Revocation of the Edict of Nantes were to be dispatched to lead these men, who were to be employed on the same terms as the Duke's regular soldiers. The Queen authorised the sum of 300,000 guilders to be spent arming the Vaudois, and in Hill's additional instructions from the Queen, dated 9 November, urged him to make haste to Turin; his presence there seems suddenly to have become urgent because the Duke was reported as quite capable of changing his coat yet again, even though he had signed the Treaty 'with the Emperor and the other Allies for the common safety against the encroachments of France'. The only thing that could be guaranteed to keep him in the allied camp was money, and Hill had to handle this. On 13 November 1703 Hill wrote to Nottingham in acknowledgement of his final orders to leave for Turin: 'my arms and my bearskins are ready for a long journey'.[18] He was to be away for almost three years.

Many clauses in Hill's instructions were secret. A highly important plan for the following spring was for Victor Amadeus to lead an army to approach and attack Toulon on the landward side while the British, and possibly the Dutch, attacked from the sea. Hill was told to say nothing of this to the Pensionary. Unfortunately, in the event, Victor Amadeus ducked out of this proposed attack at the last moment. He was not an easy man to work with and undoubtedly very devious, and he always feared a French attack on Savoy if his back were turned.

Another instruction was to press the Duke to use 'his utmost endeavours to reduce the Elector of Bavaria into the interests of the allies, to which his interest and safety, and the example of the barbarous usage of the Duke of Savoy [by the French] should be a sufficient motive and warning to him to avoid the like oppression'. The Elector had certainly got himself into a fine mess. Godolphin referred to it again in a letter written in December 1703: 'We should not think much to part with a good thumping sum of money to bring him into the interests of the allies and make his peace with the Emperor.' Hill was given very wide discretionary powers; should there be, in his judgement, insufficient time to send to London on some important point, he was authorised to discuss the matter with the Envoy from the States General and then to take the appropriate action on behalf of the government.

Hill had also been busy at the Hague planning the shipment of the Archduke's retinue, which amounted to some 450 people, to Portugal en route for Spain and his new throne.[19] This party included about sixty horses which required special arrangements for their accommodation in the transports. Considerable correspondence passed between Sir George Rooke and Hill over the departure, delays and several postponements meaning that it was much later in the year than expected and the weather had become very fickle. Sir George wrote informing Hill that the whole expedition had nearly been ruined by the 'late dismal tempest'.[20] This major storm is chronicled by Boyer in his *History of Queen Anne* and occurred on 26 November 1703 between 11 p.m. and midnight, continuing with 'almost unrelenting fury' till 7 the next morning,

> blowing down ... even whole buildings; tearing up a multitude of trees by the roots ... beating several spires off steeples; rolling up great quantities of lead like scrolls of parchment ... in this hurricane several people were killed in their beds, particularly the pious and learned Bishop of Bath and Wells and his lady ... the damage done in London and Westminster was conjectured to amount to one million sterling.

The effects at sea were appalling and several ships of the Royal Navy were lost with four ships of the line and twenty transports being dragged from their anchorages, including the flagship of Sir Cloudesley Shovel, the *Russell*. This ship was driven ashore three miles west of Helvetslys but fortunately the stores and guns on board were recovered and it was hoped to salvage the hull eventually. Rooke was awaiting word from the Dutch Admiral, Callemberg, but he reckoned at least one hundred and fifty merchant ships had gone down. Rooke added that he had always been opposed to 'our making our ships so familiar with the winter season'. Queen Anne ordered a day 'of general and public fast'. This was held on 19 January and was 'accordingly most religiously observed'. The storm has also been chronicled by Daniel Defoe in *The Storm*.

At length, Hill reached Turin via Frankfurt on 4 January 1704. He wrote immediately to Nottingham to tell him he was 'in situ' and to relate an interesting meeting that he had had in Lausanne. On arrival he was accosted by a M. Hugetan who had come 'post all night' from Geneva to catch him. That they must have had dealings before is obvious from the way Hill refers to him, but there is no mention in other letters that survive. Hill was plainly most annoyed with Hugetan and when the latter said he wanted to speak with Hill about the possibility of there being a peaceful 'arrangement' between the allies and France, Hill roughly brushed him off saying that there was not the slightest possibility of such a thing. He soon received a letter from Nottingham again pressing him on the subject of the Elector of Bavaria. The Elector had quickly fallen out with France and it therefore seemed an appropriate moment to offer him a 'carrot'. The Elector was in a tight corner. His envoy in London desired a private audience with the Queen on 22 May 1704 and said that his master found the time not right to join the Alliance as the French were too strong, but he hoped, if circumstances changed, 'a more favourable junction might offer before the end of the campaign'. The Elector was trying to keep a toehold in both camps against whatever the future might bring.

The first of the Duke of Marlborough's great victories came at Blenheim on 13 August 1704, leaving an enormous number of dead. Marlborough had marched his army from the Netherlands to the Danube, and after joining forces with Prince Eugene he delivered a crushing defeat on the combined French and Bavarian armies. Marshal Tallard was captured and invited to take his seat in Marlborough's coach, and the legend of French invincibility was shattered.

The secret plan to take Toulon was developing, and there were promises of a great fleet coming into the Mediterranean as 'early as the season will permit them to sail for Lisbon'. Thanks to the alliance with the King of Portugal, Lisbon was now a safe and useful port for the English fleet. The Archduke had finally arrived there on 24 February 1704, where he was reported by Sir George Rooke as having been warmly received by the King.

Hill had requested the services of two frigates to be placed at his disposal between Toulon, Nice, Villa Franca, Genoa and Leghorn. These ships, the *Mary Galley* and the *Lyme*, were under Hill's command, his private navy, and were intended to help Savoy in several different ways, although Nottingham was still highly distrustful of the Duke. In a letter dated 7 March 1704, Secretary of State Nottingham wrote to Captain Dolman, 'If when you arrive at Villa Franca, Mr Hill be deceased, take your orders from the Duke of Savoy. I hope this will be needless.' Fortunately it was. The two little ships arrived in Villa Franca on 6 May 1704, and Captain Dolman wrote to Hill for instructions.[21] Hill's little navy was to be very useful carrying arms and supplies, some soldiers and, of course, messages. The ships were also used to transport the vital cargo of salt. June 1704 saw letters arrive from Robert Harley, Speaker of the House of Commons and now one of the Chief Secretaries of State following the resignation of the Earl of Nottingham. (Harley was created Earl of Oxford in 1711 before spending two years in the Tower for supposed treason.)

Hill had been in Nice since early in that month but he had been in poor health, and although we learn in a letter from Van der Meer, Envoy for the States

General in Turin, that he was better, his recovery might well have been delayed by the tart letter from Victor Amadeus on his learning that Sir George Rooke had taken the fleet, which he relied on for his protection, to Catalonia and that the landing there had not been a success. Hill had, however, been assured by Lord Godolphin that the fleet would return should help be required and that he had only to send a message to Rooke. Hedges wrote to Hill saying that the Duke should not be at all concerned as to an attack from the sea, at least until the onset of winter when the English fleet would have to leave. Hedges told Hill that Savoy's fate looked like being largely dependent on Marlborough's success in either sending him some of his soldiers or by diversionary activity.

In August 1704 the Duke of Savoy showed Hill a letter he had received from the Duc de la Feuillade desiring the Duke to let him help 'accommodate his Royal Highness' affairs at the Court of France'. Victor Amadeus protested vehemently that he would not change his allegiance, and the opportune arrival of the great news of Blenheim no doubt helped convince the wily Duke that he was going to be better off with the Alliance. This view was reinforced by a victory of the English fleet under Sir George Rooke and Sir Cloudesley Shovel and their subsequent capture of Gibraltar. Hill wrote to Marlborough congratulating him on his victory and adding that even if he were to be made 'Prince of Domawert, or Schwellenburg or Hochstet' (place names in Marlborough's recent campaign), he must keep the illustrious name of Marlborough.[22] He also pressed strongly for the Duke's help, saying that Turin could not hold out once winter came, and that they were already finding the sending of couriers difficult with French troops surrounding them on three sides. The capture of a French courier carrying letters from the Pope to the Duc de Vendôme made clear to the court at Turin that there was now a treaty between the Pope and the French, with Venice being pressed to join them for 'the peace of Italy'. The letters indicated that the French were about to begin the sieges of Ivrea and Verrue, which boded ill for Savoy, and that following the capture of these frontier fortresses the army would encamp in the Plains of Piedmont for the winter before taking Turin in the spring of 1705.

In August 1704 Hill wrote to Rooke begging him to thrash the French fleet and to then remove as much salt as possible from the salt pans at the Iles d'Hyères before destroying the salt workings there.[23] He asked him to take one thousand tons of salt to Villa Franca. It would be paid for by the Duke of Savoy. He hoped the Fleet could spare three or four barrels of powder and some lead for which the Duke would also pay. He further begged him to destroy any enemy ships he could find in Antibes, Monaco and other ports containing galleys belonging to the Pope and normally based at Civita Vecchia and Neptuno, to raise papal awareness as to the Queen's feelings of indignation at the Vatican's pro-French attitude.

By October 1704 Hill's letters could only leave via Genoa, all other routes being blocked by the French. Even the Genoa route was very dangerous. Hill had hoped to go home before the onset of winter but now felt that he could not leave his post—even assuming he could obtain permission—'without the imputation of desertion'. In November he wrote to Marlborough: 'We are very deserted and still the Emperor does nothing ... the Queen loses her money and the Duke of Savoy loses his country ... the Emperor has never sent one groat into Piedmont.' Fortunately he was given permission to keep the two frigates wintering in Villa Franca, an excellent natural harbour sheltered from all but the strongest south-westerly winds and with great depth of water. Hill enjoyed commanding his little 'Navy' and begged London to send more ships to winter at Villa Franca from whence they could sally forth to burn and capture French ships. The two frigates also gave the beleaguered court in Turin some hope of escape should it become necessary for them to flee. Hill was now often at Crescentin in camp with the Duke. They hoped to hold onto their frontline stronghold of Verrue for some time longer but knew that they must finally be forced into a retreat by the sheer numbers of the enemy. On Christmas Eve 1704 Hill wrote again to Marlborough: 'Here we are at Crescentin up to the knees in dirt ever since the beginning of May; the Duke of Vendôme has never been able to draw us or drive us from this post. It is just such a place as Eton and Verrue is very like Windsor Castle, between which we preserve our bridge over the Po.'[24] It could not be held indefinitely.

In early March the enemy managed to cut the bridge connecting Verrue with the outside world and the garrison of some 1,400 men had to be abandoned to their fate. Hill reported this to Hedges and went on to say that Count Torn, who was coming from Vienna, at last, with letters of exchange for 100,000 florins and various other less valuable goods, had fallen into the hands of the enemy near Savona. He also mentioned that he now had two more frigates under his 'command' with the arrival from Gibraltar of the *Tartar* and the *Newport*. He told Hedges that the French were planning an attack on Nice and Villa Franca and pointed out that should these places be captured Savoy would be completely isolated. On 11 March Hill wrote that the keep at Verrue was still holding out and that the Duke of Savoy had organised a method of communication between the besieged fortress and the camp of Crescentin; he put his orders into an empty bomb and fired this from a mortar mounted in a redoute beside the river Po right into the castle. The governor replied by the same method, right under the nose and eyes of the enemy, and this apparently gave the Duke some degree of satisfaction.

A sudden move by the Duc de la Feuillade, who had crossed the river Var just outside Nice, caused much alarm; Hill sent urgent messages to Nice and

Villa Franca warning the frigate captains to take their ships and any stores out to sea immediately, but despite sending five separate couriers—riders on horseback and peasants on foot—he was afraid that possibly none had got through in time with his warning.[25] He also wrote to Captain Dolman, who had taken the *Mary Galley* and the *Lyme* to Leghorn, urging him to sail back with all possible speed to cruise off the coasts of Monaco, Antibes, Villa Franca and Nice to prevent the enemy ships from landing at Nice and Villa Franca; Antibes and Monaco were useful safe havens for the French at that time.[26] His messages to Captain Fisher on board the *Tartar* were urgent, pressing him to remove all possible stores that were not within the castle and to take on board, also, the pursers of the *Mary Galley* and the *Lyme* who had been left at Villa Franca to obtain provisions for their ships against their return from Leghorn. In his fifth letter to Captain Fisher, Hill instructed him to set fire to the ships in the harbour should they fail to get out in time and 'to retire into the castle where His Royal Highness [the Duke of Savoy] does not doubt but that you will do your duty like brave men'.[27] The governor of the castle was to help with men to remove all the artillery and ammunition from the ships before they were fired. In the event both ships got out to sea in time. Hill added that in Piedmont they were now completely cut off by land and could do nothing to help. The four frigates—Hill's little Navy— were proving extremely useful and even managed to take some French prizes.

Helping the Protestants being another part of Hill's brief, his correspondence contains constant reference to his efforts to succour those still left in France, in addition to those who had already escaped to Germany, Switzerland and Savoy. It was an integral aim of the whole campaign and an important part of his formal instructions, but is not easy to cover in parallel with the battle to hold on to both the country and the loyalty of the Duke of Savoy. The Duke paid only lip service to the reinstatement of the rights of the Protestants promised in return for the enormous subventions he received from both Holland and England. He welcomed the idea of using Vaudois or other Protestant refugees in his army but only because he was always frighteningly short of soldiers.

Following the Revocation of the Edict of Nantes, French Protestant families were separated and people were herded to Mass at rifle point. Numerous abuses were practised on these people, who were virtually unable to obtain employment and scratched a bare existence where they could. Several specific examples are cited in Hill's correspondence. The text survives of a petition from one Jean Salliens, a native of Montpellier (in the heart of Cevennois country), refugee in Lausanne for 15 years and resident of Geneva for five more, who with his wife, Françoise Rayne, had come to Turin to beg for the Duke's help. In March 1705 the couple lost their son. In April, by 'virtue of 25 crowns judiciously bestowed on a priest', they found that the boy, aged eight, was with a Madame St Agnes.

This woman was described as a 'godly woman whose devotion it seems lies to kidnapping protestant children'. The boy then disowned his father and said that he had a mind to be a Roman Catholic; obviously Mme de St Agnes had worked fast in her brainwashing. On 10 April the couple petitioned the Duke, who had the child moved to the house of the First President, promising to have him restored to his parents on their proving that he belonged to them. Hill and the minister for Holland obtained witnesses in Lausanne, Geneva and Toulon who could vouch for the couple, that they were legally married and had been living 'christianly' together for ten or eleven years, but nothing happened. Finally the Salliens, fearing reprisals against them if they stayed in Piedmont and having two other children, left for Switzerland. Hill reprimanded the Marquis de St Thomas, minister to the Duke of Savoy, for dismissing the matter so lightly: the Duke might refer to it as a piece of 'silliness' but, given the attention paid to the matter by the Queen of England and the States General, it was surely worthy of the Duke's consideration. By January 1706 the child had still not been returned to his parents. This was not an isolated case.

David Flotard was a Protestant who played a very active role between Savoy, the Hague and the Cevennes. Initially Hill and others were suspicious of him and reluctant to entrust him with money. It was always Flotard and often only Flotard who seemed to return safely from missions carrying both money and messages to the oppressed Protestants in the remote Cevennes. Eventually, however, all were convinced of his *bona fides*. He seems to have been a brave man and was very accusatory in letters to Hill at the beginning of their relationship, feeling that he was distrusted and that Hill had no idea of the difficulties he and others faced when trying to reach their 'brothers'. In June 1704 rumours abounded that the Cevennois/Camisards had 'made an accommodation and laid down their arms' and Hedges warned Hill that should this be true it would free up a French army which would turn its attention and forces to invading Savoy. Victor Amadeus wrote to Hill saying that it was in fact only Cavallier and his immediate band who had signed an armistice, but this also turned out to be quite untrue, the fact being that Cavallier had managed to trounce Maréchal Villars.[28]

In November 1704 Hill described Cavallier to Hedges, saying that he must now try to do more for him since it had become impossible to raise more fellow Protestants from Geneva or France to serve as soldiers: 'I should say nothing of him now if I were not amazed so oft as I see him. A very little fellow, son of a peasant bred to be a baker; at 20 years of age, with 18 men like himself, began to make war upon the King of France.' He went on to describe how Cavallier had kept a French army occupied for some eighteen months until finally the 'mighty Monarch' (Louis XIV) made an honourable settlement with him.[29] Hill described such men as being very devout and 'regular' and said that those who had left France must be returned there, where 'one Camisard is worth 100 refugees'.

Copies of letters also survive between Flotard and 'Chief' Roland, whose bravery, sadly, did not see him through the war. Roland wrote on 1 August 1704, saying that he had to have money as he was finding it very difficult to continue and that, owing to lack of funds, he was suffering desertions from amongst his own men. He said that the French had made overtures promising the Protestants a province of their own but Roland rejected the proposal outright. Three weeks later, Flotard sent Hill a long letter describing the circumstances of Roland's death.[30] It seems that on 18 August Roland was near Brignols (Brignon) in the Rhone Valley, near the Pont du Gard, with a dozen of his men, when they were approached by a man who said they should spend the night in the Château de Castlenau while he went to procure them some fish. It was a trick. He went to Uzès and reported the little band's presence to the local commandant. Early the following morning soldiers approached the castle and Roland and his followers did not have enough time to mount and gallop off. Roland was killed and five of his men captured. The five were broken on the wheel and their bodies, together with that of Roland, were burned. These horrible deaths served only to strengthen the resolve of their comrades.

The French could not manage to take Turin, and in May 1705 Hill was told that he must not yet leave as his presence was urgently required: 'It will be of great importance to the fleet that you be ready at hand to give intelligence to the Admirals when they arrive in the Mediterranean which we hope will be shortly, the fleet now being ready to sail.' It was an impressive one, with England putting 52 ships of the line to sea together with 18 supplied by the Dutch. The men of war were accompanied by a host of transport ships carrying 8,000 soldiers. Hill had obviously been planning some sort of journey, perhaps to Genoa, but not one which would take him home because Hedges plainly expected his absence only to be short. He was obviously fed up with his life in Turin and Savoy and longing to be back in England.

The fleet would eventually arrive in the Mediterranean to aid the army in Catalonia and help take Toulon and, hopefully, recapture Nice and Villa Franca. By early June it seemed unlikely that the Duke of Savoy was going to be in a position to help. This, as Lord Godolphin wrote to Hill that month, was a great pity since the French fleet, which was inferior to the English, could remain safely moored in Toulon until the allied fleet had sailed away for the winter, and then they would have the 'whole coast at their mercy'. Godolphin had written to the Duke to ask him to make this one great effort, but since the Duke had been forced to leave his territory at Chivas on 29 July, driven out by the Duc de la Feuillade after a staunch resistance lasting 42 days, this looked highly unlikely.

Nevertheless, Marlborough wrote that he was sending urgent letters to the Emperor in Vienna asking for Prince Eugene to be permitted to come to the aid of Savoy, adding that he feared any help would be too long in coming.

Correspondence flew by all means possible during the month of August between Peterborough, Secretary Hedges, Sir Cloudesley Shovel and the Duke of Marlborough. By 5 August Hill was plainly very concerned regarding Prince Eugene: 'We have heard here that P. Eugene came into Lombardy the end of April; we have heard that he passed the Oglio about the end of June. I hope he does the Emperor's business where he is; but he has done nothing for our relief here in Piedmont.'[31] At this time, Turin was virtually besieged and putting itself into a state to withstand such an event, although Hill was not convinced La Feuillade's intention was to try to take Turin at that moment. He did not consider the Frenchman had enough soldiers (no more than 17,000) so to do.[32] He wrote to Hedges and to Sir Cloudesley that he could not help suspecting that Victor Amadeus might be entering into some sort of arrangement with la Feuillade. To the Admiral, Hill wrote that he should keep this thought to himself because 'his Royal Highness has not yet given any public marks of his irresolution'. Truly Savoy was a very tricky 'ally'.

The enemy did not bother the city of Turin, and even dispatched two regiments down into Lombardy and another into Provence, which led Hill to be even more suspicious: if the Duc de la Feuillade did not require all these soldiers around Turin perhaps he really was negotiating with Victor Amadeus. In any event, Hill said they could not hold out for long without relief. Apparently la Feuillade had cheekily asked Savoy to send him rackets and balls, which did not look very threatening! Hill felt that when the English fleet (wherever it was) left for home in the winter and the French brought up some more troops from Languedoc, then Turin would fall very quickly. Although he had been told he could return home when it was appropriate, he obviously still felt he could not leave the sinking ship. He requested that his assistant, Chetwynd, be promoted and left in his place at Turin since he had already been there two years and was *au courant* with the intrigues, but this was not agreed to and someone else was to be sent from London.

Hill's letters now demonstrate that he could no longer press so hard in his requests for the fleet to come to the aid of Savoy; he felt too uncertain of Savoy's true intentions, even after Victor Amadeus came to ask him personally for the fleet to bring enough soldiers for his protection.[33] He wanted them to be landed at Nice and marched to Piedmont. Throughout August Hill wrote to London, and to Peterborough and Marlborough, saying that he was sure Savoy was negotiating with France, but that either he would not come down to their price or they would not come up to his: 'His Royal Highness, I believe, has been negotiating pretty warmly during all the month of August. Whether he would abuse his friends or his enemies, I cannot tell.'[34] Hill was now forced to send all his correspondence via Florence since the enemy was very 'curious of late to see all my letters'.

In the meantime, he was involved in a quarrel between the Maréchal de Staremberg and the Duke.[35] The Maréchal wished to return to Vienna and had even refused to undertake the implementation of some fortifications around Turin desired by the Duke. Victor Amadeus absolutely refused the Maréchal permission to leave before he received a reply to a letter he himself had written to the Emperor in Vienna. The old soldier was furious, expecting as he was the much more significant role of command of the Imperial Army in Hungary. Hill found himself caught in the middle, trying to keep the peace. He was afraid that if the row continued the Maréchal might just put himself at the head of the few Imperial troops in Savoy and march away with them to join Prince Eugene. That would have finished Savoy. Finally the old soldier agreed to await the return from Vienna of the messenger and Hill wrote, 'I think the storm is now over ... been in great disquiet this last week between two persons equally capable of the most desperate and violent resolutions.' In the end the Emperor ordered Staremberg to remain in Savoy. He did so unwillingly: 'he stays here at present, only as the Papists stay at Mass, without any zeal or devotion; and the Opus operatum has no manner of merit'.

Letters frequently fell into enemy hands, and Hill was not sure whether his own official letters of recall had been lost. He was constantly asking for official permission to leave, especially since, as of early October, the enemy seemed to have withdrawn its artillery from outside Turin and those in the city felt safe for the winter. By the end of the month, however, Turin had reason to believe that the Duc de la Feuillade was planning to return to trouble them again. In November Hill, who had had no word from Peterborough since the end of August, wrote to Hedges that Savoy was relying on the French being too busy in Spain to come and bother them. He also said they had successfully taken a French convoy near Lake Geneva. The convoy was carrying 30,000 pistoles to the army in Italy. In December Hill wrote to the Lord Treasurer that the ammunition they had been waiting for since April had finally arrived. Hill planned to send the four ships that brought it back to Peterborough fully victualled and with about 100,000 crowns sterling for the maintenance of the allied army in Spain. Hill had to arrange for this money to be available through various agents. He had also to arrange for agents in Genoa and Leghorn to give credit to the captains of these ships whilst they were being rapidly overhauled and resupplied.[36] The ships had brought news of the allied victories in Barcelona which cheered both Hill and the Duke. Hill had to travel to Genoa to make the complex arrangements, leaving

Chetwynd in Turin, and now he felt he could finally leave for home although he was patently a trifle guilty that he had not taken formal leave of the Duke. He was also concerned about the Sallien child who had still not been restored to his family. He met the parents in Genoa and learned that they were even contemplating travelling to London to petition the Queen for her protection. Hill said he hoped that would not be necessary and begged Hedges to speak to Count Maffei, the Duke of Savoy's representative in London. Hill said that, in truth, whatever Victor Amadeus might say about the matter being a cause for the judiciary of Savoy, nobody had stood in the way of the child's return except the Duke himself, who, as always, had full and total control.

Hill also described another little saga in which he had been involved. Apparently, a slave had escaped from one of the Duke of Doria's galleys and sought refuge on board one of the English ships in the harbour at Genoa. Genoa was, in theory, neutral and so ships and soldiers of both sides could be found there. This man was treated as a prisoner of war and put ashore outside the waters of the Republic. Subsequently, a warrant officer from the frigate *Newport* (one of Hill's 'fleet') was lured on board the Duke's galley and promptly clapped in chains. 'I could not bear the sight of one of the Queen's subjects here in the Duke of Doria's galleys and therefore I have got him out as well as I could. I am now studying how to be revenged fairly. Revenge is a virtue in this climate.' Hill had paid a large sum for the man's freedom and was hoping for reimbursement from the government.

He was still in Genoa in February 1706 when he wrote to Hedges saying that two of the ships had set sail for Leghorn to collect a third that they might sail in convoy back to the coast of Catalonia. They were to take especial care since the French fleet was in and out of Toulon and was said to know that the Queen's ships were carrying coin for the armies in Spain. Hill had been kept waiting in Genoa partly because his staff had not arrived from Turin, having been taken by the Spanish en route. The party was travelling on *laissez passers* signed by Prince de Vaudemont but in the name of Mr Chetwynd, who, at the last minute, had been required to stay in Turin by the Duke. Hill hoped to obtain their release shortly and this he managed two days later. He himself then set off for Bologna and then on to Venice, but his voyage was roundabout and difficult thanks to the French who had troops in the area around Padua and Ferrara. He had to travel via Ravenna and thence by sea to Venice. From Bologna he travelled in company with Prince d'Elbeuf, who having 'received some mortification at the Court of France is gone to Vienna to offer his services to the Emperor'. Another gentleman en route for Vienna was the Marquis de Langaterie, Lieutenant General of the French armies, who was also out of temper with the French military. A change of allegiance seems to have come about at the slightest provocation.

Hill reached Venice at the end of March 1706. He found the Republic in a poor state, 'devoured both by Germans and French. The only difference I can find is that the French have money and pay sometimes: the Germans have none.' Although he had no official accreditation to the Republic, Hill let it be known in his conversations with those in 'high places' that if the Republic was weary of its 'fatal neutrality', he would send to London and beg the Queen to send him her commands to treat with the Senate. He received no come back on this and accordingly left for Innsbruck, estimating that the Venetians would soon cry out for help from the Queen when they became a little more 'weary of their ill neighbours'. He was back in England by May 1706, when he wrote a paper to the Lord Treasurer setting out his appreciation of the situation in Europe.

Even as Hill wrote, Marlborough won his second decisive victory at Ramillies in the Netherlands, while events in Piedmont moved from near disaster to glorious triumph. In May 1706 la Feuillade laid siege to Turin. The Duke of Savoy escaped into open country, hoping to make contact with Prince Eugene, based at Garda. Twice French troops pursued the Duke into the Alpine valleys and on one occasion he took refuge among the Vaudois Protestants, who chose to shelter and support him against the French who would certainly destroy them should the Duke be defeated in the war. As it was, the French did not dare to enter the valleys inhabited by the Vaudois as they knew that they would be fiercely resisted and given no quarter.

In July 1706 Prince Eugene began his heroic march from Garda, up the Po valley, crossing rivers and avoiding French contingents, until, in early September, with Turin's defences already breached, he and his cousin the Duke effected a junction to the east of Turin. Their combined armies numbered 35,000 to the French 60,000, but from the top of the Superga hill the allied commanders could see that the French defences were, naturally, very weak on the west (French) side of the city. They marched round and attacked an already demoralised French army at its weakest point, while the defenders of Turin poured out to attack on a second front. The French fled and Louis XIV's dreams of dominance in Italy were at an end. When Marlborough heard of this glorious success he wrote of his feelings towards Eugene in a letter to his wife Sarah: 'It is impossible for me to express the joy it has given me; for I do not only esteem, but I really love that Prince.'

No English troops were involved when Turin was relieved—and Italy saved for the Austrians instead of the French—but English money brought by English ships had played a vital part in keeping the Duke of Savoy in the Alliance, and Richard Hill as Envoy Extraordinaire had contributed greatly to the eventual success of the grand strategy.

Although he was appointed to go to Turin once again in 1708, the journey never came to pass. The reason remains unknown, but ill health could have been the cause. In a letter written in August 1708 Hill informed the Comte de la Tour that he had come to the Hague to transact 'some little business with the authorities of the Admiralty' and that on the urgent orders of the Queen he would be continuing to Turin. He asked de la Tour to let him know what the Duke of Savoy required and told him to write to him in Frankfurt where he would be stopping en route to see the government's bankers, Couvreur. He said he would await de la Tour's reply before deciding whether or not to proceed to Turin. Hill was going to obtain the signing of a new treaty which was very secret. His health was not good and he had been constantly ill while in Turin in 1704, complaining especially of the extremes of temperature. It seems unlikely that he was looking forward to another sojourn there. In the event he did not have to proceed and the state of his health is probably the main reason why he did not undertake any further foreign missions. He was still involved with the Vaudois, and with arrangements for paying their subsidies which were described as 'royal pensions'. The last known communication on this subject is dated 1719. Following Queen Anne's death, the pensions continued to be paid under George I. Richard Hill appears to have retired officially from public life in 1708.

He had succeeded to Hawkstone on the death of his father in 1700, and after his apparent withdrawal from mainstream public affairs would have had time to plan the aggrandisement of the house and pleasure gardens, and to engage in the extensive purchase of more land and property. An ordained deacon, he is recorded in Bishop Burnet's *History of His Own Times* as taking priest's orders following his retirement from public affairs, and it is also said that he was offered six different bishoprics but declined them all. He was a Fellow of Eton College, where he kept rooms until the end of his life, and also a Fellow of the Royal Society.

Richard Hill's last years were passed under the rule of the Hanoverian King George I (1714-27). He was described by a contemporary as a moderate Tory 'of the sort who were earnest for the Succession of the House of Hanover' and evidently continued to move in the highest court and political circles despite his official retirement from public life.

In 1895, when the great bankruptcy sale took place at Hawkstone, dispersing the contents of the house which had been amassed over the preceding centuries, one of the most interesting and sought after lots was a 'fine piece of old silk tapestry (measuring 30in. x 24in.) representing a garden scene—the offerings of Flora to Venus attended by cupids and birds', according to the report in the *Shrewsbury Chronicle*. The tapestry had been mounted in walnut as a firescreen and bore the following inscription: 'This screen, the work of Queen Anne, was presented by Her Majesty to the Right Hon. Richard Hill, Ambassador Extraordinary to the Court of Turin, 1703.' It was bought for 82 guineas—a high price at the time—by a man who had come from Aberdeen for the sale.

Two of Richard Hill's major acquisitions were the purchase of the Tern estate at Atcham, in 1700, and Shenstone in Staffordshire in 1718. His purchases are detailed in an article in the *Transactions of the Shropshire Archaeological Society* written by Miss Jancey, a former Curator of the Shropshire Records Centre.[37] Tern Hall was built in 1701, even as the nations of Europe were preparing to go to war over the Spanish Succession. The estate was renamed Attingham in the 1780s. Through his brother John (described as an apothecary) and other agents, Hill also bought other parcels of land, large and small, to add to the Hawkstone estate. He was to leave Hawkstone to his nephew, Rowland, son of brother John. He also obtained a baronetcy for this young man. He was offered one for himself but, being childless, chose to request that it should go to the next generation in order that the title could be handed down.

Richard Hill must have thought carefully about how he left his property, in much the same way that the first Sir Rowland had done. He seems to have been close to his brother John, who lived at Wem and then at Lighteach. John, in acting as his brother's agent in the acquisition of property, had himself snapped up several good holdings in the area. John died in 1713, and his widow and children then moved into the Hall at Hawkstone, apparently staying there throughout the works of alteration and construction which commenced *c.*1720, with Mrs Hill taking an active part in the supervision of the work. The house as seen today dates largely from that period although every generation has had to add its own touch; sometimes happily and, on at least one occasion, disastrously.

Apart from Rowland's inheritance, Richard Hill left the other two main holdings to the sons of his twin sisters, Margaret (married to Thomas Harwood, a merchant of Shrewsbury) and Elizabeth (married to Samuel Barbour). Both heirs assumed the name of Hill.

Samuel Barbour Hill (1691-1758) received Shenstone, Staffordshire. He was educated at Eton and at St John's, Cambridge before studying for the Bar at the Middle Temple 1708. He went on the Grand Tour, where his uncle gave him introductions to most of the courts of Europe. Following the death of Queen Anne, he served as Latin Secretary to George I and entered Parliament as the member for Lichfield in 1715. He was apparently classed as a Tory 'who might often vote Whig', according to Romney and Sedgewick, and, indeed, in every recorded division he voted against the government. He apparently did not care for the business of Parliament and retired in 1722. He seems to have been close to his uncle and stayed in Cleveland Court and at Richmond while he was an M.P. He achieved a grand marriage, his wife being the Lady Elizabeth Stanhope, daughter of the Earl of Chesterfield, and Richard Hill settled more property on this nephew at the time of his marriage. Unfortunately, Lady Elizabeth died of smallpox which she apparently contracted when attending the Coronation of George II in 1727. The couple had no children and Samuel's property was divided between Hawkstone and Attingham following his death. He left a large sum of money for those days—said to be £300,000. A fine portrait exists of Samuel Barbour Hill.

Thomas (Harwood) Hill (1692-1781) was the son of Richard Hill's sister, Margaret. Margaret was first married to a Richard Atcherley, and after his death she married a prosperous draper called Thomas Harwood. Thomas and Margaret had been living in Shrewsbury but now moved to Tern. Their son, Thomas, was to found the Attingham line of the family, which was to take the name of Noel-Hill and the title of Baron Berwick at the end of the century.[38] Richard Hill sent this nephew to the continent, where he stayed in Hamburg for a time having been urged by his uncle to 'employ himself in reading, writing and arithmetic' and in learning German. He was then told to go to Amsterdam where he was articled to the great banking and merchant house of Clifford. He apparently returned home in 1721 and there are records of loans made by him to many prominent people, some very large. He sat as Member of Parliament for Shrewsbury from 1749-68.[39] His first marriage to Anne Powys, daughter of a prominent lawyer, Richard Powys, brought a son, 'pretty Dick', who died young, and two girls. Anne herself died young, and from his second marriage to Susannah Maria Noel came two sons: the elder, Samuel, who turned out to be a wild and profligate young man, died aged 23; Noel, the thirteenth child, was destined to become the 1st Lord Berwick. Thomas himself seems to have been an able man of business.

2. Samuel Barbour Hill (1691-1758), Richard Hill's nephew.

A second son of Thomas and Margaret (yet another Rowland, just for simplicity) never married, despite his uncle Richard's efforts to promote a match with a daughter of the Bishop of Coventry and Lichfield. This fell through, and Richard was reported as saying, 'I must comfort myself that marriages are made in heaven, and that my nephew has few friends there.' Rowland was the Rector of Hodnet until a rather early death in 1733. (This anecdote has also been attributed, erroneously, to Sir Rowland Hill, 1st Baronet of Hawkstone, in speaking of his eldest son and heir Richard. In view of the fact that one of the young men concerned became a priest and the other was renowned as a devout evangelical layman, perhaps they were not so friendless after all.)

Richard Hill lived at the Trumpeting (sometimes Trumpeter's) House, Old Palace Yard, Richmond and Cleveland Court, St James. The house at Richmond was part of the old Royal Palace and Hill took a lease on it in 1700 and proceeded to build a new house, which still exists. It took its name from the two 16th-century stone figures of trumpeters on either side of the doorway. He amassed a fine library and collected silver, jewellery and pictures. Most of these were sent to Hawkstone on his death. A magnificent silver-gilt ewer is in the British Collection of the Victoria and Albert Museum. It was made for Hill by David Willaume and bears the London hallmark for 1700-1. Another by the same maker, but in silver, is dated 1715. It is on view at Attingham.

Although it is frequently said that Richard Hill did not visit Shropshire for many years prior to his death, it is not possible to be sure of this. What is certain is that he took the closest possible interest, albeit from afar, in the purchases of land made there and in Staffordshire, and in the work carried on at Hawkstone in the 1720s. He also planned in detail the tomb which he had constructed for his burial in Hodnet church. William Price the mason was ordered to start work on the vault in 1722. His sister-in-law Mrs Hill ordered two coffins, one for Richard and one to contain all the bones of earlier members of the family, which sounds a trifle gruesome. Richard Hill was asked to send from London the marble for the vault steps; the rest of the vault was to have square Grinshill flags. The grey marble monumental stone was carved in London in 1726, and was carted to Hodnet with great technical difficulty and at considerable expense, owing to its size and weight.

Richard Hill certainly wrote his own inscription, in Latin, for the monument:

> Here interred amongst his Ancestors, lies Richard Hill, of Hawkstone, in the County of Salop, the Son, Grandson, Great Grandson, Brother and Uncle of the Rowlands: known amongst his relations for his paternal care: who for nine years, was Paymaster General to the Army in Flanders, under King William, and at the same time Envoy Extraordinary to many Princes: at last returning home he was made one of the Lords of the Treasury, until the death of that great King: but about the beginning of the Queen's Reign he was constituted one of the four Privy Counsellors to Prince George of Denmark, all which posts he diligently discharged, till, at last, by that Great Queen, he was sent Envoy Extraordinary with full power to all the Princes in Italy, except the Pope. He made a most happy Peace with Victor Amadeus, Duke of Savoy, afterwards King of Sicily, a Prince of invincible courage.

> Here at last, in the hope of rising again, he rests,
> Being tired with war and travel.
>
> He caused this Monument to be erected Anno Domini
> 1726, in the 72nd year of his age.
>
> I've lived, and served the Lord's anointed,
> As 'twas to me by God appointed

Richard, the 'Great', Hill died on 11 June 1727, aged 73. He rose the highest and brought the most to the Hill family in terms of material benefit. He was undoubtedly a very astute man.

CHAPTER THREE

The Evangelist Brothers:
Sir Richard Hill, Bt, MP (1733-1809) and the
Reverend Rowland Hill, Renowned Preacher (1744-1833)

THE 'GREAT' HILL had undoubtedly both continued the 'rise' begun by his predecessor, the Lord Mayor, and then 'shone'. If his 18th-century successors did not rise much further, they certainly made some mark in the world and entered their names in the history books. So who were the interesting men and women—not surprisingly, chiefly men—who followed the Great Hill?

It was his nephew, Rowland, who inherited Hawkstone and enjoyed the title of baronet which his uncle had obtained for him. He seems to have lived a fairly quiet life, embellishing and expanding his house and starting to create the great landscape park that would be completed by his son, the whimsical, eccentric and imaginative second baronet, Sir Richard. The money spent on this very grandiose undertaking—one of the wonders of English landscape architecture—was probably too great for the income of an estate that was not run competently, but, alas, this fact would be discovered far too late in the next century. In any event, Sir Richard acted charitably in employing as many labourers as he did in the creation of the Park and its follies, and if he is to be blamed for unnecessary expenditure it should be for permitting his brother, John, to take on their cousin, William of Attingham, in the 1796 Shrewsbury election contest.[1]

Sir Rowland held the position of Sheriff in 1732 and served as Member of Parliament for Lichfield from 1734.[2] A son of the Augustan age, he was father of a number of children including two remarkable sons who embraced with enthusiasm the Evangelistic outlook of their mid-18th-century generation. They became preachers, a development with which their father was clearly not at all comfortable. To be an 'enthusiast' was definitely not considered *comme il faut* amongst the upper classes. Sir Rowland would doubtless have concurred with the sentiments of Bishop Joseph Butler (1692-1752), who addressed John Wesley with the notorious words: 'Sir, the pretending to extraordinary revelations and gifts of the Holy Ghost is a horrid thing, a very horrid thing.' That the sons of Hawkstone did not share this opinion was underlined when their father sent Richard to try to prevent Rowland, his younger brother, from addressing the huge gatherings of people that always attended his outdoor meetings, and bring him home. The elder brother caught up with the younger outside Bristol, where Rowland was addressing a large crowd of miners. Many of the congregations that gathered to hear this man, possibly the greatest of the itinerant preachers, could number thousands. Instead of trying to bring his brother home, Richard preached a great sermon himself.[3] The total commitment to their faith demonstrated by both the brothers, and others of their generation, is difficult to comprehend. They were responding to the Spirit of their Age, which produced the Wesleys, Robert Raikes with his conviction that education should be offered to the labouring classes on Sundays, and men such as William Wilberforce. Richard Hill managed to remain within the Church of England, a point he frequently made, whereas Rowland, while initially trying hard to do so, did not.[4]

Richard Hill was undoubtedly an extraordinary man. As far as one can discover, almost all the Hills, and certainly all the successful ones, were deeply devout; their religion was an integral part of everyday life, an attitude which was not commonplace at that time. It appeared to sit easily with them that they also hunted, shot, fished and fought. Although Sir Richard does not appear to have been personally interested in blood sports, he was certainly totally opposed to the 'sport' of baiting. He even introduced a Parliamentary Bill at the end of his long career in the House of Commons to abolish the baiting of bulls and other animals, and received a huge quantity of letters on the subject. Fighting or baiting of dogs, bulls and cocks was widespread.

It is evident that the most successful Hills throughout the 16th, 17th and 18th centuries were highly intelligent, hard-working, religious and, with the exception of the Reverend Rowland, single; none had any children. Perhaps this enabled them to channel their energies beyond the home hearth. Rowland married within the family, by choosing Mary Tudway; her brother, Clement, was Member of Parliament for Wells and Father of the House for many years. Clement was married to Rowland's sister, Elizabeth, and the use of the name Clement within the family probably originates with him.

So what were they like, these two Evangelist Hills? Richard, the elder, inherited large estates and a title following the death of his father in 1783, and Rowland was one of several younger brothers with no land and, in comparison, very little money; just a younger son's portion. Not that he would have minded; a great inheritance would probably have been given away in a flash. Were the brothers so very different? Both were undoubtedly eccentric; both had pricking social consciences. The Hills of Hawkstone were Tory and were known to be Masons (the Attingham branch was considered Whig until Noel Hill changed his allegiance by voting for Pitt's India Bill in 1784, and received a barony for his pains!), but Richard sat in the House of Commons for nearly thirty years as an Independent, only voting as his active conscience dictated and speaking on a variety of issues. These speeches were long and full of religious allusions and quotations, and although they provoked a great deal of ridicule they were usually quite witty. When he caught the Speaker's eye other members tended to listen. He seemed peculiar to many but even his political enemies had to acknowledge that he could never be accused of wrongdoing. Sidney, his 19th-century biographer, described him as 'a man little understood because his views were far in advance of the age in which he lived'.[5]

Rowland lived to 89, dying some twenty-five years after his older sibling and preaching and working for the Lord until the very end of his life. The brothers were very similar in their personal appearance, and their leading mental characteristics were in many respects of the same kind. Richard was by nature the more studiously inclined. 'In ready wit and humour and presence of mind, they were nearly equal but in the power of imagination and quickness of perception, Rowland not only surpassed his brother but nearly every other man of his day.' It was this and such a patently innocent zeal in his faith that drew the enormous crowds to the younger brother's meetings and sermons. Congregations often stood in the rain for several hours to hear him speak.

If Sir Richard did not marry, he was certainly a 'family' man in other senses and took much interest in his younger brothers in their youth. He was many years older than Robert (born 1746), Rowland (born 1744), a number of sisters and also brother John (born 1740). The youngest of all was Brian (born 1750), yet another clergyman. Richard remained very close to Rowland and undoubtedly helped to keep him going during his itinerant life. He was also a large contributor when the Surrey Chapel was built.

John, next brother to Richard and eventual heir to the baronetcy, was the father of 16 children, and must have been of a very different cut to his older brother. He was the father of the four soldier brothers (Rowland, Robert, Clement and Thomas Noel) who contributed so much to the Peninsular Campaign in the early years of the 19th century. He lived at Prees Hall before succeeding to his brother's title in 1808, and it is likely he was the typical country squire, who enjoyed sports and country life, and found his evangelistic brothers hard to understand.

Richard's letters to his brothers Rowland and Robert when they were at Eton are fascinating. Very rarely do they contain the sort of family gossip or normal questions or news one might expect from an older brother to his siblings at public school. Instead they are long, wordy epistles devoted to saving their souls. He plainly did not turn them away from religion since Robert also took Orders and became the Vicar of Bolas. He married an heiress from Cheshire, Mary, daughter of John Wilbraham of the Hough, and founded another dynasty of Hills in Cheshire—the Hills of the Hough. Richard, himself, was educated at Westminster School in London and Magdalen College, Oxford.[6] It is not known why he went to Oxford rather than to Cambridge, where his predecessors had gone, and to which the Lord Mayor had given money.

Richard's early years involved a struggle to come to the Christian faith, and he wrote an account of his long road to conversion. 'Like his brother Rowland of whose conversion he was made the instrument, Sir Richard was designed for extraordinary purposes in peculiar times,' wrote Sidney some thirty years after his death. Richard wrote of 'first dawnings' at the age of only eight or nine years, but went on to say that this 'was but a transitory glimpse of the heavenly gift' before he 'returned to folly with the same eagerness as before'. He was surely just a normal small boy! He continued by saying that his 'superficial repentances and resolutions' continued during his time at Westminster, and altogether he wrote as if he were the most evil of boys, guilty of every sort of wickedness. He next hoped that his confirmation would help him. It did not; he still had doubts. Even allowing for the language of the time, it is a harsh self-analysis; he was alternately atheist or Christian, longing to believe totally but constantly troubled with doubts. He borrowed Dr Beveridges's 'Private Thoughts' and wrote of rejoicing 'with joy unspeakable and full of glory', but this rapture soon faded. All in all, his account gives a rather naive description of the long road he travelled. What young man does not have serious doubts on a wide variety of subjects, including religion?

After Oxford, Richard spent two years doing the 'young gentleman's tour' of the continent, returning at the age of 23 or twenty-four. Some of the houses and their landscaped grounds which he visited on his Grand Tour definitely influenced him when he continued his father's work on the Park at Hawkstone.

After several unsuccessful efforts to obtain help within the Established Church, Richard wrote to John William Fletcher, then serving as curate at Madeley, in Shropshire. Fletcher was Swiss. He had anglicised his name from Jean Guillaume de la Fléchère and came to England as tutor to a family called Burchell. In 1751 he became tutor to Samuel and Noel, the young sons of Thomas Hill of Tern Hall (later Attingham) by his second wife. Fletcher loved the country life of Shropshire. He was ordained priest in 1757 by the Bishop of Hereford and became curate to Rowland Chambré, a Hill cousin, at nearby Madeley. It was not long before his attraction to 'Methodism' upset both his patron and many of his parishioners. Richard Hill wrote anonymously to Fletcher asking for advice and requesting a meeting at an inn which he named and which was some four or five miles from Madeley. Fletcher duly arrived at the designated inn and they discussed Richard's doubts and fears at length before praying together. Initially Richard was comforted, but then slid back into his old state of mind.

Fletcher reassured him that he was undoubtedly on the road to true salvation, but Richard was still not convinced. Fletcher played a considerable part in the Evangelical Movement and in the lives of the Hill family. He was apparently a truly saintly man. On one occasion, after he had preached at Hodnet, Jane Hill wrote to her young brother Rowland at Cambridge: 'Mr Fletcher has preached at Hodnet, and given great offence. I hope his labour was not wholly in vain, though I have not heard of any good being done ...'.[7]

A stay in Oxford during Lent 1758 seems to have been a turning point for Richard, and his 'conversion', as he himself calls it, was more or less completed shortly afterwards during a period when he suffered from a severe illness. In London he also met like-minded others: 'It pleased God to make me acquainted with many of his people to whom my heart was immediately knit with the closest affection.' It was probably at this time that he met the Wesley brothers, George Whitefield, the Countess of Huntingdon, Lord Dartmouth and Lord Teignmouth, amongst many others of similar bent. Dartmouth and Teignmouth became his very close friends. The families later became inter-married when Sir Richard's nephew, Thomas Noel Hill, married Maria Shore, Teignmouth's daughter. Richard met frequently to discuss matters of faith with Dartmouth, a generous and hospitable Christian whose 'mental qualities and habits of life harmonised with his own'. Men such as Dartmouth, Whitefield and Fletcher had developed very thick skins to ignore or combat the 'sneers and contempt of most of the laity, and what is still more awful ... the virulent opposition of great numbers of the clergy in those days of darkness'. The royal family, however, approved of some of the Evangelists. Queen Charlotte described Lord Dartmouth as 'one of the best of men', and King George said of him, 'They call his Lordship an enthusiast; but surely he says nothing on the subject of religion but what any Christian may and ought to say.' True, but most others did not comprehend this and shied away from displays of 'enthusiasm'. Sidney, Richard's biographer, writing c.1840, commented 'Yet there was never a time in which vital godliness was more hated and opposed by the higher classes who were generally in a state of appalling ignorance respecting the plainest truths of the Bible and condemned as "Methodists" all ministers who even mentioned the name of Christ in their sermons.'

John Wesley did not visit Shropshire until 1761, but 'Methodism' had been developing there since 1744, and its growth in the 1750s owed much to the sanctity of John Fletcher, who had started Methodist societies in his parish of Madeley and, through his friendship with Richard Hill, in Wem. In St Mary Woolnoth Church in the City of London, of which John Newton, the converted slave trader, was rector, there is an autograph letter which Newton wrote in 1764 to Thomas Powys of Berwick near Shrewsbury, looking forward to his visit as he made his way through Shropshire fulfilling preaching engagements. He was one of the great Church of England evangelicals, and encouraged William Wilberforce in his campaign for the abolition of slavery. Hawkstone under Sir Richard became a notable evangelical centre after his father Sir Rowland's death in 1783. Sadly, a dispute during the 1770s brought about a split between Richard Hill and Fletcher.

Selina, Countess of Huntingdon (1707-91) had met John Fletcher and he often preached for her. She built chapels in several fashionable spa towns such as Bath, and patronised a seminary for the training of Calvinist 'Methodist' ministers at Trevecca, near Talgarth in mid-Wales. Her circle came to be known as 'Lady Huntingdon's Connexion' or, more briefly, 'the Connexion'.

In 1777 one William Sellon disputed the right of evangelical clergy of the Established Church to preach in an unconsecrated chapel in Spa Fields in London. The Bishop of London's Consistory Court upheld the complaint and the chapel was closed. Lady Huntingdon intervened and bought the chapel, believing that her own domestic chaplains would be protected. Sellon complained again, again successfully. The result was that her principal preachers were forced to leave her 'Connexion', and those that remained seceded from the Established Church. These chapels were then registered as Dissenting Meeting Houses with their own ministers, under the terms of the Toleration Act. Rowland Hill often preached for Lady Huntingdon in his young days, but on her death she left specific instructions that he was not to preach in any of 'her' chapels. She was apparently well-disposed towards him but there was some sort of falling-out which led to the ban.

The household at Hawkstone was not spared Sir Richard's fervour. He placed a Bible in his servants' hall, evidently a rare thing in those days, and lent books to them. His own personal servant, Giles Archer, was a most devoted Christian and both Sir Richard and his sister Jane left moving accounts of his illness and death.[8] Jane was evidently a staunch supporter of her Evangelist brothers, and she wrote to them at school almost as often as Richard did. Apparently her character 'exhibited a most attractive union of the beauty, wisdom, firmness and dignity of vital Christianity'. In Sidney's biography of Sir Richard long letters are quoted, but Sidney does not make clear to whom they were addressed. They are almost without exception totally devoted to the glory of God.

Perhaps Richard Hill was a bit of a prig![9] The Shawbury 'Wakes' gave great scope for 'mischief' and in 1768 the vicar begged Richard, who was patron of the living, to have the disorderly people arrested. However, Andrew Corbet, on whose land Shawbury sat, objected strenuously to any interference and wrote tartly to his neighbour at Hawkstone: 'When he shall stand in need of Mr Hill's assistance to regulate the diversions of his tenants, he shall then be obliged to him for the favour of it; and whenever Mr Hill shall desire Mr Corbet's assistance in Hodnet parish will readily return the compliment but would not presume to intermeddle unasked or unrequested.' The race meetings at Shrewsbury, Shawbury, Ludlow and Bridgnorth were, according to Sir Richard, the scene of much 'rioting and rabble', but they were great social affairs and, in an era when there was little scope for entertainment, offered a welcome chance for working people to have fun. The horse racing was usually accompanied by other diversions such as cock fighting, pig chasing, foot races and other bizarre contests; in 1796 at Shawbury there was a carthorse race, and in 1799 a race for 'turtle and buck' (tortoise and hare?).

By 1767 Richard Hill was taking an increasing interest in the efforts to promote 'the cause of truth at Oxford'. The university authorities had demonstrated that they wanted none of this and made clear their intention to suppress any attempt of this kind, together with its authors. The Hill brothers received most of their information from John Hallward, a young and somewhat impetuous man who had begun preaching under the auspices of Richard at Hodnet and carried on a busy correspondence with Rowland; he evidently suffered the same sort of parental opposition to his work as the younger Hill. A group of young men, rapidly growing in numbers, met on Sunday evenings in a private house in Oxford for prayer and conversation and, on occasion, to hear a sermon. The Bishop of Oxford protested and accused the revivalists of schism and Antinomianism. This disapproval in high places did not serve to discourage those who attended the meetings and they continued to grow in number until the university began a real persecution.[10] In the following year, 1768, charges were laid against some of these enthusiasts by a tutor of St Edmund's Hall called Higson, initially naming six students of that college. He complained to the Principal of St Edmund's Hall, Dr Dixon, and was rather annoyed when the good Doctor said he could not find any fault with the students 'for having adopted expressions that were Scriptural and authorised by the offices of our own Church'. Higson then set about finding valid complaints against the students and the charges were heard by the Vice Chancellor of the University and his Assessors. The students were declared 'guilty' of crimes worthy of expulsion and were forthwith expelled. It now appeared that the young men had deviated in certain respects from university rules, but not in anything connected with religious observation. Later, Dr Dixon told Richard Hill that he 'never remembered in his own or in any other College, six youths whose lives were so exemplary and who behaved themselves in a more humble, regular, peaceable manner'.

Richard Hill now spoke up for these victims. He published a pamphlet, *Pietas Oxoniensis*, that was to become very widely read. Unfortunately, as was often the case with his publications, his arguments and the language he employed aroused hostile feelings even in people who might have supported him. The charges brought against the students to which Richard Hill drew attention were threefold: first, that three of the accused were bred to *trades* and that both these men and two of the others were 'destitute of such a knowledge in the learned languages as is necessary for performing the usual exercises of the said Hall, and of the University'. It seems a pity that none of this had been discovered before the students began their studies. The second accusation was that all six were 'enemies to the doctrine and discipline of the Church of England' and, thirdly, young Middleton was accused of being 'an enemy to the doctrine and discipline of the Church of England as appears by his officiating as a minister in holy orders, although a layman'. There were further accusations of disrespect to their tutor, etc. The only things that were proved were illiteracy, with Mathews declared guilty of being a weaver and of ignorance, Jones of being a barber and not proficient in Latin and Greek, and Shipman of being a draper and illiterate. Middleton was held to be 'guilty' of Methodism, Kay of attending Mrs Durbridge's, which was where the Sunday meetings were held, Grove of preaching and Methodism, and Blatch of being a gentleman without any school learning, although he was not expelled. In other words, if you were an ignorant 'gentleman' you could remain. Controversy raged and Richard Hill frequently (perhaps too frequently) picked up his pen to support the wretched students and to expose the prejudices of their accusers.

In 1769 William Romaine, a saintly and religious man, was invited to preach at St Chad's Church, Shrewsbury, the original church, which collapsed in 1788. Mr Romaine 'did not lose that opportunity of declaring the gospel of Christ without reserve, which excited, as it did at that time ... all over the kingdom, the bitterest hostility against him'.[11] Apparently the vicar of the parish, Dr Adams, followed him into the vestry after he had delivered his sermon, and said in a very angry voice, 'Sir, my congregation is not used to such doctrine, and I hope will never hear such again.' Mr Romaine meekly accepted Dr Adams' stern rebuke and the Doctor took the opportunity, two weeks later, to deliver a violent sermon in reply. It was thought this would end the matter, but Adams chose to print his sermon and it went on sale in London. Sir Richard was moved to respond. His reply, in the form of a letter to Dr Adams on his Sermon, was duly published and bought by a wide public and quickly ran to four editions. The tract was publicised as being by the author of *Pietas Oxoniensis*.

Apart from his religious activities, although he did his best to involve the one with the other, Richard Hill was much involved in the political life of the time, entering Parliament as Member for Shropshire in 1780, at the height of the American War of Independence. After the British Army, led with poor judgement by General Burgoyne, had been defeated at the Battle of Saratoga in October 1777, the English saw that their American colonies were not going to be easily subdued and an order was issued in March 1778 for the Shropshire Militia to be put under orders. Noel Hill of Attingham was Lieutenant Colonel of the regiment and he and his wife, Anne Vernon, seem to have rather enjoyed the social events that went with the life in cantonments or camp in Kent and later in Devon.[12] In the event, the regiment was never sent to America and finally marched back to Shropshire without having seen any action.

War dragged on until October 1781 when Lord Cornwallis together with his whole army surrendered at Yorktown to an alliance of French troops and a largely untrained militia, poorly armed but brilliantly led by George Washington. It was against the background of these unfolding events, when the strength of Lord North's leadership of the government was waning, that Richard Hill was returned to Parliament in the election of 1780. He was the first Evangelical to sit in the House. He declared his motto to be 'Pro Christo et Patria' and he always 'conducted himself in the strictest sense of the expression, as a Christian senator'. According to Sidney, 'No man was ever more thoroughly divested of all fear of the ridicule of the world and if at times he unnecessarily exposed himself to it, he acted upon an honest principle and with a view to prove that religion was falsely accused of generating moroseness and gloom.' He, himself, was certainly never gloomy.

It was a time of great orators in the House: Burke, Fox, Sheridan, Pitt, Wilberforce. Hill was a Member who was always heard attentively, even if his constant religious allusions were often derided. At the end of a debate on peace negotiations with America he rose to speak. Sir Richard declared himself to be in favour of peace and that nothing else could save the Empire, but as to the coalition between Fox and Lord North he had heard of that night, he reprobated it in the most ironical terms, and declared 'that the coming together of Lord North and Mr Fox would, like the meeting of an acid and an alkali, cause only a violent fermentation which would destroy them both'.[13] The King himself, who had long supported North and refused to consider his frequent requests to be relieved of office, and who disliked Fox intensely, could see that if the two were joined in a confederacy, Fox's talents would leave Lord North with little or no influence. At this time, when King and country were coming to terms with the loss of the American colonies, politics entered a strange, unsettled period. Lord Rockingham died late in 1782, to be followed in office briefly by the unpopular Lord Shelburne; then followed the short-lived Fox/North coalition. In 1782 Sir Richard voted against the government saying, 'he was a supporter of government; for he maintained just government by removing bad governors'.[14]

After Fox's India Bill was defeated in the Lords by 75-57 the King invited young William Pitt to form a government in December 1783. He was just 24 years old, son of 'the Great Commoner', the Earl of Chatham. Pitt was generally popular with the Tories despite the first mumblings of reform and anti-slavery measures. In 1784 he introduced a revised India Bill, bringing the East India Company under British Cabinet control, although it retained its trading monopolies. Noel Hill, also a member for Shropshire, received his peerage as a result of his support for Pitt at this time, becoming 1st Lord Berwick.[15]

Richard Hill was a friend and supporter of Pitt, but that did not mean he approved of all his Bills by any means. One to which he took great exception, and spoke against at great length, was the proposed tax on bricks. Wittily and, as usual, at length, he proposed other items that might be taxed that would not bear so heavy a burden on the poor. The first was a Sunday toll to be paid at all turnpikes throughout the kingdom. At the time it was only imposed around the largest towns and was the source of much revenue. Hill suggested that it be extended nationwide, adding that it would certainly only affect the commerce of Sabbath-breaking. He estimated at the very least it would bring in £15,000 p.a. Then he proposed a tax on corks, a third on shot, powder, guns and pistols, except for the use of the Army or Navy, another on pins, needles and fans, a fifth on prints and printed music, and a sixth on places of entertainment such as the Ranelagh Gardens, Vauxhall, Sadlers Wells, or Astleys, home of the famous circus. He proposed that such taxes would affect neither the poor nor the industrious, injure no business and take nothing out of a man's pocket but that which he could spare. He had many other items to propose for taxation including newspapers, although he was aware of what a tender subject that was! Newspapers seldom appear in a man's epitaph, but they did in Richard Hill's. He seems to have held a remarkably contemporary suspicion of them.

William Wilberforce entered the House of Commons in the same session as Richard Hill. A close friend of Pitt since their Cambridge days, he was also a great friend of both Richard and Rowland Hill, though 26 years younger than Richard. In 1785, during a tour of the continent, he became 'converted' to Evangelicalism while staying in Nice. His decision led him to withdraw for a while from fashionable society and to lead a strictly religious life. He became deeply devout and gathered round him a group known as 'the Saints'. He seems to have been a genuinely good man and it is said that his charm and transparent kindliness and simplicity made him popular even with his political enemies. He is best known for his work in bringing about the eventual abolition of the slave trade in 1807 and of slavery in all British colonies in July 1833 just six days before his death. This came into effect one year later in 1834. Many of the rich and influential people had vested interests in seeing that the Bill made agonisingly slow progress thanks either to their ownership of slaves on West Indian plantations or their activities in the transport of the wretched human cargo.

There is some family correspondence relating to this topic. Sir Richard's nephew John had married Elizabeth Cornish. The Cornish family lived in the West Country, where Elizabeth's father was a surgeon, and owned land with slaves in Jamaica. A letter dated 12 August 1828, only five years before the Bill's final passage, was addressed to her by a Mr Smith in Spanish Town who wanted to settle her share in the Cumberland Plantation.[16] He proposed that she settle it on her niece, Mary. There were apparently 34 slaves and if she wished to keep her share there were various formalities to be gone through involving the wretched slaves being 'valued', 'an unpleasant proceeding to them and leading to doubts as to who is their owner and what is their destination'. Her portion was so tied up that he recommended she convey her rights for a full consideration which she could then dispose of for Mary's benefit and enquired whether £500 would be acceptable.[16]

Wilberforce also pressed for a more humane criminal system and founded, in 1787, the Proclamation Society, which was replaced in 1802 by the Society for the Suppression of Vice. Both were the subject of much derision ... but not by his fellow Evangelicals! He was a member of the 'Clapham Sect' which included John Shore, created Lord Teignmouth, and Zachary Macaulay. Teignmouth (1751-1834) had spent his early career in India where he was Governor General in 1792. He was the first President of the British and Foreign Bible Society and took an active part in the religious controversies of the day. He voted to remove /exclude all apocryphal books from the Bible. Teignmouth was not a brilliant man but an able administrator. His daughter, Maria, married Thomas Noel Hill, nephew of Sir Richard and brother of the 1st Viscount.

This period has been called the Age of Revolution, and the new peace with a now independent America was shortly followed by the violence of revolution in France. The English, including Pitt, seem to have been initially rather indifferent to the upheavals across the Channel and Sir Richard and brother Brian set off for Sicily in late 1790 without any qualms, when much of Europe looked on with mounting apprehension at political developments in France. The Paris massacres of 1792 horrified the English and early enthusiasts like Wordsworth rapidly revised their opinions. Once started, the movement generally gathered momentum, becoming unstoppable during the aptly named Reign of Terror (1793-4).

By this time, Sir Richard Hill was actively engaged in the landscaping of the Park at Hawkstone, already a well-established tourist attraction.[17] This aspect of his life's work shows a side of his nature that contrasts with the fervent Evangelist. He was certainly a romantic and the various beauties of the Park, both natural and man-made, were often the subject of his poetry and prayers.

Another event in the 1790s was the founding on the estate of Industry Hall, designed to give some education and training to children of the estate workers.[18]

Needless to say, the school was founded on sound religious principles and each day began with prayers. Some of the prayers were the work of Sir Richard, others of his youngest brother, Brian, who took an active part in the running of the school. It seems that the main activity was the working of wool. According to Sidney, the fleeces were sent to the Hall to be 'picked' by one set, 'carded' by another, 'spun' by a third and finally knitted as stockings or made into rugs. Proceeds from the sale of these items went to buy supplies for the school and help clothe those children that needed it. The Reverend Brian Hill was then Vicar of Weston under Redcastle, just outside the Park, and was described as being a 'man of elegant mind and of engaging manners'. For all these attributes he was yet another Hill who never married! He was a neighbour and close friend of the well-known hymn composer Bishop Reginald Heber, who was Rector of nearby Hodnet before going to India where he served as Bishop of Calcutta. His family, the Heber-Percys, still live in Hodnet. He was in the habit of trying out his compositions on Brian Hill, of whose literary judgement he is said to have held a high opinion.

All through this part of his life Sir Richard employed scores of men on the estate. Many of these were engaged in creating the Hawk Lake and the Caves, or forming the terraces and other fantastic and romantic scenes that are to be found in the Park. In employing so many labourers on the construction of the landscaped features of the Park he kept bread on the tables of these men and their families. Hawkstone was one of the early houses to open its park to the public, and the great numbers who came to enjoy the 'sublime' experience inspired the construction of the *Hawkstone Inn*, where visitors might stay while they explored the Park.

In 1791 Sir Richard and his youngest brother made a tour through Sicily and Calabria.[19] We have some of Sir Richard's letters home, and Brian kept a journal of the trip. It was not without its moments of danger, which is hardly surprising, given the part of the world they travelled through, well-known for its robbers and bandits. The party spent Holy Week in Rome and was duly shocked by the 'Popish' celebrations of Easter. They must have left England in the autumn of 1790 because we know they had reached Loreto in Italy by 11 December. In February 1791 Sir Richard wrote a long letter to his brother Rowland and his wife Mary, describing the first part of the journey. The ceremonies they had witnessed at Loreto were of great magnificence, it being the period of the *santa casa* ... or 'holy house'. This festival commemorated the story of when the Turks overran the Holy Land and angels carried the house of the Virgin Mary to Dalmatia, where it was left for a few years, but then, insufficient respect being shown it, the angels returned and carried it to Loreto. Here it remained on top of a hill until some time in the 15th century, when the Virgin appeared to a holy man in his sleep and told him of the miracle. Word reached the Pope, who ordered that a magnificent church be erected on the site. The Hawkstone party were amazed by the glitter of the ceremonies which commemorated 'this nonsensical tale'. The celebrations ended with a two-hour long cannonade in the middle of the night to announce the arrival of the 'holy house', at which point Sir Richard thought their ancient, crumbling inn would collapse.

Sir Richard describes their arrival in Rome on 14 December, when they had the luck to see the Holy Father (Pope Pius VI) in St Peter's, but the party was shocked—again—by 'the blessed father repeatedly making the lowest obeisance that his old body could stoop to; he then kissed the feet of the image (of the statue described as being that of St Peter) and rubbed his head against them just like a purring cat when she is pleased, then kissed and bowed, and bowed and kissed again.' Sir Richard continues: 'After a few more childish ceremonies, the Man of Sin left St Peter's and got into his carriage which was waiting at the door with four mules, to take him out an airing.' The Hawkstone party only stayed ten days in Rome as they intended to stop again on their return journey.

Next they went to Naples, where they spent five weeks and saw Vesuvius together with every other place of interest. They left Naples at the end of January and arrived in Palermo 25 hours later. The boat had contained a strange group of passengers consisting of Italians and 'Sclavonians', two priests, a madman and a murderer. The last was being taken back to Palermo to be hanged; Sir William Hamilton, British Minister at Naples and husband of Emma, had told them that although as many as 6,000 people were assassinated a year in Naples, only two executions had taken place in 12 years. Palermo was therefore thought to administer more rigorous justice.

In 1807 the Hills' diplomat cousin, William Hill of Attingham, was posted to Italy. From 1824-32 he was resident in Naples and Palermo (Sicily) in the diplomatic service and formed an important collection of pictures, furniture and *objets d'art* which were eventually to find their way to Attingham. William was to succeed his brother as the 3rd Lord Berwick in 1832.

Sir William Hamilton having given the Hawkstone party a letter of introduction to the Viceroy of Sicily, Prince Caramanico invited them to dine. He lived in great state and, having served as Ambassador in England, had returned with some 'English' habits—including a fireplace. Sicily was an extraordinary place at that time. The aristocracy lived in great style and were driven in their impressively accoutred carriages along the seaside promenade each evening: 'Hyde Park in its glory could not shew as gaudy an exhibition of trappings and horses ... The dresses of the ladies were exceedingly magnificent and in good taste but their morals were detestable ... Much of this laxity was considered to arise out of the spirit of Popery whose first object being to keep up the authority of the Church absolved immorality much sooner than the neglect of an *ave-maria* or eating flesh on a fast day.' Very censorious!

It was the number of assassinations, not surprisingly, that both fascinated and horrified the Hawkstone party. It is even recorded that there was a hospital for the stabbed. Sir Richard bought himself a stiletto, 'much ornamented and of elegant make', which the vendor described as being a weapon for the use of ladies who might want a weapon of that sort. They did themselves witness several murders and seem fortunate to have escaped unharmed

Sir Richard wrote home that to 'give you a description of the roads and inns in this country would take up much more time and room than I can allot'. The inns were filthy and verminous and it was necessary to bring one's own supplies— fortunately there was an abundance of food and wine to be had and they even cooked a turtle once, with Sir Richard being the chief cook. The method of transport was a sort of litter, a type of closed sedan coach which they climbed into via the window. It was supported by two poles and carried by mules. Their escorts were themselves banditti, which patently offered the best protection. The travellers were fascinated by the novel scenes through which they passed, although there were abundant checks to their gratification: the legions of fleas seem to have ranked high on this list.

The King of Naples and Sicily, Ferdinand IV, was a strange fellow who loved hunting and had an extraordinary taste for *macaroni* which he devoured in vast quantities. (At Attingham there is a painting by Jakob Philipp Hackert of an enormous boar which the King had killed.) He had also ordered the killing of all cats which had, not surprisingly, led to a plague of mice and rats, so that the people had had to petition him to rescind this law. 'When some of his dogs went mad, he caused his whole kennel to hear mass.' The party also had an introduction to the Convent of San Martino, a magnificent place founded to cater for the sons of the nobility who were bound either for the Church or to be Knights of Malta. There were no longer many inhabitants but those who were there were divided into two sets which never intercommunicated. The Hills dined in some state thanks to an introduction from Prince Caramanico, a Freemason like Sir Richard.

In Syracuse they were driven from their inn by the fleas. They were attacked by bandits en route to Catania but despite the mules of one *litiga* bolting they survived. On their return to Palermo they fell in with two unknown English gentlemen and asked if there was any news from Naples. The strangers replied, 'Yes, great apprehensions are entertained for the safety of Sir Richard Hill and company who are supposed to have been taken by the Algerines.' This was highly entertaining to the Hawkstone party and Sir Richard replied, 'I am happy to be able to give you ocular demonstration to the contrary.'

From Palermo, they returned to Rome for Holy Week, being celebrated even more brilliantly than usual due to the presence of the King and Queen of Naples and 'Mesdames de France', the two elderly and very religious aunts of Louis XVI. Despite the party's professions of shock at Roman pomp and show, the Hills seem to have attended most of the most important events of the week. We have descriptions of services in the Sistine Chapel, in St Peter's, High Mass said by the Pope, several *misereres,* the illumination of the great Basilica and fireworks, benedictions galore and the canonisation of a female French saint. Religious ceremonies apart, there was an extraordinary horse race in the Corso. 'The horses ran without riders and were urged to madness in their course by prickly balls fastened to their backs, which acted sharper and sharper as the poor animal's speed increased ... every art was called forth to give splendour and éclat to the worthless scene of superstition, revelry and folly.' The party returned to England, collecting soldier nephew Rowland, who was studying at a Military Academy in Strasbourg, on the way, and was much shocked by the news from France.

In 1795 Sir Richard actively opposed Pitt by voting for an amendment introduced by Wilberforce. His speech included the following: 'How, Sir, could I again look my constituents or my countrymen in the face, were I to vote the money out of their pockets and the blood out of their veins, in support of a war which has hitherto been disastrous in the extreme, and which if persisted in, I am persuaded will be most awful in the event!' He had originally voted for war but now he said,

> Is there an honest, independent man in this House who will ask, 'Is there, or is there not, an opportunity of making peace on any tolerable terms?' If it be said *yes,* then in God's name let us endeavour to do it without delay; if no, then let us withdraw our forces from the continent and keep them to defend ourselves. Let Old England add to her wooden walls by which she has ever proved herself mistress of the ocean and shouted in the vast theatre of the globe, 'Britannia rules the waves'.[20]

Indeed, Britain did add to her Navy and she was soon to need it. War did continue, of course, and would only end twenty years later at Waterloo.

In 1790 the Hawkstone estate steward, George Downward, was found 'negligent', but instead of being dismissed he continued in his employment and his failures were probably one of the factors contributing to the overspending and poor management that eventually led to the collapse of the Hawkstone 'empire'.[21] Downward was living in the Citadel—before its rebuilding and aggrandisement—and was still there in 1804. He left in 1814.

In October 1806 Parliament was dissolved and Sir Richard, who was in poor health, decided not to stand for re-election. He appears to have lived fairly quietly at home for the remaining two years of his life. One of the activities that he loved to organise was the band of musicians made up from his servants. He would invite his guests to be rowed down the new lake—about two miles in length—to a spot known as 'Neptune's Whim' while the servant orchestra played.[22] After dining in the cottage which resembled one in North Holland, but was rather strangely embellished by sculptures of Neptune and his neriads, the company would be rowed back to the Hall listening to the music again. On occasion, cannons were fired from the nearby *Hawkstone Inn*, as it was then called.

On 28 November 1808 Sir Richard died and was buried in Hodnet church. A strange and obviously eccentric man, he was highly principled and occasionally too impetuous in reply, but a true Christian. His place in the work of the early Evangelical Movement has been rather overlooked, perhaps because his writings and thoughts did not produce anything really original, but he vigorously promoted his interpretation of Christian belief—based on the 39 Articles—throughout his life, without leaving the Established Church.

Sir Richard is represented by two pictures in the National Portrait Gallery: one is a pastel by John Russell dated 1780 and in the other he appears in a painting of the House of Commons made at the time when Pitt announced the French Declaration of War in 1793. It is by Karl Anton Hickel. Also visible are Canning, Alexander Hood and Charles James Fox. His backside also appears in a Gillray cartoon which depicts the Headmaster of Westminster School flogging 'Master Billy', William Pitt; others waiting to be flogged including Burke, Sheridan and Hill. Brother Rowland is found in no less than five different depictions, amongst them another pastel by Russell, and an oil by Samuel Mountjoy Smith painted not long before his death, in 1828.

Sir Richard left his soldier nephew, Rowland, of whom he was enormously proud, the estate of Hardwick, near Hadnall in Shropshire, and £2,000. Rowland learned of this bequest while leading his troops on the terrible retreat to Corunna in December 1808. All the other nephews and nieces received bequests, Tom receiving the London house. Sir Richard died too soon to see the major successes that crowned Rowland's military career or to know that he would receive the peerage that Richard had felt himself to be more deserving of than his cousin, Noel Hill, in 1784.

His epitaph on a white marble plaque in Hodnet church reads:

In Memory
of Sir Richard Hill Baronet, of Hawkstone in this County,
Eldest son of Sir Rowland Hill Baronet,
and in several successive Parliaments one of the Representatives of the same,

> who in the lively hope of a blessed Resurrection
> through the alone Righteousness of Christ his Redeemer,
> resigned his Soul into the hands of his heavenly Father
> on the 28th day of November in the year 1808,
> and the 76th of his own age.

> He desired that as little as possible might be said of him
> in Newspapers, or on his tomb stone.

> The Character he most delighted in was that
> of a Sinner freely saved by Sovereign Grace.
> His religious Sentiments were those established
> in the Church of England at the time of the Reformation,
> as expressed in the doctrinal Articles of that Church
> to which he was always steadily attached,
> though maintaining a truly Catholic Spirit
> towards all good Men of different Persuasions.

The Reverend Rowland Hill (1744-1833)

'Rowley', as he was known within the family and amongst his friends, was 12 years younger than Sir Richard but they evidently became very close in their desire to spread the word of God. Rowland was sent to Eton, where he was a King's Scholar. He demonstrated a ready wit allied to a generous disposition and this, together with his great ability at sport, probably helped him to avoid too great a degree of ridicule amongst his fellow pupils. At school 'he began to reap the first fruits of the abundant harvest of his future ministry', according to the Rev. Charlesworth, one of his biographers. A handwritten note against his name in the Eton College Register[23] notes he 'excelled in athletic sports and is said to have swum from Cambridge to Grantchester in October 1757'.

In October 1764, at the age of 20, he entered St John's, Cambridge (endowed by his ancestor the Lord Mayor). He obtained his BA in 1769 and his MA in 1772. It had been planned that he would take Holy Orders and be given the living of a parish in Norfolk in the gift of the family. However, he chose to follow a far more difficult and interesting path. His sister Jane wrote to her great friend Lady Glenorchy, 'I trust that he will ever stand faithful to the cause of his crucified Master, whether he be admitted as a Minister of the Gospel, to preach in his Name or not.' He was to have a great deal of trouble over ordination.

During his time at Cambridge he met John Berridge, who was to be a strong support and influence in his life.[24] Rowland preached in villages around the city wherever he could find an audience, and also visited prisons and the sick. The university authorities tried to stop his 'irregular' activities but George Whitefield

3. The Rev. Rowland Hill

strongly urged him to persist. Whitefield had become the leader of the Welsh Calvinistic Methodists, having returned from his ministry in America and separated doctrinally from his friend, John Wesley. Whitefield told Rowley that 34 years earlier he had himself been taken to task by the Master of Pembroke for visiting the sick and those in prison. He added that should Rowland 'be denied his degree or expelled, it will be the best degree you can take'.

At home in the long vacation of 1767 Rowland found himself in trouble with his parents who, sadly, took the same view as the university authorities. In his later years he wrote that, as a young man, he had often paced the terraces of Hawkstone in the knowledge that most of his family thought him a disgrace.[25] The opposition no doubt came principally from his staid and conventional father, Sir Rowland, since we know that brother Richard was responsible for his 'conversion' and that sister Jane was of the same persuasion.

When he returned to Cambridge in October 1767, the case of the six Oxford students referred to above was in the news. Naturally, Rowland joined in the fray. There were more difficulties ahead when he sought ordination after his graduation in 1769. He was refused by six different bishops. His father reduced his allowance to try to force him to change his way of life and his itinerant preaching but it made no difference; his feet were firmly planted on a certain path and opposition only served to stiffen his resolve. He had virtually no money and set off on his journeys on a small pony bought by the Rev. Cornelius Winter with money donated for the purpose.[26]

In May 1773 he was married to Mary Tudway, who must have been an extraordinary character, although we know little about her. Immediately following his wedding, he was finally ordained deacon by the Bishop of Bath and Wells, probably at the request of Clement Tudway, his new brother-in-law, who being the Member of Parliament for Wells must have known and had some influence with the Bishop. Rowland then spent a year in the parish of Kingston near Taunton as curate, where not all the parishioners approved of him. Next he was promised ordination as priest by the Bishop of Carlisle, but this failed to take place, the Bishop receiving explicit instructions from the Archbishop of York not to ordain Rowland on account of 'his perpetual irregularity'. He was disappointed, but continued his work, saying that 'he ran off with only one ecclesiastical boot on'!'[27]

Mary accompanied him on most of his journeys and they were once held up by highwaymen; apparently Rowland stood up in the carriage and made such an appalling noise that the ruffians ran off, fearing they had held up the Devil himself. He preached all over the country and especially enjoyed doing so in the open air. He must have known John Fletcher from childhood, but this did not stop him siding with Augustus Toplady when he split from the faction of John Wesley and Fletcher. The latter preached salvation through grace but Rowland and Toplady held the Calvinist belief in predestination of the elect. Toplady was fiercely controversial in his time but today he is best known as the composer of the hymn 'Rock of Ages'. Berridge tried hard to keep Rowland out of this controversy but he failed. It was a period that saw bitter dissent between men of passionate beliefs who were, at the same time, all exceptional Christians.

Rowland often addressed enormous congregations, sometimes up to twenty thousand people. At the time most of the dissenting chapels were in the north of London so Rowland made a great effort to cover the southern half of the city. In 1780 some of his supporters, including his brother Richard, raised the funds to build a chapel for him: the Surrey Chapel in Blackfriars Road was opened on Whit Sunday, 8 June 1783, when Rowley preached on the text 'We preach Christ Crucified'. He was just 40 years old. The Trustees of the Chapel confirmed him as Minister, but it was clearly understood that he would be there for only six months of each year; he had no intention of abandoning his itinerant teaching. Rowland also had a house in Wotton-under-Edge in Gloucestershire, where another chapel, 'The Tabernacle', was built for his use, and here he spent about three months each year. The church on the site is now a thriving auction house and a plaque commemorating Rowley sits high up on the wall. His own 'manse' still stands immediately behind the Tabernacle. It is a charming small classic Georgian house with Palladian-style windows. Unfortunately the garden around it has been built over. His name is also commemorated by a row of almshouses although they are not the original ones.

The Surrey Chapel flourished. There were 13 Sunday Schools attached to it with more than three thousand children enrolled. Rowley was the first Chairman of the Religious Tract Society, which was formed during a meeting at the Coffee House in St Paul's Churchyard in May 1799, and he was deeply involved with the British and Foreign Bible Society. He was also connected from its foundation until the end of his life with the London Missionary Society, and was proud of the fact that the Surrey Chapel's contributions to this society were the largest of all the missionary contributions, seldom averaging less than £400—an enormous sum at the time and one that very few churches could hope to equal even on a great feast day today.

Rowland took an interest in the development of the practice of vaccination with 'cowpox' (in this he was influenced by Edward Jenner). According to Charlesworth, he published an article on the subject entitled 'Cow Pock inoculation Vindicated and Recommended from matters of fact', and not only had himself vaccinated but personally treated thousands of people.

Following his death, the Cabinet Registry for 1833 contained a long piece:

> It is quite true that Mr Hill both said and did things, occasionally, which few other men could have said with good effect or done without imprudence. But the unimpeachable integrity and purity of his intentions, the sanctity of his life, the charm of his manners, the dignity of true breeding, which

rescued from vulgarity his most familiar phrases and his most eccentric actions, conspired to secure for him, through life, the affectionate veneration of all who enjoyed the privilege of his acquaintance or understood his character ... As a preacher Mr Hill was unequal as well as systematically unmethodical; generally rambling, but pithy, often throwing out the most striking remarks and sometimes interspersing touches of genuine pathos amid much that bordered on the ludicrous.[28]

Rowland died aged 89, an immense age in his time. Only a week before he had preached to Sunday School teachers in the Surrey Chapel and his mind remained clear to the end. His body was buried in front of his pulpit in the Surrey Chapel. The funeral sermon was delivered by the Rev. William Jay of Bath, who took as his text 'Howl, fir tree, for the cedar is fallen'. He was undoubtedly one of the greatest preachers of his time.

Unfortunately some legal problem arose with the lease of the Chapel, which Rowland had intended to be a renewable instrument, and the congregation was forced to move. They took the body of their founder with them to Christchurch, opposite the entrance to the Lambeth underground station, where he was reburied under the Lincoln Tower. Christchurch was bombed in World War Two but the tower remains standing. Recently it has been used as a practice venue for acrobats; the adjoining Hall is called 'Hawkstone Hall' and contains a showcase with memorabilia of the Reverend Rowland. The man himself would have probably found this amusing.

The anecdotes concerning him demonstrate a wonderful quick wit allied to the profound faith that he clearly never questioned, and a loathing of bigotry and false piety. He left behind hundreds of sermons and verses. His *Village Dialogues*, published in 1810, was immensely popular and ran to many editions.

Jane Hill, sister (1738-96)

Jane Hill, who has already appeared as a staunch supporter of her brothers in their Christian faith and zeal, and who seems to have been a formidable lady, left an account of a visit to the continent in about the year 1788. It is of great interest, not least because it recounts her presentation at the French royal court at Versailles a short time before the King and Queen were forced to abandon Versailles for Paris and subsequent imprisonment and execution.

The party consisted of Lord and Lady Montague travelling in a huge coach drawn by six horses and 'driven by postillions in the grotesque accoutrements and boots then so common in France'.[29] Miss Hill and her friends followed in a smaller vehicle of her own, but the postillions wore scarlet and gold with immense pigtails and ear-rings. One of the first sights Jane noted was a pedlar pulling his own cart but dressed in crimson velvet lined with green silk and wearing a bag wig, ruffles and silk stockings. Jane commented very unfavourably on the way in which the Belgian lower orders treated their wives in those days. She frequently saw three or four great fellows sitting in a barge, smoking at their ease, while their poor women were drawing it along. Men were also seen to load their women with heavy trunks on a journey while they only carried some extremely light parcels.

Arriving in Brussels on the Feast of the Virgin, the 'pure protestant feelings of the party' were surprised and shocked by the magnificent ceremonies of the festival. Jane recorded a detailed description of the decorations of the church and of the figure of

> the Virgin ... dressed in an enormous bell hoop with a train of rich blue and silver and coloured tissue. Her petticoat was pink under silver gauze and over her shoulders was thrown a mantle of the same colour covered with fine point lace. Round her neck were two large rows of pearls and in her ears were an immense pair of glittering ear-rings. On her head and on that of the figure of the infant Jesus were crowns of gold set with precious stones; the faces of both were black.

She continued by describing the procession through the town with the lamps, the priests, the music. 'I felt greatly shocked,' said Miss Hill.

They continued to Spa where they were received by the Capuchins, who appear to have warmly welcomed the English party and permitted them to walk in their gardens. She compared the behaviour of the Capuchins favourably with an English service that they attended in the house of an English 'Milord', where they were shocked by the congregation 'in a constant titter'.

From Brussels they continued to Paris and then to Versailles. They were at the Palace on the Feast of All Saints, and witnessed the King and Queen attending High Mass: 'She is in general reckoned beautiful but she did not at all strike me in that light; her person and face are *dollish*, though she has a sharp wanton look. She appeared affable and good-humoured.' Jane was not impressed by either of their Majesties: 'The king has a countenance of all others the most vacant and bloated. He is fat and very awkward—quite destitute of the graces. Not so his brothers and sisters, who are elegant and fashionable in their appearance.' They were to become fat too, in due course! The poor ill-fated Queen addressed a few civil words to Miss Hill, who then little thought of the 'sobs and groans that ere long were to stifle her gentle voice, or that the dungeons of the Temple and the horrors of the scaffold were to succeed the luxurious chamber of the Petit Trianon and the splendid luxury of the finest palace in the world'.

Jane's time in Paris was spent in verifying facts about Voltaire. What had led this pious woman to become so fascinated by this 'dreadful enemy of religion' is unrecorded, but she had done a translation from the French author and wished to authenticate some of the facts 'respecting the despairs which gather like a thunder-cloud around his dark and awful end'—not, she assured her readers, 'in the way of contemptuous triumph but of Christian pity; that they might become a warning to those who hate the only light that can comfort and guide in the gloomy vale of the shadow of death'. A serious lady.

Sir John Hill, 3rd Baronet (1740-1824)

This man, who was brother to the above and sired 16 children, seems to have steered clear of religious controversy, and it is easy to imagine him attending church regularly if only because it was what you did as lord of a great estate. John Hill was educated at Shrewsbury; there is no mention of his having gone to university. He married a cousin, Mary Chambré, daughter of John Chambré of nearby Petton, and he lived at Prees until the death of his brother, Richard, in 1808. John Hill represented Shrewsbury in 1784 as a follower of Pitt. He is recorded as having voted for Parliamentary Reform in April 1785. For an account of his memorable battle with his cousin William of Attingham for the Shrewsbury seat in 1796 see Chapter Seven.

He is buried in Prees church with a splendid memorial erected by his grandson, Sir Rowland, 4th Baronet and 2nd Viscount Hill. The inscription reads, 'To future ages this marble will point out the spot where rest the remains of a good man'.

CHAPTER FOUR

General Rowland, 1st Viscount Hill
Part 1

> Surely old Rowland and Sir Rowland Hill
> have done enough to gain the world's goodwill.
> Each in his calling makes his foes retrench—
> one thumps the cushion,
> *t'other thumps the French!*

No history of the Hills of Hawkstone could fail to include a lengthy piece on 'the General', not eccentric, not the greatest builder, money-maker or by any means the 'showiest' of this family, not even a great heroic figure in stature, but certainly one of England's 'heroes' of the Napoleonic era.

Rowland Hill was an unassuming man, totally lacking the mien of a successful soldier, but he inspired affection and respect in all who came in contact with him. In many ways he appeared the antithesis of a fighting man. He was sincerely religious, scarcely ever swore, used no foul language and, although he must have had ambition, he never put personal aspiration before the good of the Army. It is also impossible to find any trace of jealousy amongst his fellow officers at his success and rapid rise. Nobody, certainly, begrudged him his peerage (together with Graham, Beresford, Hope and Stapleton Cotton) at the close of the long Peninsular War in 1814, although one or two such as Picton felt that they, too, should have been ennobled. The fact that Hill was not a 'flashy' and charismatic figure probably explains why he has never inspired a proper biography save that written by the family chaplain, Edwin Sidney.[1] Sidney's book is poor. Perhaps the only excuse is that it was written when a good many of those mentioned were still alive. There is virtually no family background, very little personal information, and no more than passing references to his brothers, three of whom were with him in the Peninsula and also at Waterloo. Clement was his brother's faithful ADC for many years, when he could almost certainly have advanced much further if he had chosen to pursue his own career. On the other hand he was at the centre of the action, and had the distinction of carrying his brother's dispatches to London at least twice. He eventually became a Major General with a command in India, where he died. Robert and Thomas Noel are only mentioned in passing and yet Robert was still alive when the book was written. Sidney had no understanding whatsoever of military life or campaigning, and never mentions anything that could possibly be construed as critical. There is no mention of the extraordinary problems Hill had with James Brudenell, 7th Earl of Cardigan when at Horse Guards, and very little is made of the Chartist riots, the control of which fell to the Army in the absence of a civil police force. Even the background to Rowland's decision to abstain from voting on the Reform Bill receives scant notice. After making due allowance for the language employed in the mid-19th century, it must be judged an obsequious and tiresome book, only worthwhile for the family letters it quotes. These letters, together with contemporary accounts in the books of such fellow soldiers as Rifleman Harris, Sergeant Robertson, Moyle Sherer and, of course, Colonel Napier, among many others, have left us a fair and vivid picture of campaigning life during the Peninsular War.

In appearance Rowland Hill was of medium height and rather portly—even Pickwickian—in later life at least. He was florid in complexion and resembled more the country squire than the fighting soldier. Indeed, his nickname in the army was 'Daddy' Hill, due both to his benevolent appearance and his care for his men. Most of the portraits of the General are the usual head and shoulders churned out by journeymen painters at that time but there are one or two of more interest. One very large canvas shows the General with his charger. It must have been bought by the *Hawkstone Park Hotel* at the dispersal sale along with a 'pair' representing the Duke of Wellington. These hung in the hotel until the recent sale of the golf club.[2]

Rowland was born at Prees Hall, Shropshire, the second son and fourth child of John Hill and Mary Chambré of nearby Petton. The family was, by this period, firmly established as one of the county's leading families, with something in the region of 16,000 acres making up the Hawkstone estate. Judicious marriages had added to the land left by the first Sir Rowland in 1561, and this had been increased by the 'Great' Hill at the beginning of the 18th century. Mary Chambré was the grand-daughter of the Francis Chambré who had overseen much of the building work at the house in the 1720s. Francis had married Richard's niece, Elizabeth Hill.

John Hill was the quintessential country squire, representing Shrewsbury in Parliament and enjoying field sports in the conventional manner of the time. He was brother next in line to Sir Richard, the 2nd Baronet at Hawkstone, and brother also of Rowland, the famous evangelical preacher. The relationship between soldier Rowland and preacher Rowland was very close. John and Mary Hill's son Rowland's position as a younger son of a younger son meant that no country seat could be expected, although he enjoyed a comfortable upbringing with all the rural pleasures available to a family living on a great sporting estate.

Rowland Hill's early education was at small schools, first at Ightfield in north Shropshire and then in Chester. The latter was run by a Rev. Winfield and Rowland became very fond of this man and his wife. As a young boy he was not robust and could not stand the sight of a wound or blood—he was even known to faint! He was soft-hearted and would help the younger boys with their studies and games. Apparently a good pupil, he never experienced 'supple jack' or 'Dr Birch', and the warmth and kindness he demonstrated as a schoolboy indicate an almost feminine personality, not the steely resolve and incisiveness of the soldier he would become, and both are early signs of the compassionate nature for which his soldiers loved and respected him.

The structure of the British Army in the 18th century was extraordinary, and even more extraordinary was the fact that the system worked, and continued to do so for nearly two hundred years. In order to become an officer, a man had to be able to purchase his commission and, what is more, had to continue to pay as he sought promotion. Lieutenant Colonel was the highest rank open to purchase. 'Brevet' promotion was possible, but it only gave army rank and was not relevant to regimental rank and was usually given for service in action. The purchase system provides the reason why men frequently transferred into different regiments possibly using the services of one of the many agents who assisted in such transactions. It was a system open to abuse, and it led to many good men remaining as junior officers whilst less able men gained positions of command. In the main, other rankers did not take kindly to one of their own being commissioned. They may have disliked many of their officers but, as Rifleman Harris stated in his *Recollections*, they understood that 'gentlemen' had more natural authority, to which they responded.

Few officers in the Army during the Napoleonic era had any special academic qualifications, and very few had gone to university. The sole requirement was basic literacy. Rowland was probably better educated than most of his peers, but in all likelihood had little appreciation of the arts apart from what he may have absorbed from life in and around a great house such as Hawkstone.

Rowland's elder brother, John, was in the Royal Horse Guards Blue and then the 25th Light Dragoons until his marriage, when he resigned his commission to become a country squire, although he did continue to apply his military training to the Shropshire Militia. The Hills were to figure prominently in the Royal Horse Guards Blue in the first half of the 19th century. Since five of John Hill's sons in all were in the Army and serving in good regiments, considerable sums of money would have been required to establish them. Their mother was co-heiress of John Chambré of Petton, but it is possible that Sir Richard may have contributed to the purchase of commissions.

Rowland's parents had destined him for the law, perhaps because of his relative frailty as a child. The boy was adamant, however, that his was to be a military life, and his father graciously acquiesced, saying that he feared Rowland was unlikely to make a mark in the Army such as he might have done in the law.[3] John Hill immediately began to make enquiries as to the best route to be followed and, the family being well connected, an ensigncy in the 38th Regiment was soon obtained. John Hill researched the best path for his son to pursue a successful career, and it was recommended that he undertake further study. He was given permission by his regiment to attend a Military Academy in Strasbourg and Rowland was one of very few soldiers to undertake study of a formal military nature.

He did not stay in Strasbourg for very long. Revolution in France made it an uncertain spot, and when two of his uncles, Sir Richard and the Reverend Brian Hill, came through Strasbourg at the end of their exciting and rather dangerous tour of Italy and Sicily in 1791, young Rowland was told to return home with them.[4] The journey seems to have been fun; the two devoutly Christian uncles were also extremely good company and they all enjoyed the journey down the Rhine and through Holland. Once back in England, Rowland rejoined the 38th which was stationed in Kent. Before long, following the now established career pattern, he transferred in January 1792 into the 53rd then stationed in Edinburgh. The constant changes make it hard to understand how regimental loyalty became established. The 53rd stayed in Scotland until the end of the year, and at the start of 1793 Rowland raised an independent company of Salopians and was promoted to Captain; he was 21. Having delivered his men to the 53rd in Belfast, he travelled with Francis Drake, a diplomat who was going to Genoa as Minister Plenipotentiary. Hill served as Assistant Secretary to Drake for a short time but, keen to see action, he obtained permission to go to Toulon. Here he was successively ADC to Lord Mulgrave, General O'Hara and Sir David Dundas. He had met Dundas during his brief stay in Ireland and this presumably led to the appointments. Toulon was to give Hill his first taste of battle and also brought to prominence Napoleon Bonaparte, then a young artillery officer.

The British had been welcomed by the people of Toulon on their arrival in August 1793 to open a front in southern France and exploit the possibilities for civil war against the Revolutionary government led by the Jacobin, Maximilien Robespierre, but their numbers were too small to hold the port. Mulgrave returned to England and General O'Hara took over the command until he was seriously wounded and captured.

Under the command of Sir David Dundas the young Hill received his first commendation: Dundas referred to him as one 'whose intelligence, activity and courage rendered him of great service to me'.[5] He was granted the special privilege of carrying dispatches from the Admiral Commanding the Channel Fleet, Lord Hood, and Sir David to England, and sailed on 13 December 1793. The news he carried underlined the impossibility of holding Toulon with the force at the Commander's disposal. En route Hill met the Duke of York in Flanders; it was the start of a warm acquaintance that would last until the Duke's death in 1827. In fact, Toulon was lost within days of Hill's departure, Napoleon's inspiring leadership of the French troops causing the British fleet to slip away during the night of 18 December.

Rowland Hill was now on a fast track upwards and was invited to join Thomas Graham of Balgowan's independently raised regiment—the 90th—with his Majority if he could bring a certain number of soldiers with him. He seems to have had no problem in raising the company and Graham was to become a life-long friend.

Thomas Graham was a most remarkable man and another unlikely soldier.[6] He took up a military career very late in life following the death from consumption of his adored wife in 1792. She had died in the south of France, where they had gone for the sake of her health, and he had decided to bring her body home for burial. Crossing France he was set on by a group of National Guardsmen who were pursuing supposed royalists in a bloodthirsty fashion. Breaking open the coffin, they found the body of Mrs Graham. Thomas was so shocked by this act that he joined the British Army to fight against the barbarian French when war broke out between the two nations a few months later in February 1793.

He helped Hill at the start of his career and they became close friends, despite Graham serving as a Whig member of Parliament when all the Hills were Tories. Graham was already 44 years old when he embarked on his military career but had great success and was created Lord Lynedoch in 1814 at the same time that Hill was granted his peerage. By that date Graham was 66 years old; he died, aged 96, a year after Hill in 1843. By the time that the 90th reached 1,000 men, Hill had become a Lieutenant Colonel at the age of 23; he would be a full Colonel by the age of twenty-seven.

The French pushed the Duke of York and the British Army out of Holland in January 1795, forcing the Stadholder to flee to England. Whilst there, William visited Hawkstone, where he was royally entertained by Sir Richard.

That year saw Hill stationed on the Ile Dieu off the western coast of France.[7] The French were too busy elsewhere to bother the English invaders and from the military point of view life was unexciting. Ever resourceful in organising their entertainment, the young Colonel and his Commanding Officer Thomas Graham managed to enjoy a variety of the field sports in which the Hill family were always active participants. Their principal recreation seems to have been coursing and shooting and Hill was even asked to try to procure shooting dogs through his family at Hawkstone. Brother John duly obliged, sending out pointers and setters.

In the summer of 1800, Hill obtained permission to accompany the diplomat Francis Drake, with whom he had travelled to Genoa in 1793, to the continent via Switzerland. He was hoping to rejoin his regiment, the 90th. Departure was delayed until, finally, Hill abandoned Drake and sailed from Spithead on board a troopship, the *Pegasus*. Finding himself the senior officer on board, he had various obligations and, when he met an outward bound East India convoy and heard that the French fleet was out, organised the troops on board to act as marines. In the event they met only one enemy vessel and the *Pegasus* was so slow that she was unable to take her. On arrival in Gibraltar Hill found that O'Hara was still in command.

His Mediterranean travels then followed a roundabout route covering Majorca, Leghorn, Corsica and then back to Minorca where Hill finally caught up with Sir Ralph Abercromby, commander of the expeditionary force. Having joined the main Army, Hill became very unwell in September and had to be taken to Gibraltar where he recovered ashore.[8] A large fleet was assembled carrying approximately 25,000 men. It sailed for Cadiz, the troops being employed in various manoeuvres designed to keep the French and Spanish guessing as to the real intentions of the British. These proceedings enraged General O'Hara, who demanded to know the point of all this activity.[9] 'It is a diversion, General.' 'Diversion!' O'Hara exclaimed, ''Tis a diversion for all Europe is laughing at you. Why, your commander cannot see the end of his nose [Abercromby was apparently very short sighted] and as for your fighting cock, Moore, he has trimmed his tail.' (Sir John Moore had recently acquired a modern haircut—a crop—and even paraded with his hair uncurled and unpowdered, which old General O'Hara thought very shocking. At last, in 1808, an order was given to the troops to cut their 'queues' which received almost universal approval; the heavily powdered hair had been uncomfortable and unhygienic. The Duke of Wellington had adopted a crop as early as 1800.) The fleet sailed to and fro off the North African coast, suffering from very poor food and terrible weather. Hill was still unwell and spent the time they were in harbour at Minorca ashore. On 17 November they finally sailed for Malta, where the regiment was gratefully disembarked for a month. Hill's diary makes mention of the shipwreck of St Paul; he made frequent and unaffected mention of his beliefs and sincere faith.

January 1801 found the fleet in the safe harbour of Marmoris on the southern Turkish coast. They spent the best part of two months here. Sergeant Robertson describes the awful storms with their enormous hailstones, winds so violent that boats were torn from their moorings, and a gunboat struck by lightning. All the tents having been torn away, there was no shelter and the cold was appalling, especially at night.

Sergeant Robertson, serving in the 92nd (Highland), fought alongside the 90th for much of the Egyptian affair. His account of events includes experiences that were similar to those of Rowland Hill. Owing to the violent weather, the fleet could not leave the shelter of the bay of Marmoris until late in the winter of 1801. Finally they set sail and dropped anchor in Aboukir Bay on 2 March, disembarking a few days later. Hill's diary records that they moved towards Alexandria on the 12th and on the 22nd were attacked by the French army left behind by Napoleon after he returned to Paris three years earlier, then 'defeated them and gained a glorious victory. Was wounded …'.[10] A more detailed account was written later. His regiment, the 90th (forming part of Major General Cradock's brigade), had been in the vanguard together with the 92nd Highlanders when they were attacked by a band of French cavalry, which they repulsed. The fighting was very fierce, and both the 90th and the 92nd took heavy casualties. 'I was wounded by a musket ball which struck the strong brass binding on the peak of the helmet.' The force struck him unconscious and he was carried from the battlefield. The celebrated piece of headgear, that probably saved his life, was preserved at Hawkstone. Hill's wound must, however, have been more serious than his pocket diary would suggest, since he remained out of action for three weeks and was taken on board the flagship of Admiral Lord Keith, the *Foudroyant*, which sounds as if she must have been a French prize. Whilst Hill was recovering, Sir Ralph Abercromby was brought on board and placed in the same cabin. After a week of suffering he died of gangrene from the thigh wound he had received. While Hill was still recuperating he received a visit from a Turkish Captain who presented him with handsome gifts including an elaborately decorated sword, a valuable gold box and a 'shawl' which was probably an elaborate type of cloak.

On 2 May the British Army together with their Turkish allies moved forward on the road that would bring them to Cairo. Water was very short and the troops suffered severely in the early summer's heat, which often reached 130 degrees; many died from dehydration. They had several skirmishes en route although the greatest scourge was probably sand blown by the *khamsin* wind. Food was available, however, with corn in abundance, this having been abandoned by the French. On 21 May the French agreed to evacuate Egypt and surrendered the Citadel in Cairo.

Despite his duties in command of the 90th, Hill managed to make a sightseeing tour of the Pyramids, Cairo and Alexandria before sailing on 23 September for Malta. Here the regiment stayed for several months, which must have been a relief to the men. In October 1801 the Peace of Amiens gave the combatants much-needed respite from war, though both Britain and France knew that the peace was merely an interlude. On 28 February 1802 the regiment embarked once again, but during the passage between Malta and Gibraltar the fleet was hit by a violent storm, finally limping into the harbour at Gibraltar on 12 March. Here Hill was devastated to learn that his friend, General O'Hara, had died during his absence.

Once back in England, he returned on leave to Shropshire where his uncle, Sir Richard, gave a 'fête' in the Park at Hawkstone to celebrate his homecoming. A huge tent, formerly belonging to Tipoo Sahib, that Hill had bought in Egypt from an officer returning from India, was erected for the occasion and housed a large number of guests.

He had fully expected the regiment to be reduced or disbanded, but with more rumblings of war this was not to be, and Hill spent the winter of 1802 in Scotland recruiting men. Napoleon had got himself elected Consul for life in August 1802, and under his direction, but not by him personally, a stable government had been established and reconstruction begun. This was the period when Napoleon used some of his boundless energy to draw up the *Code Napoléon*, creating the *départements*, founding the Banque de France and establishing the *Légion d'Honneur*. By 1804 Bonaparte was sufficiently sure of his position to crown himself Emperor and then began his short but most glittering period. He set out once again to seize the rest of Europe and expand his new empire.

Hill and the 90th were sent to Ireland in the spring of 1803 and did tours of duty in Belfast, Ballinasloe and Mullingar. Here he heard that he had been promoted Brigadier General—at the age of 31—and was appointed to the Staff of the Army in Ireland in August 1803. The promotion to the Staff meant that he had to leave the 90th, which he had been with since its creation, and he received a very handsome tribute from his officers.

Ireland was in a state of unrest following the Rebellion of 1798 and the Act of Union in 1800, and Pitt's failure to persuade the King to agree to Catholic Emancipation. Napoleon had established a vast fleet at Boulogne and the threat of invasion by the French kept the British on a permanent state of alert. Rumours that part of the French fleet had sailed and was heading for a landing in Ireland were frequent, but all proved false. Hill had much to occupy him in Galway, where reorganisation was badly needed. In early January 1804 he reconnoitred the coast together with Captain Currie. Currie became a favourite with Hill, who was most put out when the 90th sailed for the West Indies and the Captain had to rejoin the regiment. He was to return to Hill's staff later and remain with him until he was killed at Waterloo. It was very fortunate that Hill had left the regiment; service in the West Indies would almost certainly have severely affected his health.

Hill made detailed plans to be implemented in the event of a French landing, and instructions were given to landowners to blow up bridges. He also arranged for the Athlone Militia to be raised to combat any unfriendly action by local groups ill-disposed towards the English and likely to welcome French invaders, and saw to the creation of a signalling system between Loughrea and Galway. The mechanics of this were devised by a Royal Navy officer, Captain Trench. An excellent system of look-out towers was put in place, but they do not seem to have been required since there was no sign of the French, although Bonaparte's great invasion army remained encamped at Boulogne. It was finally dispersed in 1805.

Such was Napoleon's success on land that Great Britain decided to send troops to support her allies attempting to stem his apparently irresistible progress. A letter from Frederick, Duke of York, Commander in Chief, to Lord Cathcart, in his role as Commander of the Forces, directed him to put in train arrangements to send a force to the continent and specified the regiments to be embarked at Cork. The letter added that the General Officer in charge was to be Brigadier General Rowland Hill.

This—the Hanover Expedition—was another of Pitt's military initiatives that would end in disaster. The waging of war and foreign affairs was not his strongest suit; he was much more successful dealing with the economy. Napoleon was heavily involved in Austria and Pitt and his Russian, Prussian and Swedish allies believed that it was an auspicious moment to try and break the Corsican's grip on Europe. En route from Cork Hill put into Falmouth, and the ships then anchored off Deal. Here Rowland Hill met Sir Arthur Wellesley for the first time and Wellesley took over command. Despite the bad weather—the fleet had to turn back three times—the ships set sail in mid-December. Hill arrived in the Weser on Christmas Day 1805, but many ships had been wrecked either on the Dutch coast or on the treacherous Goodwin Sands and some 2,000 men had drowned.[11] The Russians had decided not to wait on the arrival of Wellington and had pushed on to attack Bonaparte. The Emperor duly gave them a thrashing at the Battle of Austerlitz. The expedition was an ill-conceived and miserable affair. Having received word of Napoleon's success at Austerlitz, Pitt died in January 1806 and the Weser expedition was recalled. It was the only time that Hill (and indeed Wellington) was to return from service abroad without distinction; there had been no opportunity. His arrival coincided with the news of his mother's death. Altogether it was not a happy time.

Hill served in Kent until December 1806, when he left once more for Ireland, but now as a Major General and with his young brother, Thomas Noel, serving as his ADC. Headquartered in Fermoy he spent the whole of 1807 in this appointment, responsible for suppressing local disturbances and sifting information to discover which of the many rumours in circulation were false and which were true, although there was no longer any serious threat of invasion.

In 1806 Napoleon gave to his brother Joseph the Kingdom of the Two Sicilies, and to his brother Louis the throne of Holland. Neither would last long. England was now isolated. Napoleon realised that he could not defeat the British at sea and, the better to enforce a trade blockade, turned his attention to the last, or almost the last, part of Europe that continued to trade with England. He aimed to annexe the Iberian Peninsula and, by seizing Portugal, to close the port of Lisbon which had long been a supply base for the British fleet. In 1807 the Emperor ordered the invasion of Portugal and Canning sent a British fleet to rescue the mad old Queen of Portugal, her son, the Regent, and senior government officials and transport them to safety in Brazil. They sailed on board a British warship on 29 November, just ahead of Junot's arrival at the head of a French army in Lisbon. The fleet escorting the royal family carried most of the contents of the Portuguese Treasury, works of art, the national archives and many of the nobility. In the months immediately following, Napoleon forced both King Charles IV and his weak son, Ferdinand, to give up their rights to the Spanish throne, sending Charles into exile in Italy and Ferdinand to Talleyrand's château at Valençay in France. In their place he installed his brother Joseph, whom he loved, and of whom the best that can be said in these circumstances was that he, at least, understood there was probably not a single Spaniard who approved of him.

4. Rowland, 1st Viscount Hill.

Before his own departure for the Peninsula Hill found himself back in England, an England with a new government following the death of Pitt at the age of forty-seven. A scheme for an expedition to South America having fortunately been scrapped, Rowland Hill was ordered to embark for Portugal with a small force of some 9,000 men under Sir Arthur Wellesley. The first recorded letter from Sir Arthur to Hill was written on 23 June 1808 from Dublin Castle, where Wellesley was serving as Chief Secretary for Ireland: 'My dear Hill, I rejoice extremely at the prospect I have before me of serving again with you, and I hope we shall have more to do than we had on the last occasion on which we were together'— the disastrous Hanover Expedition. This was certainly going to be true. The first troops bound for Spain embarked from Cork on 12 June 1808. They totalled 9,505 'rank and file', 550 sergeants and 227 of the all-important drummers. Ever impatient, Wellesley decided to leave the main transport fleet and sailed ahead in HMS *Crocodile* to the disembarkation point, the fishing village of Figuera da Foz in Mondego Bay, midway between Porto and Lisbon.[12] Arriving on 1 August he prepared for the arrival and disembarkation of the main body of men. At that moment in his career, Wellesley found himself to be the most junior of seven Lieutenant Generals; this would change shortly. Mondego Bay was not an ideal disembarkation point, with the rolling Atlantic waves picking up the long boats and hurling them onto the shore, where the wretched men were plucked from the boats and carried up the beach by naked sailors. Some 180 horses had been pushed overboard from the merchant transports and had to swim for the shore, where they galloped wildly up and down until finally caught. The whole scene must have been one of utter chaos. Some of these wretched chargers had lost the control of their hind legs, due to the long weeks at sea, and it took some time for them to be rideable.

Hill's first encounter with the enemy at Rolica, on 17 August 1808, involved driving General Delaborde back through the difficult mountain passes with considerable loss of life but with, for the British, the important capture from the French of three pieces of artillery. The diary of Rifleman Harris records Hill's first battle: 'It seemed to me that few men could have conducted the business with more coolness and quietude of manner, under such a storm of balls as he was exposed to. Indeed, I have never forgotten him from that day.' 'Quietude' of manner summed up Hill's personal style. Harris also described the kit the foot soldiers had to carry. He was not a big man and the huge, awkward, poorly designed and heavy pack was almost too much for him. He swore that many a soldier was defeated more by his pack than by the enemy.

The Battle of Vimeiro followed on 21 August. Unfortunately, at the point of the battle when Wellesley was succeeding in pushing the French back and had the possibility of arriving in Lisbon ahead of the enemy, he was superseded by Sir Harry Burrard as Commander of the Army. The latter, a cautious fellow, lost the opportunity that had been offered, preferring to wait for reinforcements with the imminent arrival—the next day—of a new commander, Hew Dalrymple, who could take the blame if all failed. The French took advantage of his caution to retire in good order.

Madrid fell to the French in November 1808 so Sir John Moore decided to go onto the offensive and confront the French rearguard with 30,000 British troops. However, news soon reached him that Napoleon was approaching with a huge force of 80,000 men to annihilate the British, and thus began the famous retreat to Corunna. The plan was to evacuate the British army by sea, and in the event part of the army left from Vigo and the rest from Corunna. The midwinter retreat was appalling, and it was a tattered, exhausted and reduced force that actually reached the boats. Unfortunately the transports had been delayed by bad weather and mismanagement, and the only small boats available when the army arrived were quickly filled with sick and wounded. Moore fought a desperate action against Marshal Soult (inevitably known as 'old Salt'), to whom

Napoleon had entrusted the pursuit of the British when he left Spain hurriedly to protect his Austrian front. In the struggle the British managed to blow two gunpowder magazines. Embarkation was scheduled to begin on the evening of 16 January but the French attacked at noon. Sir John was killed, but the main part of the tattered army escaped. Hill's brigade, consisting of the 1st Royals, and the 5th, 14th and 32nd Regiments, was the last to go on board ship, having been required to protect the troops in their retreat and embarkation. This episode provides the first record of Hill's care and consideration for his men and especially for the sick and wounded. The evacuation fleet docked at Plymouth and the city was not to forget him: he was given the Freedom in 1812 and later served as Governor in the 1830s.

It was in early January 1809, at Lugo, in the middle of the demoralising retreat, that Hill received a letter from Hawkstone informing him of the death of his uncle, Sir Richard. Rowland's father, John, had succeeded to the estate and the baronetcy, and Rowland himself was to inherit Hardwick Grange and its farms, and £2,000 in cash. He immediately wrote his will on the back of the letter! On a short leave in England he had hardly time to visit the family in Shropshire and take possession of his new estate before he was given a new command and ordered back to the Peninsula, proceeding once again via Cork. He was to serve initially under another cautious general, Sir John Cradock. Morale amongst the troops was very low, but the rapid departure of Cradock and his replacement by Sir Arthur Wellesley was a great tonic. Wellesley is often described as being an arrogant, harsh and bullying character where his enlisted men were concerned, and indifferent to the welfare of 'the scum of the earth'—'it is really wonderful that we should have made them the fine fellows they are'—but the men certainly held him in great respect.

By the time that Wellesley and Hill were together again in Portugal, in April 1809, the Emperor was fighting a somewhat uncertain, though ultimately successful campaign against the Austrians, and had issued orders to Soult to capture Porto, which he did just before Wellesley arrived in Lisbon. When Hill disembarked at Lisbon in early April 1809 he little thought that, with one short break in 1811 due to illness, he would remain abroad until 1814. The Army was destined to march back and forth, advancing and tactically retreating (at which Wellington was a master strategist) until finally, in winter weather at the end of 1813, the British and their Portuguese and Spanish allies would drive the French back through the rugged terrain of the Pyrenees, with Hill gaining his final victories of the campaign.

Wellesley moved swiftly, in May 1809, to push the French out of Porto and the fertile Douro valley, which was such an excellent source of supply for an army. Soult had destroyed the bridge over the Douro, which was flowing fast at that time of year, and retired, leaving only 11,000 men to hold the city. He thought he had ensured there were no boats on the side from which the British were approaching. Hill, leading the 3rd Infantry Division, commandeered some little boats used for harvesting seaweed and, brigade by brigade, transported his men through the delta lagoons to the main road into Porto. Other troops crossed the Douro in wine barges which had been overlooked by the French and attacked the city.[13] In the ensuing engagement Hill replaced Edward Paget, who was seriously wounded, and held the north bank until the French were driven off in late morning. They retreated north-east, hotly pursued by Hill. Soult managed to escape but he left 58 of his guns in Porto. It is said that Wellington sat down to eat the dinner that had been prepared for 'Old Salt'. Hill, together with his younger brother, Clement, and his other ADC, Captain Currie, were all mentioned in Wellesley's dispatches. He wrote many letters to his sister, Mary (known in the family as Maria), and it seems that following their mother's death she took on the role of 'mother hen' to the family. In the letter he wrote from Porto on 22 May he described the capture of the French guns and a great part of the baggage train, including much ammunition. Clement added that he had been hit by a musket ball on his hip 'where my sash was tied' and was bruised and stiff, but reassured Maria that the wound was not serious. Rowland went on to report that his precious greyhound, Dido, was safe. Dido was at that moment the proud mother of a litter of puppies and the letter describes how, when the baggage was being assembled to be sent off before the battle, she herself brought the travelling basket for her pups to be put in. Such was the news from the war front.

Hill wrote to Maria on 30 July 1809 with a long description of the battle of Talavera. First he reassured her that both he and Clement were safe. It had been a bitter struggle, starting with a preliminary skirmish on the evening of the 26th when it was almost dark. Hill was established on the Cerro de Medellin when, at 9p.m., the French attacked most unexpectedly.[14] Hill, who had been riding back to his brigade from dinner and hearing a commotion, rashly rode to investigate the cause, never dreaming that the enemy had made such a bold move. He only just escaped either death or, certainly, capture after his horse was shot and he was seized by a French soldier. He broke free when his horse plunged forwards as it fell. The French were repulsed and the night passed quietly. At dawn the French army was drawn up in lines of battle immediately opposite Hill's post. Battle began at sunrise. Hill lost one horse and was hit by a musket ball near his left ear and the back of his head and had to leave the field, but the battle was almost over by that time and the French were in retreat towards Madrid. Hill later recounted that this was the second time his headgear had saved his life: 'My hat saved my life; it has suffered as much as my helmet did in Egypt.' He added that Clement had been hit by three musket balls (he seems to have been wounded frequently) and lost his horse, as had the other ADC, Currie. The re-supply of horses was evidently a real headache. Hill told his sister that he thought his two wounded animals would recover—one was wounded in the belly and 'the other had 2 shots through its withers and one in the saddle'. It is amazing that the wretched beasts survived. Casualties had been very high and out of 18,000 men the Army had lost 200 officers and around 5,000 men were killed, wounded and taken prisoner. It was a victory dearly bought, but the success saw Wellesley raised to the rank of Viscount Wellington of Talavera.

Mild Rowland Hill inveighed against the Spanish and their total failure to support their allies—the British. Wellesley also was enraged by the cowardice of the Spaniards. He wrote, fuming, to Castlereagh, 'Nearly 2,000 ran off, on the evening of the 27th from the battle of Talavera, not a hundred yards from the place where I was standing, who were neither attacked nor threatened with an attack, and who were frightened only by the noise of their own fire. They left their arms and accoutrements on the ground. Their officers went with them; and they and the fugitive cavalry plundered the baggage of the British army which had been sent to the rear.' Hill's reading of the situation made it clear that he could not see a satisfactory outcome. At the time the British Army in the field numbered about 13,000, although fortunately it was thought by the French to be at least twice its actual size. He wrote to the family that there were no fewer than 10,000 sick and wounded in hospital and men were dying at the rate of fifty a day from exhaustion and disease, usually a form of malaria. Rowland himself, while living pretty rough, seems to have enjoyed surprisingly excellent health. He was of the opinion that Napoleon's possible return to Spain posed a real threat and that the British could still need to retreat to Lisbon and take ship for England. News of the peace signed between Austria and France made this eventuality all the more likely.

The youngest soldier brother, Thomas Noel Hill, served as an officer in a Portuguese regiment from November 1809. The Portuguese army had proved far more professional and reliable than the Spanish, and most of their regiments had British officers, with Marshal Beresford in command. For a time, after Talavera, the brothers had the chance to meet frequently, and if not able to do so often had news of each other, with Rowland in Montejo only some twenty miles from Wellington's HQ in Badajoz. Day-to-day life was fairly quiet outside of normal duty, and they were able to enjoy the more sophisticated society of Badajoz in addition to coursing several times a week. Clement wrote in one letter home, 'I should not wonder if Bonaparte gave us a chase of another sort some of these mornings.' Clement and Rowland had also acquired some sheep, which were destined to accompany the milk goats in the baggage train until they could be transported to England, where the brothers thought they could be used 'to improve the Shropshire breed', not by their looks so much as the fact that they gave good mutton, which was far more important. In one of the sale catalogues at the end of the century there is mention of some 'Spanish' sheep—descendants of these beasts?

In late November 1809 Hill's division was inspected by the C-in-C, now the Viscount Wellington, and Hill himself was promoted to Lieutenant General, a promotion that the Duke had been urging on Horse Guards for some time. He was thirty-seven. At the end of November Hill wrote home saying that the Spanish, having rashly marched on Madrid, had been crushed by the French and suffered enormous loss of cannon, about 8,000 killed and 15,000 taken prisoner. The figure for prisoners demonstrates that the Spanish preferred to give up than to stand and fight. It was a difficult moment, and Hill again expressed his uncertainty as to the future in his letters to Hawkstone.

Wellington was now busy defending Portugal from another invasion and wrote to Hill on 15 December 1809, telling him that he proposed to form two principal corps, both mixtures of British and Portuguese troops. He intended to command the larger corps, to operate in the north of the country and to offer the command of the 2nd corps to Hill. It would be a semi-independent command (was there ever such a thing as a totally 'independent' command under Wellington?) based on the Tagus at Portalegre, on the Spanish-Portuguese frontier, and placed to prevent the French army in the south from advancing on Lisbon. Wellington asked for an immediate reply by messenger. Naturally Hill was delighted to accept this sign of confidence in him. By early January 1810 the entire British force had left Spain to winter in Portugal. Everyone apparently felt much better for the change of scene.

Command of this secondary force—his own wing—gave Hill the opportunity to demonstrate his efficient organisation and his ability to respond to changes in circumstances.[15] He also showed considerable tactical skill and was capable of taking initiatives and operating under pressure, something that he showed himself to be less good at when in an administrative role at Horse Guards twenty years later. At times Wellington sent him orders that expressed his own opinion as to how they should be implemented, but usually with the rider that 'you on the spot must be the best judge whether you can effect your object ...'.

In June 1810 the French captured Ciudad Rodrigo after Marshal Ney had blockaded the city for months. Hill had not expected that it would hold out so long, but Clement wrote to his sister, 'The Spaniards often fight longer than they are expected when they get behind a wall.' Eighteen months later, in January 1812, Wellington retook the fortress. Hill felt confident in his troops and was agreeably surprised by General the Marquis de la Romana's abilities in the field, and also by his very fair written English. The British generals had also been pleased by the Portuguese cavalry regiments, which had performed well. Hill's letters mention occasions when he was in communication with his French opposite number, General Reynier, over the exchange of prisoners. He described one visit made by a member of his staff to the French: 'We are very civil to each other as far as words go.' The officer had been well dined in the French mess and understood from the conversation that the French army was pretty fed up with being constantly provoked by the British and seldom receiving any word from Paris. The French certainly suffered much from desertions.

Perhaps the British armies had more camp followers than the French and this was a deterrent to desertion; certainly it was not a major problem amongst British soldiers in the Peninsula, although not unknown. The number of hangers-on was considerable and Wellington, although complaining frequently, does not seem to have tried very hard to put an end to this practice. The women probably made life marginally more bearable for their menfolk (not always, or even often, husbands), and if their 'fellow' was killed they normally had little trouble in attaching themselves to another. This was to pose a huge problem at the end of the war, when women who could not prove they were married, and did not have any children, were not permitted to go to England with their 'man'.

Officers seldom brought their wives although there were exceptions, such as the famous Juana (Juana Maria de los Dolores de Leon), wife to Harry Smith. She was only 14 when Harry rescued her amongst the disgraceful scenes following the taking of Badajoz in April 1812, married her and lived happily ever after! Another well-known drum follower was the wife of Captain Currie, senior ADC to Rowland Hill. She must have been a brave and indomitable character, given to organising 'tea parties' and 'receptions' whenever a suitable moment arose. A sketch made by a French colonel while a prisoner at Elvas in 1812 shows an English officer (almost certainly Currie) riding at the head of a little group consisting of the officer's lady, her maid, baby, cage of canaries, etc. with a servant in the rear to 'encourage' the mules on the road. On the whole, such practices were not encouraged.

In September 1810 Hill crossed the Mondego and took up his position on the right flank of Wellington's army, already in position at Busaco. The army included 25,000 Portuguese soldiers. Thomas Noel Hill, now a Colonel at the age of 27, was present in command of his regiment. The Portuguese had been turned into excellent soldiers under the direction of Marshal Beresford and his British officers. The French, numbering 65,000, were commanded by Marshal Masséna (Duc de Rivoli and Prince of Essling), with Ney and Reynier in support.

The Battle of Busaco was fought on 27 September. The Anglo-Portuguese army was well placed on a mountain ridge, the main body hidden from the

French by the lie of the land—a strategy frequently employed by Wellington—so Masséna was deceived as to the number of English and Portuguese soldiers lying in wait for him. The allies fought a defensive action and had relatively few losses, but the French lost five general officers, killed or wounded. Thomas Noel was mentioned in dispatches following the brave showing of his Portuguese regiment. Clement Hill wrote home that, following Busaco, 'Marshal Beresford and Lord Wellington have not forgot his [Tom's] name amongst others that are mentioned'.

An intercepted letter from Napoleon to Marshal Masséna showed that the Emperor had underestimated the Portuguese as a fighting force, although he seemed now to have a fairly accurate idea as to the number of English troops available to Wellington. It was the Emperor's urging that had driven Masséna to attack at Busaco, forcing the enemy into the sea, but after the battle Wellington withdrew southwards, removing all produce and livestock as he went, to shelter behind the lines of Torres Vedras, the system of fortifications which he had prepared with great care during the preceding year. Masséna made the mistake of following him, little aware of the horrors to come.

On 12 October Clement wrote to the family at Hawkstone that he and Rowland were comfortably established in a Palace at Alhandra about 18 miles from Lisbon: 'We are both quite well. Tom is not far from us but I have not seen him lately. We hear almost every day of his being well.' And a week later: 'He [Tom] made us a morning call.' It is rather charming that in the middle of this tiring and often exasperating campaign, the brothers were in such frequent touch with each other; their shared experiences must have forged a great bond. Hill had expected to be attacked by the French, but Masséna could make no headway against the strongly defended British positions. With his forage parties experiencing harassment at the hands of the guerillas in the wasted country, and his army facing starvation, Masséna's position became untenable, and on 14 November Hill woke to hear that the French had disappeared during the night. Masséna's retreat in winter was harsh and brutal for both his soldiers and the Portuguese peasantry in the villages, and resulted in his ignominious recall by Napoleon.

By mid-December 1810 Rowland was laid low by a fever. It seems likely that it was a form of malaria. The low-lying country along the Tagus was not healthy, especially in the damp autumn, and many of the men suffered from disease. Hill was taken to Lisbon, where he stayed in the Duke's house and appeared briefly to be recovering, but he remained very weak. As reinforcements seemed to be reaching the French he was loth to leave, but following a severe attack of jaundice he agreed to return to England to recover. He was accompanied by two of his ADCs—brother Clement and Captain Currie. Clement was promoted Captain in April 1811. Hill must have been very happy to spend a few months at home but was anxious to return to the Army and finally did so at the end of May 1811. He arrived too late for the fierce battle around Badajos, which the French were hanging on to grimly, but expressed the hope in a letter home that the allies would retake it very shortly. In fact the French sent such strong reinforcements that Hill drew back and the city was resupplied and reinforced. At about this time Digby Mackworth (later Sir Digby), an ADC to Hill and a young man whom he appears to have held in high regard, was released by the French on the intervention of Lord Wellington. He had been well-treated in captivity—generally, though not invariably, the experience of British prisoners of the French.

Hill remained near Elvas at Vila Vicosa for some weeks, enjoying hunting and rides in the park surrounding a royal palace formerly favoured by the royal family. Here he could obtain excellent supplies, including the wines of Borba which were considered amongst the best in Portugal. He wrote to Maria asking her to thank their eldest brother John for the hounds which had arrived safely and which would 'afford great amusement to the officers of this part of the Army, who I am persuaded, are entitled to every recreation circumstances will admit of'. He also promised to find his young nephew Rowland, John's son, a beautiful Spanish horse. It was this nephew who would succeed his grandfather Sir John (3rd Baronet) to the baronetcy and to Hawkstone—and in 1842 to the title of Viscount Hill on the death of Rowland, Lord Hill—and who by dint of his extravagances was to begin the irrevocable decline of the family.

In the middle of October 1811 it seemed that a French force under General Girard was about to attack Hill's corps, but after being forced to withdraw from Caceres on the 26th, the whereabouts of the French army became unclear. Intelligence finally revealed that they had gone to Torremocha and Hill decided to pursue them, cut them off and try to defeat them. It was a forced march in terrible weather, but the soldiers pressed on regardless and on the evening of the 27th the British corps encamped only four miles from the French at Arroyo de Molinos.[16] The French were unaware of their arrival and, to ensure that they remained undetected, Hill forbade the lighting of fires despite the pouring rain and the cold at an altitude of 6,000 feet. For the fifth night in a row the wretched soldiers slept in the open. Some had been sent into the surrounding villages to prevent the local people from giving any warning to the French; the locals were in fact pro-British but there would always be the odd person wanting to profit from passing on intelligence.

The troops were assembled before dawn broke—not a bugle sounded—and after a short march fell on the unsuspecting French. Hill, as was his habit, led from the front. The second brigade commanded by General Howard had circled the village of Arroyo to prevent the French from escaping by the other side.

The French tried desperately to form into 'squares' but they had no time before being mown down by artillery fire. They fled, leaving piles of equipment. Girard was wounded, but escaped. Some high-ranking prisoners were taken including the Prince d'Aremberg and General Brun, who was second in command to Girard. Hill's own losses were trifling. It was a triumph, and in his *Recollections* Major Sherer wrote, 'One thing in our success at Arroyo de Molinos gratified our division highly; it was a triumph for our General—a triumph all his own.' Hill had taken an initiative and was well rewarded by success. This victory earned the 2nd Division the nickname of 'The Surprisers'. Wellington recognised it and begged the Prime Minister, Lord Liverpool, to obtain some recognition for Hill from the Prince Regent. He said that Hill's service had always been 'meritorious' and very distinguished, and 'he is beloved by the whole Army', which does underscore Hill's reputation for humanity in an age when such a virtue was certainly rare in the Army. This was an important part of his character and an attribute that would make it almost impossible for him to understand Cardigan's behaviour many years in the future.

Writing home on 5 November 1811, Hill gave the family his account of the affair. Clement, who was commended for bravery in the battle, was granted the privilege of carrying the official dispatches to London, always a mark of approbation for meritorious conduct since it brought the messenger into direct contact with very senior government officials and often even the royal family. Hill received letters from numerous colleagues, all of whom appeared genuinely delighted at his success. Not least, news of the victory gave a boost to the morale of Wellington's army during a period of relative inactivity.

Clement had a rough sea voyage to England but was warmly received by Lord Liverpool at his country house. The Prime Minister then sent him on to the Prince Regent at Oatlands. The Prince being sick in bed, Clement actually met the Commander in Chief, the Duke of York, which was probably more congenial for two soldiers. The captured Prince d'Aremberg, a prince of the Imperial family through his marriage to the ex-Empress Josephine's niece, was a prisoner of considerable consequence. He was sent to England and kept at Oswestry in Shropshire, only a few miles from his captor's home at Hawkstone. Officers were usually well housed and put on parole. Hill had not forgotten his own staff. ADCs Currie and Squire were both promoted Major, with the same rank to go to Clement shortly after. The General himself was given the Order of the Bath.

In January 1812 Wellington recaptured Ciudad Rodrigo. The fortress had changed hands several times because of its strategic location on the northern border between Spain and Portugal. Thomas Noel led his Portuguese regiment in the assault, in which his men distinguished themselves. It was a bloody affair with the French garrison putting up a strong defence. Casualties were very high, and many participants demonstrated conspicuous bravery.

Sir Thomas Picton and 'Black Bob' Crauford led the attack; the latter was killed. He had been a tough and ruthless commander, foul-mouthed and bullying, but one who enjoyed the respect if not the affection of his men. The soldiers' conduct after entering the town was appalling—not the British Army's most shining hour. Wellington's 'scum' pillaged and raped in a drunken orgy that lasted for some three days. Wellington was generally totally opposed to such behaviour but perhaps he felt that a slackening of the reins was essential after such a bloody affair, when the men had seen so many of their fellows killed alongside them. In truth, the troops were probably totally out of control.

Similar scenes were to occur after the fall of Badajoz, to which Wellington laid siege on 18 March. He needed to capture this southern border stronghold, but it was only late at night on 6 April, after increasingly anxious hours of desperate and bloody struggle, that the city fell, and once again the troops ran amok. They were not brought under control until 11 April. On this occasion Hill's role was a supporting one, his corps lying north of the Guadiana river towards Merida. He eventually fell back to Merida to avoid confrontation with Soult, who was bringing up his Army of the South from Andalusia. To the consternation of the town's inhabitants, Hill had to destroy the bridge, but he promised the Mayor it would be repaired, which it was some weeks later. The British Army was, on the whole, much respected for its dealings with the local people.

Hill's next success—destined to be lastingly remembered as it formed part of his title when he was elevated to the peerage—was at Almaraz. In April 1812 Wellington ordered Hill to attempt the capture of the French position guarding a bridge at Almaraz. By mid-May, having moved his force with the maximum possible secrecy, Hill hoped to mount a surprise attack, but the French garrison in the castle of Mirabete, which lay on the route to Almaraz, was prepared and defended with vigour.[17] The terrain was too mountainous to deploy artillery and Hill called off the attack. He had, however, discovered a narrow goat track leading to the river down which he led a brigade under cover of darkness. By dawn part of his force was concealed beside the bridgehead at Almaraz and the rest descended below a hill hidden from the French on the south side overlooking the bridge—Fort Napoleon. On the north side Fort Ragusa occupied a similar position. Hill's men stormed Fort Napoleon, catching the French off guard as they were watching a diversionary attack against Mirabete. The captured cannon of Fort Napoleon were then turned on Fort Ragusa while those French soldiers who could attempted to cross to the north side. At the same time the British captured the bridgehead. The French cut the link of boats forming the bridge, thus causing many of their fleeing soldiers to be taken prisoner. The garrison of

Fort Ragusa abandoned the fort and retired northwards. Retrieving the French boats, Hill destroyed the two forts, the river defences, and whatever stores and ammunition they could not carry away with them. Last of all, they destroyed the boats. The most important result of this engagement was that it cut the lines of communication between the French armies of Portugal under Marmont and of the South under Soult.

After the action, Wellington asked Hill if he could not also have destroyed the fortress of Mirabete itself. Hill replied that he had considered it too big and strongly defended for an assault without heavy losses, and had contented himself in the knowledge that it was now at least cut off with the bridge destroyed. Later in the year, at the end of August, Hill passed the great fortress once again on his way to cross the Tagus at Almaraz and was rather pleased to find that his initial estimate of the strength of Mirabete, now abandoned by the French, had been accurate, and that the force he had had with him in May could never have breached the huge, circular tower.

This time it was Currie who bore the dispatches to London and who wrote to the General thanking him for the 'kind and considerate manner in which you have put me in a fair way of promotion'. Hill certainly always looked after his 'family'. ADCs were very much regarded as family—which they frequently were—and formed a close social group around their general. Good generals kept their faithful ADCs for years.

The Army was busy in the summer and autumn of 1812. Despite his great victory at Salamanca and a three-week occupation of Madrid, Wellington was forced to the conclusion that with the means at his disposal he could not oppose the more numerous armies of King Joseph, Soult (Duke of Dalmatia) and Suchet (Duke of Albufeira). He abandoned Madrid and moved north-west to Burgos, where he was forced to abandon his attempt to capture the citadel and retreat into Portugal. The year had seen large areas of Spain freed from the French and the dispatch of at least 20,000 prisoners back to England. The number of prisoners created a huge logistical problem for the British.

The retreat from Burgos was a hasty and desperate affair, a disappointing end to a year of conspicuous successes, but the war in the Peninsula was tilting in favour of the allies, and as the Army recouped its strength in the friendly territory of Portugal in the winter of 1812 it learned of Napoleon's much more devastating retreat from Moscow, and prepared with renewed energy for the implementation of Wellington's grand strategy of 1813.

CHAPTER FIVE

General Rowland, 1st Viscount Hill, Part 2

TERRIBLE WEATHER drove the British into winter quarters at the end of 1812, and this gave everyone a chance to rest, repair their gear and generally recover from the exertions of the previous months. Rowland Hill's army was in cantonments at Coria. Word was beginning to filter through of Bonaparte's disastrous Russian campaign and his ignominious and ghastly retreat from Moscow through a countryside laid waste first by his own troops on their advance, and then by the Russians. Hill even sent French outposts copies of dispatches he had received from London describing the retreat—a good morale-sapping move! Movements in the French armies led to speculation that they were going to retreat to France, but this was not to happen yet. Hill was kept busy preventing his men from plundering the neighbouring villages. The local people, Spanish and Portuguese alike, had had a truly wretched time as the two opposing armies moved back and forth ravaging their country. The French lived off the land and did not pay for the supplies they took from the people, and this contributed to their unpopularity. On the whole, the British Army did pay and were as a result the favoured 'invaders'. It cannot, unfortunately, be said that the soldiers behaved so well; payment may have been made by the quartermasters for provisions and fodder taken from the locals, but the men were quick to plunder and were frequently so drunk they were slung across the back of baggage mules to prevent their being captured by the enemy. Every now and again Wellington issued directives about troop behaviour, and from time to time made an example of men caught in an act of loot or rape, but it was a hard job, given the origins of most of the enlisted and pressed men.

Hill now took a Cheshire man called Egerton into his 'family'. Officers on the Staff of the Generals were usually either the sons of friends or members of the general officer's own family. Egerton was to remain with Rowland to his death and was at his bedside when he died. In his turn Rowland asked the Duke of Wellington to ensure that Egerton wanted for nothing since he had sacrificed his own career to work for the General.

Hill was elected to Parliament for the Borough of Shrewsbury in 1812. His kinsman, William Hill of Attingham, having decided not to stand again for

Shrewsbury, Rowland had been proposed as the Tory candidate.[1] His father John, who had fought the self-same William in the bitter and notorious contest of 1796, managed his son's campaign, even composing his address to the electorate. Voting went on for five days, a long period considering how few people were eligible to vote, but it was intended to allow time for those in outlying districts to walk in. The hustings were set up in front of the old Shire Hall. Poll Books published by rival publishers do not agree as to figures, as seems frequently to have been the case in those days, but Hill was returned alongside the Hon. Henry Bennett. In the event, Rowland never took his seat in the House of Commons due to his elevation to the peerage at the end of the Peninsular Campaign in 1814.

In spring 1813 Wellington decided on a big push. Hill wrote in his correspondence of the cavalry, which did not in fact play a very prominent role in the whole campaign, due mainly to the terrain which often proved unsuitable for their deployment. Wellington always considered that the French cavalry was superior to his own and there had been various incidents of 'galloping at everything' which had ended in disaster. It was only in the southern part of Spain, Estremadura, to the east of Ciudad Rodrigo and Salamanca, that cavalry could be properly deployed. In many events cavalry were used for scout and piquet duties, for which they were very useful.

In June 1812 came perhaps the worst cavalry battle of all from the British point of view. It involved General John Slade and his Dragoon Guards, Slade having already come to notice through his errors of judgement. Hill was engaged in putting pressure on D'Erlon: he sent a Spanish troop off on a recce with Slade, heading towards Maguilla but with strict orders not to engage. Whatever the truth, and there are no conclusive accounts, Slade chose instead to pursue Lallemand. He followed him for a few miles before being brought up short by a narrow passageway. The main French force erupted from the defile and General Slade turned tail and ran. Some say Slade offered money to any man who would stay and fight. He was not a good commanding officer, too nervous and jittery, and Hill was furious. He instigated an enquiry and Wellington was extremely angry. There are different versions of the affair but 'Black Jack' Slade's career in the Peninsula was over when he returned home in April 1813.

By this stage of the war the mounted regiments were, on the whole, in a much better state, and in a letter to his father written in March 1813 Hill reported that the cavalry was now in high fettle and that his brother Robert, Colonel Robert Chambré Hill, had been commended by Wellington for his regiment (Royal Horse Guards Blue) of 'donkey wallopers'.[2] The 'Blues' were not officially integrated as Household troops until 1820. The cavalry as a whole had gained a poor reputation early in the Peninsular War for frequently being out of control when attacking. A considerable amount of artillery and other equipment, not to speak of men and horses, was lost through this lack of discipline.

Rowland wrote an amusing account of a dinner given by the 28th Regiment to celebrate the second anniversary of the battle of Albuera, which had been fought by Beresford in May 1811 during Hill's absence on sick leave in England.[3] Refinements might have been missing. There were, for example, not enough tables and chairs. But campaign life had made the officers very resourceful. The length of a table to seat 100 guests was marked out on a piece of flat ground, two trenches were dug in parallel lines a table width apart, and the sods piled up on the 'table' top and then levelled out so that the guests could sit with their feet in the trench. They all brought their own plate, knife and fork plus, no doubt, a mug or glass. The food was described as being 'of the substantial' order with vast roasts, boiled meats, pies, soups, etc.

At the end of May 1813 Hill's corps arrived at Salamanca and marched on to Burgos in early June. This town had been vacated by the French in September 1812, but they had held on to the great fortress and the British had failed to take it. In October 1812 Wellington had abandoned the siege and retreated, but the fortress was a strategic target controlling the main Madrid/France road and he knew that he must return to capture it before long. Thomas Noel Hill had been in the force attacking the stronghold. In June 1813, as the Allies pressed on with their triumphant outflanking of the forces of King Joseph and his marshals, Rowland's men heard from a distance a mighty explosion. The French had blown up the fortress, regarding it as being no longer of any strategic importance to them as they retreated northwards towards Vittoria.

Hill's Military Secretary, Captain C.H. Churchill, kept a number of papers relating to this period and they give yet another view of life in the Peninsular Army.[4] A great deal of Churchill's time was occupied in dealing with requests for promotion, the exchange of prisoners, and so on. In August 1813, for instance, the French wanted a Monsieur (Colonel) Anthoine, ADC to Marshal Suchet (Duke of Albufera), exchanged, but a letter from Lord Fitzroy Somerset, Military Secretary to Wellington, instructed Hill that they must first receive an accurate list of the names of the English prisoners they were going to be sent in the exchange, as it was the frequent practice of the French to include 'peasants, vagabonds and not true prisoners of war'. Numerous letters to Hill requested that he should not forget various officers who had been captured when such exchanges were being negotiated, and careful note was kept of money sent to prisoners on both sides. There was mention of 1,000 francs being sent by Drouet (Comte d'Erlon) for Colonel Anthoine, and requests for the return of money sent for prisoners who had died. There are also requests to search for officers who were missing.

An interesting letter was written by a French Captain Floquerel. His wife, Maria de Las Navas, had vanished on 21 June, the date of the battle of Vittoria. Unfortunately, there is no indication as to whether the lady was ever found. A happy ending to another domestic affair followed the discovery of a small girl wandering in the baggage train on 21 June. It transpired that she was the daughter of a Captain Guillet who was on the staff of the 'Duke of Dalmatia' (Soult). The child was cared for in the English lines for two months before she could be returned to Marshal d'Erlon's HQ. She was taken on 6 September to an advanced post of the British Army, where she was collected by her happy father.

In November 1813 Hill wrote to a French General Le B. Abbé asking for a search to be made for official papers that had vanished following an engagement between the two armies at Puerto de Maya on 10 November, the 'livres publique' of the 14th Regiment. Hill's letter also asked if the General had the 13th Regiment's paymaster, who was taken prisoner at the same time. General Abbé replied that he had instituted a search but so far had no news of the paymaster, or of a Captain Harman. Had the good Captain vanished with the regimental funds? Sadly, there is no record of the outcome of this affair either. Another episode involved correspondence between Lieut-Colonel John Fitzgerald and his General, Stewart. Fitzgerald had been commanding an advanced reconnoitring sortie on 6 August 1813 when he got lost in a wood, was seized by the enemy and stabbed and had everything taken from him. He asked Stewart to try to arrange for him to be exchanged but, in the event that this prove impossible, he needed his clothes! There is something engagingly civilised about these exchanges in the midst of a bitterly fought war.

21 June 1813 saw one of the most decisive encounters of this long and tough campaign, the Battle of Vittoria, in which Hill commanded the right wing. In the days leading up to the battle there were endless problems over provisioning, but this time it was the Portuguese and not the Spanish who begged for help. Wellington had long ago instructed that the Spanish and Portuguese allies must be responsible for provisioning themselves. Hill was informed that the Portuguese had literally nothing to eat, and was driven to request permission from the Duke to supply them with some meat. The C-in-C replied somewhat crisply that he might help if he wished, but on the strict understanding that it was an exception.

The Battle of Vittoria proved a turning point in the war. On the morning of the battle the Allied army was on the move early and, emerging from a narrow defile into open ground, found itself faced with some 70,000 French troops and a hundred pieces of artillery. Hill's corps had the right, Wellington the centre and Graham the left. The fighting stretched over a vast area—approximately eight miles wide—but Wellington had faith in both Graham and Hill. Hill dispatched his Spanish troops under Morillo to occupy the high ground of La Puebla. It was a bitterly contested affair and the British success was largely thanks to the French neglecting to destroy or even guard a bridge at Tres Puntes, which allowed Picton to cross and surprise two French divisions who had been looking the other way, attacking Hill's position.

The French were driven back in total disarray but the casualties were very high; the British lost some 5,000 men and the French more like 7,500. The spoils that were being carried back to France by the fleeing 'King' Joseph Bonaparte offered rich pickings to his conquerors. It is recorded that there was so much loot—grand 'toilettes', uniforms, money, jewellery, plate, paintings, even the 'royal' chamber pot—that the Allied army's baggage train was literally hung with the spoils.[5] The baton of Marshal Jourdan was found lying on the battlefield. Not content with his crushing victory, Wellington gave orders for the fleeing French to be pursued towards Pamplona. The pursuit was a little more half-hearted than usual because the troops were so busy collecting loot from the scattered remains of 'King Joe's' baggage. All four Hill brothers had taken part in the engagement and all had come through unscathed.

With the French on their way back into France, Hill was put in charge of the blockade of Pamplona. He began to make life uncomfortable for the inhabitants by cutting off their water supply, and firing on anyone who risked obtaining water from the river. As soon as he had put in place all the necessary measures to seal off the city, Hill turned the management of the blockade over to the Spanish. A letter home from Clement written on 1 July reported that they were on the march for France and that the French had fled so fast the Allies had taken few prisoners. Clement went on to say that the mountain countryside was 'the most delightful part of Spain I have ever seen for summer' (and he had certainly seen a lot of it) but added 'it must be bad in winter'. The British Army had its tail up and, in addition, the soldiers were now enjoying good food, including the luxury of French butter.

After a rapid advance involving a number of small *fracas* with the French, the Allied army was now within sight of the border in the Pyrenees. The end was not to come for many months, however, because at this point the French rallied strongly under the energetic command of Marshal Soult, who arrived to take command on 11 July. Hill's men were subjected to fierce attacks and there was fighting almost without cease at Roncesvalles, Sorauren and Maya between 25 July and 2 August. Hill was forced to retreat, but the setback was temporary and the lost ground was quickly retaken. On 29 July the French had tried to relieve Pamplona but Hill's corps forced their withdrawal, his generals Dalhousie and Byng playing the major roles and the latter also capturing a convoy of French

5. Rowland, 1st Viscount Hill (from a miniature).

supplies. Hill estimated that Soult had lost 15,000 men during the three weeks of fighting in the mountains. He also told his family that captured French officers were anxious for peace. They were fighting with ever reduced numbers, albeit still greater than those of the Allied army, because the Emperor constantly needed more soldiers on his eastern front.

Hill received a letter from his old friend, Thomas Graham, whose attempt to take San Sebastian had proved impossible with insufficient guns. It was not one of Graham's most successful affairs, and he lost a large number of men. At length, following an attack on 31 August across the estuary at low tide, the town fell to the British, but not the Citadel, which the French surrendered only on 8 September after a two months' siege. Thomas Noel Hill was involved in the siege and was thoroughly fed up with being 'detained here by this abominable place'. However, when the town did eventually fall to the British Thomas Noel was commended for distinguished services. He was still serving with the Portuguese and was obviously a highly successful soldier and perhaps a little unlucky to have been born in the same generation as his elder brothers, although, apart from Rowland, Sir Thomas is the only brother to feature in the *Dictionary of National Biography*.

On 7 September Wellington learned that Austria had re-entered the war a month earlier on the side of the Allies. This welcome news relieved him of the anxiety that if Napoleon made peace with his adversaries in the east, he might return to fight the British in the Pyrenees. This fear was one of the reasons for Wellington's delaying too precipitate an entry into France.

During October the British crossed the Bidassoa and entered France. In Wellington's battle plan Hill again commanded the right wing. On 9 December 1813 this corps pushed its way across the river Nive in flood conditions. Hope (later Hopetoun), arriving somewhat late, was in command of the left wing between the sea and the river, and was attacked by a huge force under Soult but stood firm. On 13 December a battle was fought at St Pierre de Port, where Soult attacked Hill's tiny force of only 14,000 men. Hill knew he would have to hold out for some time since the pontoon bridge that had been erected to help the army cross the Nive was out of action. It was a bitter battle, with Sir William Stewart, divisional commander of the troops in the centre, distinguishing himself by his bravery. Not so the newly arrived commander of the 71st, Sir Nathaniel Peacocke.[6] Perhaps this man had never previously been involved in such bitter close combat, but he was to be remembered as a coward on the field and a bully in barracks. He ordered his battalion to retreat at a most crucial moment and when Hill went to discover what had led to this great gap in his centre, he found Peacocke in the rear pretending to inspire the Portuguese ammunition carriers to advance while carefully keeping himself well out of danger. Hill was furious and, demonstrating his own bravery, he personally led the 71st and his final reserve, Le Cor's reliable Portuguese, into action.

Conspicuous bravery was shown by many of the commanders and in particular Major General Edward Barnes, Colonel John Cameron and General Byng. Both armies were exhausted and the French finally withdrew just as Wellington arrived. Hill had held his position until Wellington could bring up his reserves. It is often said that this battle was only the second occasion on which Rowland Hill was heard to swear.[7] The death rate was appalling but the 'thin red line' had held through almost the entire day, Hill in constant personal danger as he rallied his men from the front again and again. Soon after the arrival of the reinforcements, the French retired to Bayonne. Wellington wrote to Sir John Hope that, 'Sir Rowland Hill has given the enemy a terrible beating.' The Duke wrote the same, in French, to General Castanos and added, 'It is a long time since I saw so many dead on a battlefield.' He rode up to Hill when victory was certain and caught his hand saying, 'Hill, the day is your own.' Peacocke had retired a second time to the rear, not wounded but shocked after a ball passed through his coat tails! He was subsequently informed that the King (in fact, due to George III's madness, the Prince Regent) had no further use for his services. He was very fortunate not to suffer a worse fate. Clement Hill again had the honour of carrying his brother's official dispatches to England.

While the two armies faced each other across the river Adour a certain trade was established between the men which seems to have consisted largely of the French supplying brandy to the English: a useful rock in the middle of the river had a large canteen placed on it where the British put money to be replaced with the brandy. It did lead to some trouble: one day the English soldier sent to fetch the brandy obviously drank rather too much of it and the French had to shout to his comrades to come and fetch him! On another occasion, in early 1814, an English squaddie called Patten was so enraged when he found the canteen empty and his money gone that he charged straight on across the river to an enemy outpost, seized an amazed sentry whom he stripped of his gear, and rushed back to the British lines.[8] A flag of truce appeared on the French side and a young Captain begged for the return of the stolen kit saying that his own commission and probably the sentry's life would be at stake if it could not be recovered. Patten reluctantly relinquished the gear and was sentenced to 300 lashes. Sir Rowland now demonstrated something of the judgement of Solomon. He had the wretched Patten paraded for punishment and the soldier felt, perhaps not unnaturally, very ill-used. The General delivered a stern homily on the stupidity and danger of Patten's conduct but then, unexpectedly, listed some of the man's previous acts of gallantry and, beaming in his usual paternal fashion, quashed the sentence.[9]

Whilst his army prepared for its next action, Wellington took pains to try to ensure that his men behaved reasonably well to the civilian population. In fact, the wretched peasants were not used to troops that actually paid for their provisions, and once the locals realised this was the case they lost little time in making money out of the occupying force. Wellington knew the Spanish troops would not be able to resist plundering and looting, though, so he sent most of them home.

Early in February 1814 Hill wrote, 'We are again in motion ... but I do not expect any serious resistance.' After a week of active campaigning he wrote on 20 February to Maria, saying that he was very tired and so were his men, but that they now looked forward to a period of quiet and indeed to a lasting peace. He was wrong. Inactivity did not last long. Orders came to push the enemy back north and the next battle on 27 February was at Orthez, where Hill again received a warm commendation from Wellington. He had threatened Soult's rear by crossing the river Gave de Pau by means of a convenient ford, but when Soult decided to retreat Hill just failed to prevent the French from reaching a bridge over the Luy de Béarn at Sault de Navailles despite his racing for it. Following his defeat at Orthez, realising that he was already cut off from retreating north to Bordeaux, Soult headed north-eastwards for Toulouse.

As they advanced towards the 'rose' city, Rowland Hill learned from Clement, then at Hawkstone, of the death of their oldest and apparently much-loved brother, John. A memorial on the north wall of Hodnet church extols his virtues. It was his son, another Rowland, who would eventually inherit Hawkstone with the title of 4th Baronet (after the death of his grandfather, another John, in 1824) and, later, his uncle's viscountcy. There would have been little time to grieve, as the armies continued to skirmish and a minor battle was fought at Tarbes. By 3 April the British had managed to cross the swollen waters of the Garonne, and the scene was set for Wellington's final action, even as Napoleon accepted the inevitable and signed, on 6 April in Fontainebleau, a deed of unconditional abdication.

The Peninsular War was almost over. The campaign had made the career of Wellington, who would go on to become Commander in Chief of the Army and Prime Minister. On Easter Sunday, 10 April 1814, he initiated the final action of the war, the Battle of Toulouse. It lasted for two days, and was fought mainly on the east side of the city, with Hill and his men providing diversionary activity on the south side, attacking a division in the St Cyprien area and engaging in heavy hand-to-hand fighting. On the Monday night Soult abandoned Toulouse under cover of darkness and retreated south-east towards Carcassone. Hill marched his troops through the city in watchful pursuit.

On Tuesday 12 April Wellington made his triumphal entry and on the 13th word arrived from Paris bringing news of the abdication. The citizens of Toulouse wasted no time in fêting the victors, and Rowland found himself enjoying a ball where he also saw his brother Robert. In a letter to Maria, he wrote that the Duke had left for Paris leaving him in command of the Army, a part of which was to be readied to embark for America. He added that he would not accept the command in America if offered it.[10] He was tired. On his eventual arrival in London in May he was told 'it was the particular wish of the Government' that he should take this appointment. He saw Lord Bathurst the following day and was told that he need not leave immediately, but was pressed to go and probably would have felt it incumbent on himself to do so, except plans were changed and in the end only a small force was sent which did not merit the appointment of such a senior general.

The peace celebrations were now in full swing and Sir Rowland became Lord Hill of Almaraz and of Hawkstone (eventually changed to Almaraz and Hardwick), and was awarded a pension of £2,000 a year. He took his seat in the Lords on 1 June. On 6 June, Tsar Alexander, the King of Prussia, Metternich, the old warhorse Prince Blücher and the young Prussian princes all crossed the Channel to join in the celebrations. Twenty years of war provoked by the ambition of Napoleon Bonaparte were over. The English public gave an extraordinary welcome not only to all the foreign leaders but also to their home-bred heroes and, superficially unheroic figure though he might appear, Rowland Hill was very much in the front rank of these men. A truly modest soul, he felt that he had only done his duty, but he was to be garlanded and fêted all the same. Together with Lord Beresford, he was given the Freedom of the City of London at a ceremony at the Guildhall at the beginning of June. Both were presented with handsome swords and a gold box containing a parchment scroll with their Freedom inscribed. His old uncle, the Rev. Rowland Hill, attended this ceremony. The new Lord Hill hankered after his family and Hawkstone, but the public expected to pay tribute to its heroes. He also received a sword from the city of Birmingham accompanied by the words, 'Take it, my Lord, and it will not fail you.'[11] He accepted it, apparently saying, 'Trust it to me and I will not disgrace it.'

The next stop was Shrewsbury, where he looked likely to be overwhelmed by the public's enthusiasm. Thousands poured into the town. The Yeomanry paraded for his inspection and formed part of the procession that escorted him. He was accompanied by Lord Kenyon, another illustrious Salopian whose grand-daughter, Charlotte, was to marry John Hill, clergyman nephew of Rowland Hill (and the author's great grandfather). Owing to the recent death of his elder brother, John, Rowland paraded with his charger 'dressed' in black trappings. Houses were bedecked with flowers and shops were closed; it was truly a hero's return, and the hero was accompanied by his three soldier brothers and his faithful ADC, Cheshire man John Egerton, all of whom had served throughout the long campaign.[12] Freedom of the Corporation of Shrewsbury was voted to Rowland and his brothers and is still the right of male descendants today. The ceremony took place in 'the Quarry', Shrewsbury's beautiful public park on the banks of the river Severn, and such was the press of people wanting to touch Lord Hill or shake his hand that he had to be rescued, saying, 'I never did fly from the fury of my enemies, but I have been obliged to do so from the kindness of my friends.'

Rowland was relieved that plans to send a large force to North America were cancelled and he also declined the offer of commanding the Army in Scotland, which left him in a position to enjoy, for the first time, his estate at Hardwick Grange, and to participate in his favourite field sports. The shooting seasons found him at many of the great houses such as Belvoir and Chatsworth.

As early as 1813 Shrewsbury determined to erect a monument to celebrate the achievements of its favourite son.[13] Much debate ensued but it finally took the form of a Grecian Doric column erected in Abbey Foregate. It is huge: 15 feet in diameter—the same as London's Monument—and 133 feet in height. This made it the tallest such column in the world at the date of construction; after all, it had to exceed Bonaparte's column in the Place Vendôme in Paris! The figure of the General is some 16 feet high and was designed by Panzetta and cast by Coade and Sealy of London. The lions lying at each corner of the plinth were made by John Carline, a local architect and builder. The cost was mainly borne by public subscription and construction was carried out by members of the Salopian Lodge of the Masonic Order. Many of the Hills appear to have been masons. Certainly Sir Richard, 2nd Baronet was, and it thus seems likely that others were too. The first stone was laid on 27 December 1814 and the foundation deposit inserted into a block of some four tons in weight contained a bottle with silver and gold coins of the realm and a copy of the *Shrewsbury Chronicle*. The internal staircase was designed and constructed, at his own expense, by Mr John Straphen and has 172 steps. The column was completed in June 1816, by which date yet another battle could, of course, be added. Two sides of the plinth were inscribed with the General's battles, a third with a sort of eulogy to Lord Hill's achievements and the last with the full list of his titles, in Latin. It cost a total of £6,000 exclusive of John Straphen's work.

The General was asked to nominate a veteran soldier to act as caretaker to the column. He wrote in September 1817 from his post at Cambray with the Army of Occupation in France to put forward the name of a Sergeant Davies of the Royal Welsh Fusiliers. This man died in 1820 and his widow was permitted to continue his guardianship. In 1835 Trooper George Okeley of the Royal Horse Guards Blue was appointed her successor as Keeper of the Column. Lord Hill was then Colonel of the Royal Horse Guards Blue and Sir Robert Hill had commanded them at Waterloo. Younger brother Clement was to become Colonel of the Blues.

The peace was all too short-lived. In France too much had changed since the storming of the Bastille in July 1789 and the benevolent, clever but entirely ineffectual Bourbon King Louis XVIII, younger brother of Louis XVI, was unable to rise to the political challenge of the times. There was appalling poverty amongst Napoleon's veteran soldiers and the backward state of the country shocked English visitors. The French had hoped for relief from the tight conscription that had existed for so long, and also from the heavy war taxes imposed by the Emperor. The wily Talleyrand had negotiated excellent terms at the Congress of Vienna, and Napoleon's former Marshals were 'forgiven' and permitted to keep all the titles and perquisites they had been awarded, but the poor and the ex-soldiers were not so fortunate.

Barely were the countrywide celebrations over in England when Napoleon escaped in March 1815 from the very poorly guarded island of Elba and landed in Golfe Juan near Cannes in the south of France. The famous 'Hundred Days' had begun. The recently restored King Louis XVIII, probably best known as a *bon viveur*, took to his heels as his army rallied to Bonaparte, including Marshal Ney who had initially sworn to bring his old chief back to Paris in a cage; such was Napoleon's amazing ability to attach and command. Ney was to die for his disloyalty to the King.[14]

Rowland was on a pleasure visit to London with his sister Emma when he received an urgent summons to Downing Street. Wellington was at the Congress in Vienna and the British government was most anxious to keep the young Prince of Orange from doing anything stupid following King Louis' flight to Ostend. This young man had served on the Duke's staff in the Peninsula and was well-liked but impetuous and inexperienced. The idea of 'Slender Billy' being at the head of an army was definitely worrying even to his closest friends. Lord Bathurst spelled out the government's wish to handle the young Prince as tactfully as possible and that is probably why the avuncular Lord Hill was chosen for the role. The plan was to keep all quiet while the Allied Army was assembled and the Duke would arrive from Vienna to command it. Things did not look too promising for the Allies: the first battalions of most British regiments were either in America or in Ireland, and the available troops were by no means the experienced and battle-hardened men that had survived the long, arduous Peninsular Campaign. Fortunately it turned out that a number of seasoned generals were ready. Rowland arrived in Brussels on 1 April. Three days later old 'Douro', Wellington, arrived. He put Lord Hill out at Grammont, where he was opposite his old enemy from Arroyo de Molinos, General Girard, and very near the home of the Prince d'Aremberg, whom he had captured at Arroyo.

The Iron Duke had time to pester Horse Guards on behalf of Lord Hill, and he wrote to Lord Bathurst saying that Hill was at the head of what amounted to an international army and maintaining of necessity a large staff. His pay was only that of a Lieutenant General, although he had several of that rank serving under him, and his expenses were beyond his means. Wellington asked that he should be given the pay and allowances of a General on the Staff and this was agreed to.

Rowland had written to his diplomat brother, Sir Francis, that he might find it interesting to spend some time in Brussels at this momentous hour, and Sir Francis arrived together with Charles Shore (brother to Maria, later to become the wife of Sir Thomas Noel Hill), later Lord Teignmouth. Shore's father had been a close friend of Rowland's uncle, Sir Richard, sharing his Evangelical beliefs and being a staunch supporter of the Bible Society. The two men stayed until the eve of battle, when the General thought it politic for them to remove themselves to Antwerp.

By this time Napoleon had amassed a large fighting force, whereas the Allies—British, Russian, Prussian, Austrian and Dutch/Belgian—were widely scattered. In the event, the Russians were not to join the Allies until after the Battle of Waterloo. Old Prince Blücher was at the head of the huge Prussian army of 100,000 men which was holding the Franco/Belgian border from the Ardennes to Charleroi. Wellington tried to hold the border to the coast with a mixed bag of Dutch, British, Hanoverian and Brunswickers. This was the short but socially glittering interval in Brussels of which so much has been written: the parties with balls, picnics, troop reviews, 'breakfasts' and hunting in the forests which were organised principally by the upper-class English society families who had flocked there that spring. The English were still enjoying the freedom that Napoleon's first abdication and the subsequent peace had brought to people who had been virtually prisoners in their own island for 20 years.

On the night of the Duchess of Richmond's famous ball, held on 15 June, Rowland Hill was not present; he was with his corps preparing to take up a position at Merke Braine to the right of the Nivelle road at first light on the next day. He had monitored the enemy's movements carefully since Napoleon had taken everyone by surprise with the speed of his advance. On 15 June Ney attacked at Quatre Bras. The battle for the crossroads was continued on 16 June, ending in a hard-won victory for the Allies. On the morning of the 16th, Hill visited Wellington at his HQ at Quatre Bras. Sergeant Robertson (92nd Highlanders) wrote, 'We all stood up and cheered ...'. Wellington rushed out to see if the French were coming and laughed when he saw the cheering was for

Hill. Meanwhile, Napoleon inflicted a defeat on the Prussians commanded by Prince Blücher at Ligny on the same day. In the course of this engagement the 72-year-old General was knocked down and ridden over by the French cavalry. One of his staff remarked it was lucky he had such a thick head after he emerged from the affair more or less unscathed! Old he may have been, but Blücher was to prove a most reliable ally. It is highly unlikely that Waterloo would have ended as it did without the Prussians.News of this defeat for the Allies arrived swiftly in Brussels, causing panic. All roads to Antwerp and the other Channel ports were clogged with fleeing civilians, mainly British, their carriages and carts loaded with possessions. Fortunately Blücher was a seasoned campaigner and did not panic but drew back towards Wavre in order to maintain contact with Wellington. He had sustained casualties of between 15,000 and 20,000 men, which was a serious loss for the Allies and a severe blow for morale.

The next day Wellington withdrew from Quatre Bras to his chosen position at Mont St Jean, near the hamlet of Waterloo, Blücher to Wavre, and Napoleon fatefully despatched Marshal Grouchy with 33,000 men in vain pursuit of the Prussian army.

The night of 17/18 June was dreadful for the men in the field. It poured with rain and the soldiers were unable to keep dry or light cooking fires. Hill and his staff fared only marginally better in a small cottage beside the Brussels road. On 18 June Hill, in command of Wellington's main reserve, was posted behind and beyond his right (western) flank. Being the Duke's most reliable and experienced commander, his task was to safeguard the western lines of communication to the ports on the coast, in case a swift retreat became necessary. His command comprised the famous Light Brigade (under General Sir Frederick Adam), the 23rd, the 51st and the 14th under Colonel Mitchell, and the 1st Brigade of the King's German Legion, composed of very reliable troops. Because of his position at the beginning of the battle, it has been assumed that Hill took little part in the engagement, but this is quite untrue. Sir Digby Mackworth, one of Hill's ADCs, described his General's actions at 'the grand crisis of the day':

> He placed himself at the head of his Light Brigade, 52nd, 71st and 95th, and charged the flank of the Imperial Guard as they were advancing against our Guards. The Light Brigade was lying under the brow of the hill, and gave and received vollies within half pistol shot distance. Here Lord Hill's horse was shot under him, and, as he ascertained the next morning, was shot in five places. The General was rolled over and severely bruised, but in the melée this was unknown to us for about half an hour. We knew not what was become of him: we feared he had been killed; and none can tell you the heartfelt joy which we felt when he rejoined us, not seriously hurt.[15]

Mackworth also recorded his experiences of the day's conclusion at greater length later that night:

> At last, seeing all their efforts vain, all their courage useless, deserted by their Emperor who was already flown, unsupported by their comrades who were already beaten, the hitherto Invincible Old Guard gave way, and fled in every direction. One spontaneous and almost painfully animated 'Hurrah' burst from the victorious ranks of England. The line at once advanced, generals, officers, soldiers, all partaking in one common enthusiasm. The battle was over ... Lord Hill and staff retired to a small cottage where we now are. We have but one room between nine of us, including his Lordship. All but myself are asleep.

They had dined on soup made from two fowl scrounged by Rowland's servant, John Holding. These soldier servants were amazing fellows and could almost always be relied on to conjure something out of nothing. The Emperor, who had boasted that he would finish off the Allied Army and its sepoy General, Wellington, before lunch, was finally crushed.

Letters from Rowland and Thomas Noel to Maria at Hawkstone impart some of the exhilaration that they felt. Thomas wrote: 'We gained a complete victory yesterday, Boney in person commanding the French,' and the wounded Clement added a postscript to Tom's letter: 'We are all in high spirits at the complete drubbing Boney has had, towards which I hope the Blues (commanded by brother Robert) did their share.' Clement had been pinned to his saddle by a sword thrust through the fleshy part of the thigh and was later to maintain that his life had been saved by his wearing his dressing gown because, in his haste to dress, he had not been able to find a shirt. Robert Chambré Hill had been wounded by a musket ball passing through his right arm and slightly grazing his chest. Both were initially recorded as being seriously wounded, but were removed to Brussels where they made rapid recoveries.

Rowland went with the Duke to visit Blücher on 23 June, by which time the armies had advanced into France.[16] They found 'the old Marshal amusing himself with Bonaparte's hat, stars and personal baggage which, together with his carriage, had been taken by the Prussian cavalry'.

It soon became apparent that victory had been dearly bought and that the battle had given victory to the Allies by only a whisker. There were the sad statistics of the friends killed or badly wounded. Of Rowland's own 'family', Colonel Currie was dead after nine years on the staff; he had served as Assistant Adjutant General to Rowland at Waterloo. Currie came from a military family and had been commissioned by the Duke of York at the age of thirteen. Young Orlando Bridgeman, who hailed from another well-known Shropshire family, was wounded, although not in danger. They buried Currie, and also the remains of Rowland's horse. Despite the fact that he is frequently described as rallying his men from the front, the General appears to have been wounded only twice, once in Egypt and the second time at the end of the Battle of Talavera, and both times he was saved by his headgear.

Wellington's dispatch to London contained a paragraph relating to Lord Hill: 'I am also particularly indebted to General Lord Hill for his assistance and conduct upon this as upon all other occasions.' Probably no other officer received such constant commendations from the Iron Duke as Rowland Hill.

Awards were conferred on Rowland, his brothers and his ADCs after the battle. Major Churchill was promoted by brevet to the rank of Colonel. (Some of Hill's papers were kept by Churchill; his daughter Louisa Anne married a Major General John Michel in 1838 and, at some point, the Michel family deposited them with the Dorset County Record Office.) Rowland, Lord Hill was made a member of the Russian Order of St George, 2nd Class, a Commander of the Order of Maria Theresa and, in January 1816, the Prince Regent declared by Letters Patent that Lord Hill was to be styled a Baron of the United Kingdom and of Great Britain and Ireland, and heirs male of body lawfully begotten, by the name, style, and title of Baron Hill of Almaraz and of Hawkstone and Hardwicke in the county of Salop and in default of such issue, to the heirs male lawfully begotten of his late brother John Hill Esq., deceased, of Hawkstone, in the said county of Salop. Thus Rowland Hill's newly acquired dignity could be passed on despite his childlessness. This was a rare privilege; a new creation can only normally descend by direct line for the first generation. The Prince Regent also bestowed on him the Guelphic Order for his distinguished exertions in leading the Hanoverian troops at Waterloo. Shortly afterwards the Duke of York announced that Rowland was to wear a gold clasp in commemoration of the Battle of Orthez which had been one of his final victories of the Pyrennean Campaign in 1813/14.

Robert Chambré received the Military Order of the Bath, became a Knight of the Order of Maria Theresa and received from Russia the Order of St George, 4th Class. Thomas Noel, KCB, was made a Knight of the Order of Maximilian Joseph by the King of Bavaria.

Clement? Nothing. This brother served Rowland loyally and long, probably too long for the advancement of his own career, although later he would become a Major General.

Lord Hill rode into France and on to Paris to take possession of the city, establishing himself in the *Hotel Montesquieu*. The English flocked across the Channel and the celebrations began, with the Allies holding balls and entertainments of every sort, together with troop reviews. Louis XVIII returned to his capital. He was often referred to by the French as Louis 'dix huitres' in reference to his gluttony and, especially, his taste for oysters!

Rowland was longing to return to Shropshire but his rank required his attendance at many functions and he himself gave a big party. He said to Maria that he feared the Bourbons were not popular; he was right. In December he wrote that since both Paris and the countryside were peaceful the Army was to withdraw from the city and go into quarters at Cambray in the north. He commented on the execution of Marshal Ney (the Prince of Moskowa) that month.[17] Ney had served Louis XVIII as War Minister after Napoleon's first abdication but following his rapid defection to the Emperor at the start of the 100 days the Royalist faction was unwilling to forgive him a second time, although it is said that Louis desired a different outcome. Rowland seems to have considered his execution appropriate. With the exception of Murat, executed in Naples in October 1815, Napoleon's other leading generals were pardoned and permitted to retain both their grandiose titles and the perquisites that they had received under their old leader. Rowland disapproved, feeling that all trophies and plunder should be returned to 'its proper owners'. He, personally, never helped himself to 'loot'—the only recorded plunder being some hams that his manservant obtained from the baggage train of King Joseph. He also expressed strongly his opinion that 'the allies ought not to leave without so completely clipping the wings of France as to render its government, be it what it may, totally incapable of disturbing the peace of Europe again'.

February 1816 found Rowland asking the Duke for permission to go home on urgent family business. He explained the problem to Wellington: it arose from his uncle, Sir Richard, and then, following *his* death in 1808, Rowland's father, Sir John, together with his cousin, Noel the 1st Lord Berwick, and then, on *his* death, Sir John Powell, being 'bondsmen' to Thomas Eyton. They had apparently stood surety for their fellow Salopian and on his death the Exchequer demanded £300,000; no wonder the family was in a state. Wellington immediately granted him leave for as long as was needed and his reply does seem to confirm the Duke's genuine respect for Rowland.[18] He pressed Hill to accept a personal loan from him, as he feared that in the existing financial climate it would be impossible to borrow such a sum. Hill was touched but luckily did not need to call upon the Duke for help. The case took several years to settle, but when the Exchequer finally came to an agreement, in 1820, Sir John Hill on the one hand and Sir John Powell on the other had only to pay £5,000 each. Rowland patently felt himself to be pretty much head of the family with his father now an old man and his nephew, young Rowland, not yet of age. During the protracted negotiations, Lord Teignmouth, father of Maria Shore who was shortly to be married to Thomas Noel, was in talks with the Chancellor, Vansittart, on behalf of the family.

Back in Cambray, Lord Hill lived at the Château Maniers where his life was made comfortable by his devoted aide, Colonel Egerton, and his wife. Early in 1817 he suffered another severe attack of the illness that had struck him down in Portugal—probably a form of malaria. Once he was well enough to travel he went to England for a short time to convalesce. On his return to Cambray there was plenty of time for hunting, coursing, etc. Hill's favourite sport was boar hunting, and he had a close shave when he was attacked by a furious boar flushed from the woods by the beaters; apparently he plunged his spear into the beast but the shaft broke off with the head embedded in its skull. Wellington sent him a replacement, and the tusks and skull of the animal were kept at Hawkstone alongside the helmet that saved his life in Egypt.

In September 1817 a group set off to visit the battlefield of Waterloo. Rowland was accompanied by Clement, Colonel Egerton, sister Emma, Colonel Abercromby (son of Sir Ralph, his former commander in Egypt) and his nephew, George Hill, who was the son of Robert Chambré Hill. They visited the tiny cottage where Hill, Clement and John Egerton had spent the nights before and after the battle, and visited an even meaner one where Clement's wounds had been dressed immediately following it. They also found the spot where Colonel Currie's body had been found after the battle and where John Egerton and Hill's servant, John Holding, had buried the body the following morning. Emma made several sketches and wrote a description of the landscape of the battlefield with the help of her brothers. This is in the Shropshire Records Office.

In the Creevy diaries that inveterate gossip reports going to dine with Lord Hill at Cambray in 1818.[19] It was apparently a big party and they all dined in a tent. Creevy reports 'Miss Hill'—presumably sister Jane, who acted as her brother's hostess—as a more likely figure than her brother to be second in command of the Army, Lord Hill's appearance being so unmilitary. General Sir Edward Barnes, the Adjutant General, told Creevy that the Army could not have a better No. 2 than Hill and 'the Diarist', in turn, recorded his favourable impressions of the General and his formidable sister.

The Army of Occupation was finally withdrawn in 1818 and Lord Hill had no official military duties for a time, although he was in regular attendance in the House of Lords. He was also chosen by George IV to carry the Royal Standard at his Coronation in 1821. Nephew Rowland was now of age and had taken his seat as MP for North Shropshire, the first appearance on his feet being the moving of an address at the request of Castlereagh. William Wilberforce, who was a family friend, wrote a letter to Hawkstone saying that he had acquitted himself well. This young man had come into a large inheritance at a very young age; his father had died when he was a schoolboy and it seems probable that he was rather spoilt. Although he appears to have been a popular figure in the

County and liked by his tenantry, most of the blame for the family collapse must be laid at the door of his enormous expenditure on the 'aggrandisement' of the estate over many years.

Rowland, Lord Hill was constantly being offered prestigious positions, but he appears to have been reluctant to accept anything that would take him from home for long. He was at heart a countryman and after so many years away campaigning, with only very brief periods of leave at home, he was obviously anxious to help the family and to spend time at Hardwick improving his own house and farms. A splendid anecdote of these times appeared in the local paper headed 'extraordinary fox chace'.[20] This lasted some two hours, ending with the beast holed up in a house belonging to a Miss Langford in the village of Dodington. The fox ran up the stairs and hid himself in a cupboard pursued by the pack of hounds, terrifying the owner and her maid. Jack Mytton was the owner of the pack and was, it is reported, quick to compensate the two poor ladies. The paper described Sir John Hill as the 'father of heros' and he was reported as being a bruising rider who was almost always in at the death. Not bad at the age of 80. There were apparently five Hills (including Lord Hill) riding that day, and the brush was awarded to one of the late Colonel John Hill's sons. Jack Mytton of Halston was a notorious sportsman who ended his life an alcoholic, held in the King's Bench Prison for debt.

Lord Hill was shown the first designs for the alterations to Hardwick Grange in 1820 by Thomas Harrison of Chester; he found them too elaborate and in 1821 the architect sent a simplified drawing. Harrison wrote to Carline, the Shrewsbury architect/builder: 'The elevations in outline are, you will perceive, more or less simplified ... and as his Lordship appears to wish a useful rather than an ornamental mansion, the same plan might be executed at much less expense by preserving the old front and adding the dining room etc. in a way more or less to agree with it.' This sums up Rowland's personality; he did not wish to be flamboyant in his way of living. One detects perhaps a faint note of disappointment in Harrison's letter; his creative skills were obviously not going to be heavily employed on this commission. Work was carried out between 1822 and 1824. The General's total outlay came to £7,482, with 'chimney pieces and bells' costing two-thirds as much as the new lodge (£348)! An additional £1,027 was spent on the grounds. The house was demolished in 1931, but a Gothic lodge remains, as do the stable block and the outline of a landscape garden.

In 1825 Lord Hill was promoted to the rank of full General, and in 1827 was asked to take command of the Army in India. He declined on the grounds that after service in the Mediterranean and in the Peninsula he already knew that heat did not suit him. He was next offered the senior post of Master General of the Ordnance, an important position carrying responsibility for the manufacture of all arms and artillery. Hill had previously turned down the Lieut-Generalship, giving as his reason the fact that he was not accustomed to sitting in an office and that living in the city permanently would adversely affect his health.

Finally, in 1828, came an offer no soldier could refuse, the Command of the Army, which Wellington, on becoming Prime Minister, was obliged to relinquish. Officially Hill was appointed 'Senior General on the Staff, General Commanding in Chief'. This was slightly different from being 'Commander in Chief' in that it did not include a seat in the Cabinet. Hill, even now, was by no means the most senior general on the Army list, but it was a very gratifying appointment. If the Duke had once written of him, 'But I am not sure that he does not shrink from responsibility', Hill had patently borne a great deal of responsibility during his long years at the top of his soldiering career, although, in most cases, the buck had always finally rested with Wellington. And Rowland had had no experience of the politics of an office such as he was to encounter at Horse Guards. He certainly preferred to avoid angry words and direct confrontation, despite his reputation as a stickler for discipline. One of his letterbooks is headed 'soft words turneth away wrath but grievous words stir up anger' (from Proverbs 15:1). His appointment caused severe disappointment to others who had coveted the post.

At the end of 1830 England had a new monarch, William IV. The former Duke of Clarence, 'Billy' was not an intelligent man and could be counted on to 'put his foot in his mouth' when making speeches. One of his early acts was to confer the Colonelcy of the 'Blues' on Lord Hill when the Duke of Cumberland resigned on a point of etiquette. It was customary for the C-in-C to command the entire Household Brigade. The appointment was apparently a crushing blow to the Marquis of Londonderry, who had been lobbying heavily for the appointment. The Marquis felt that Lord Hill would not be given yet another 'juicy' appointment so soon after receiving the governorship of Plymouth, the City of Plymouth having held Rowland in the highest esteem since he had demonstrated such care for the sick and wounded in the evacuation following Corunna. Considering his very long service at the top of the military tree, the rewards that came his way were really not that numerous and there is certainly no likelihood that he sought them himself.

Once installed at Horse Guards, Rowland rented Westbourne House at Westbourne, then still a suburban area of London. Today Lord Hill Street—a very dreary thoroughfare—is to be found beside Paddington Station. The new King, William, said to Hill shortly after his accession, 'I do not dine with any body in London, you know, but you do not live in London and I shall come and dine with you'—and he did so at least once. One party included prominent names such as Wellington, Combermere, and the future Prime Minister Robert Peel. Rowland had taken on one of his nephews, Alfred, son of his brother Robert

Chambré, as one of his ADCs. In May 1832 he wrote to say that he considered Alfred would require £500 per annum to cover the cost of maintaining three horses, a trooper and a private servant, which gives some idea of the costs borne by officers, although for young Alfred it was probably cheaper to be his uncle's ADC than have to meet heavy mess bills in the Royal Horse Guards Blue.

Writing in his *Personal History of the Horse Guards (1750-1872)*, published in 1873, J.H. Stocqeler described Lord Hill as 'decidedly the most distinguished of the generals who had served under the Duke in the Peninsula'. He went on to say, 'His services in Spain and Portugal had been beyond price. Individually he was beloved by the Army. When the soldiery looked on him in the Peninsula they thought of "home", for he was the type of a country gentleman; homely, kind, frank, and courageous.' Stocqeler also described Hill's commitment to military loyalty, and the swift retribution that fell on any officer deemed to have failed in fulfilment of his duty or the maintenance of discipline. On the other hand, he was always anxious to recognise good service and to support his officers when in difficult situations.

Hill's period of tenure at Horse Guards saw trouble in Canada, a slave mutiny in the West Indies, the ongoing problems in Ireland and domestic unrest with the Chartist Movement, which caused the militias and other troops to have to act as 'policemen'. Hill's loyalty to the Throne and to the Army led to a political opponent, Sir Rufane Donkin, testifying in Parliament to the honest and impartial manner in which he had distributed the patronage of the Army. Donkin believed that never for one moment since that Noble Lord had taken office had he given way to private feeling or political bias in his distribution of the Army patronage at his disposal. He continued by saying that, although opposed in politics to Lord Hill, he felt it his duty to bear testimony to the impartiality always manifested by the Noble Lord. Nobody who knew Rowland would have been surprised at this. Indeed, in March 1828, immediately after he took up his position as GC-in-C, Rowland apparently held out for his own choice as the new commander of a crack Scottish regiment, 'a tip top one—one of those beautiful Highland regiments'.[22] It produced a ten-day 'battle' between the King and Lord Hill, the latter threatening to resign if he were overruled, and involved the appointment of Major General Ferguson instead of Lord Glenlyon, second son of the Duke of Atholl, whose appointment had been sought through Court connections. King George IV was much opposed to Ferguson, who had indeed been in various scrapes. Rowland obviously thought he was worthy of the command or he would never have stuck his neck out, but his staunch opposition to the King—'and yet little Hill has carried him thro'—surprised everyone.

One of the major thorns in Rowland's side proved to be not an enemy in the usual sense but rather a most extraordinary soldier, James Brudenell, 7th Earl of Cardigan. Rich, spoiled, domineering and extraordinarily good-looking but, above all, possessed of a terrifying and ungovernable temper, the only profession this man wished to pursue from an early age was soldiering. Being an only son, however, his parents forbade him a military career which merely served to frustrate his energies. Marriage to Elizabeth Tollemache (following elopement and a scandalous divorce from her first husband, who was apparently highly relieved to be rid of her) proved a disaster. Finally in 1824 his parents agreed to his entering the Army and he was commissioned in a Hussar regiment at the age of twenty-seven. Cecil Woodham-Smith in *The Reason Why* describes his early years as 'comparatively serene'. It did not last and he soon acquired a bad reputation; he was impatient of any correction, becoming easily enraged and prone to duelling. Thanks to court intrigues, and supported by the patronage of the Duke of York, Brudenell rapidly climbed the promotion ladder. In 1832, just four years after Hill became General Commanding, he bought the Lieutenant Colonelcy of the 15th Hussars for the enormous sum of £35,000. A happy, successful regiment was soon quaking under the new regime.

His attitude to the command of men was completely alien to Rowland Hill. Hill was a Tory of the old school, a staunch supporter of the aristocracy and one who believed that, in general, military authority was best vested in that class. Long experience had taught him that it was very difficult to commission men from the ranks, such men having neither the educational background nor the natural authority to direct and take charge. But he certainly did not hold cheap the non-commissioned officers, whom he considered to be the true 'backbone' of the Army. James Brudenell, however, was a snob.

In much the same spirit, Hill did not support the Reform Bill. He had even refused to budge on his decision when pressed by the King himself. On his accession William IV had confirmed Hill in his position at Horse Guards and assured him that it was not to be regarded as a political appointment, and it was this assurance that gave Lord Hill the ability to abstain. Creevy wrote that Lord Hill was forced to vote by Lord Grey, as he was a member of the government, even though this put him in direct opposition to his 'patron' the Duke of Wellington.

It is clear from Rowland's personal correspondence that he did not vote on the passage of the first Reform Bill. Wellington was always bitterly opposed to parliamentary reform; he was terrified that revolution and unrest of the type rearing its head again in France might be transported across the Channel. The King and Queen Adelaide held Hill in high regard and both bachelor brothers, Rowland and Clement, now Lieut-Colonel of the Blues, were frequent and popular guests at Court. Following Rowland's refusal to vote, William even gave him a sword as a mark of his esteem. The Bill was passed only after serious opposition from the House of Lords.

The elections following the passage of the Reform Bill were bitter. James Brudenell was returned as Tory member for the Northern Division of Northamptonshire after a bitterly fought campaign in which all the worst characteristics of a violent reactionary were evident. His obvious contempt for the local people was so patent that on one occasion he had to be rescued by the Army in order to prevent a riot. It was only the beginning of a strange career and one that was to give Hill a great deal of anxiety.

The court martial of one of Brudenell's officers, Captain Wathen, was an extraordinary affair in the course of which Brudenell simply ignored Hill's ruling. Wathen and his deportment, which his Commanding Officer considered very sloppy on parade, were severe provocation to Brudenell. In 1833, after yet another harangue—these were frequently delivered on the parade ground in front of the entire regiment and then followed by even worse beratings in the office—the Captain was arrested prior to a court martial. Hill read the papers and, only too aware of Brudenell's temperament by now, ordered the release of Wathen and recommended that the officers of the 15th Hussars should learn to live together. After a long trial Wathen was reinstated. It was not long before Brudenell managed to find another reason for the arrest of the unfortunate Captain; the issue of stable jackets is a long and complicated story. A court martial was convened in Cork just before Christmas 1833 and provided the press with rich pickings. In February 1834 it was announced that Wathen had been acquitted and Brudenell was accused in the court martial report of 'conduct revolting to every proper and honourable feeling of a gentleman'. He was dismissed from his command. But Lord Hill thought he had seen the last of James Brudenell he was sadly mistaken. During the course of the trial his conduct had been violent and bizarre in the extreme, but coming from a family of courtiers he once again managed to wriggle out of trouble. His first action on hearing the verdict was to rush off to London and demand an interview with Lord Hill. The relative peace of Hill's days at Horse Guards was now shattered. Perhaps he had failed to remember that Brudenell was brother-in-law to Earl Howe, one-time Chamberlain and long-time confidant to Queen Adelaide.

After staying relatively quiet until 1835, Brudenell applied to the Duke of Wellington for help. Wellington, obviously having no time for the firebrand, dismissed his request for help with reinstatement. The Court connection was now brought into play and Hill allowed himself to be pressed, following the personal intervention of the Queen, into agreeing, albeit reluctantly, that he would approve Brudenell in another command if he could obtain one.[23] Hill said, 'I have consented to this step because I am unable to endure the distress of this noble family [the old Earl of Cardigan, Brudenell's father, had begged King William to help his son with tears in his eyes] and because I hope that the author of this distress is now sensible that he cannot be permitted to follow the dictates of his ungovernable temper. I trust this lesson has not been thrown away.' By dint of paying the enormous sum of more than £40,000 Brudenell became commander of the 11th Light Dragoons. Wellington was to campaign for the abuse of purchase to be brought to an end and for the established price for such transactions not to be exceeded on pain of dismissal. A great furore broke out when news of the appointment became public and Lord Hill was much criticised in the press.

The 11th Light Dragoons had been in India for many years and perhaps Lord Fitzroy Somerset and Lord Hill felt Brudenell's departure for foreign parts might help solve their problems. The new Colonel sailed to join his regiment in India in 1837. During his very short stay he managed to avoid most of the hardships encountered by the Army there and alienate his men, and by the end of the year the regiment was ordered home.

The activities of Lord Cardigan, as he now was, continued and nobody, let alone the GC-in-C, appeared able to control him. By the year 1840 Cardigan did not even bother to reply to letters from Lord Hill, which demonstrated a contempt and arrogance which Hill seems to have been totally unable to deal with. The conflict between Hill and Cardigan serves to illustrate the General's lack of toughness when hard, unpleasant decisions had to be made. Perhaps Wellington's 'I am not sure he does not shrink from responsibility' is more apt apropos Hill at Horse Guards than it could ever have been regarding his merits as a soldier in the field.

With the death of King William in 1837 Rowland Hill lost a good friend. In the seven years of William's reign Rowland spent much time at Buckingham Palace and Windsor. The sons of George III were notorious for their scandalous personal lives, extravagances and indiscretions. William IV was the last of them to reign as king. Lord Hill carried the Royal Standard at the funeral.

The paternal figure of Rowland Hill now had a different type of sovereign to deal with, the 18-year-old Victoria. She seems to have liked the elderly soldier.[24] Lord Melbourne, however, thought him a bore. They came from somewhat similar backgrounds, but while one was a suave politician the other had spent most of his life campaigning abroad and probably did not have the same drawing room manner, although there is no question that he was lionised in the salons of Mayfair. Hill in his turn thought Lord Melbourne had too much influence with Victoria and he was not alone in this. Undoubtedly he felt at a disadvantage with a Whig government in power, although, he was very impressed with the young Queen's application to her work.

Towards the end of the 1830s Chartism reared its head and the Army began to be involved in a certain amount of civil control. The Chartist leader Jack Frost even led a band of followers into Newport, Shropshire, just down the road from Hawkstone. He was apparently on his way to Monmouth, with the intention of freeing some of their number who had been imprisoned there.

Hill's time was also much occupied with events in Canada, where Upper and Lower Canada were about to be brought more closely together. Since the beginning of the century there had been unrest, and in 1837 there were two rebellions, one by the French in Lower Canada, who had no intention of being ruled by a minority of English, and the other by English settlers in Upper Canada, who demanded an elected Legislative Council. The only thing these two groups had in common was their wish not to be absorbed by the United States. John Lambton, 1st Earl of Durham, was sent to Canada in 1838 to report on the situation and advise as to a solution. This man had been a pro-Reform minister and Ambassador in St Petersbourg and was highly able. After only six months he returned to England and made his report in 1839. It was controversial and initially did not find favour with the government. He made three recommendations: that Upper and Lower Canada be amalgamated in a United Province, that responsible government be granted to the Colonies, and that French Canadians be assimilated. Durham was certain that in order to keep the whole of Canada on the side of the 'Mother Country' it needed to have more control over its internal affairs. The French in Lower Canada were furious. In fact the government virtually sacked Durham—he actually resigned—and the first Bill was thrown out by the House of Lords. It was eventually implemented under Durham's successor, Lord Elgin, the fusion of the Upper and Lower Provinces by an Act of Union in 1840 creating a new Province of Canada.

Gradually Rowland's health began to fail and at the beginning of 1842 he was forced to absent himself from several events in London at which he should have been an honoured guest, including the visit of the King of Prussia. His appearance was the subject of adverse comment when he made the effort to accept an important engagement to dine with the Duke of Sussex, and he refused dinner and parties with the Buccleuchs and the Duke of Cambridge. As the summer wore on it was obvious that he must resign. In July he transmitted his formal resignation to the Queen through Sir Robert Peel, Prime Minister. He still had sufficient presence of mind to write to Wellington begging his help and support for Colonel Egerton, his long-time friend and aide-de-camp. Wellington was swift to assure him that he would do everything necessary to ensure the officer was treated in accordance with Rowland's wishes. At the end of August he received a letter from Peel informing him that he was to be created Viscount with remainder to his nephew.[25]

His condition must have deteriorated very quickly because by October he could no longer write but stayed mainly in bed where he received visits from

6. Rowland, 2nd Viscount Hill. Painting by Richard Jones.

all the family and took especial comfort from the presence of the Rev. John Hill and the Rev. Francis Hill, son of his diplomat brother Francis. His valet, Calderwood, reported to John Hill that his Lordship 'never wakes day nor night but he prays earnestly', and one of his last utterances was, 'I have a great deal to be thankful for; I believe also that I have not an enemy in the world. With regard to my religious feelings, I have not power to express much and never had; but I do trust I am sincere; and I hope for mercy.' He died on Saturday 10 December 1842.

The funeral was private, by his express wish, although the Corporation of Shrewsbury had been anxious to give him a grand ceremony. The service was held in St Chad's Church, Shrewsbury, and the procession then wound its way to St Mary Magdalene, Hadnall where he was buried under the church tower. The tower was new, the original built of wood having disintegrated, and had been built with money given by the Hill family. Lord Hill had selected the site for his own burial in a crypt under the tower; his sisters Mary (Maria) and Emma were also interred here. Maria left a sum of money to found the Church of England School and sufficient to pay for the teacher. She also left a sum to clothe poor children. A large monument to Lord Hill with the figures of a shepherd and a soldier flanking a couched lion and his Lordship's coat of arms behind can be seen inside the church. There is also a long inscription ending

> the earthly honours conferred upon him did not blind him to his spiritual wants and necessities, nor render him insensible to his deep need of a saviour. He passed the brief evening of his repose in sincere penitence and prayer and died in peace looking unto Him alone who is the way, the truth and the life.

On the morning of the funeral and, apparently, just as the bells started to toll, his sister-in-law, Elizabeth, the widow of his brother John, died at the Citadel. It was a sad time for the family.

Letters of condolence addressed to his nephew Rowland were received from the Queen and Prince Albert and, of course, from the Duke of Wellington who referred to its being 'thirty five years since I had the satisfaction of being first connected with and assisted by him in the public service; and I must say that, from that moment up to the latest period of his valuable and honoured life, nothing ever occurred to interrupt for one moment the friendly and intimate relations which existed between us'.

Disastrous mismanagement of the Hawkstone Estate later led to its sale, and all the General's Orders, Decorations and Medals were sold. At the first sale, in Shrewsbury in 1895, they were apparently bought on behalf of the Hon. Francis (Frank) Hill (later the 5th Viscount) by Spink. He, in turn, sold them at a sale at Sothebys on 19 April 1910.[26] The collection was acquired for the Maharajah of Patiala and can now be seen in the Sheesh Mahal Museum in Patiala. The enormous sum of £1,010 was paid for the decorations. The collection contained some vary rare pieces such as one from the Egyptian Campaign of 1801, Gold Medal (large size) of the Imperial Order of the Crescent in its original black embroidered case, and also a General Officer's Peninsula Cross with clasps listing his Peninsula Battles. The long list included orders from Portugal, Russia, the Netherlands and Austria in addition to his British decorations. It is an example of the strange outcome of human affairs that the decorations of this most English of Generals should end up in India, where one imagines they cannot evoke much interest.

That Hill was an excellent general is certain. He was both well liked and admired for his abilities and for his transparent honesty and integrity. This was often demonstrated during his life and is aptly summed up by an anecdote. On an occasion in 1813 towards the end of the Peninsular War, Horse Guards asked the Duke if he would release Hill to command the army in Holland. 'Had you better not take my right hand?' was his reply. When given his head in the field Hill never failed to attain his objective, but he was probably just too nice a man to succeed at Horse Guards—not tough enough and totally unaccustomed to office life. Unquestionably an old-fashioned Tory, who felt that there were divisions between the classes and that each had its own contribution to make to society, he shared Wellington's views on reform. Had Wellington not existed, though, it seems unlikely that we should ever have seen Rowland Hill as Prime Minister.

Rowland was imaginative in his command of men, is credited with the innovation of the Sergeants' Mess, and also provided a school for his regiment, the 90th. He was concerned to provide books for soldiers in barracks and offer them alternative entertainment to drinking. One of his officers wrote of him when in Spain: 'He never under any circumstances forgot that he was a gentleman', a statement that then, and by many today, would be regarded as a sincere compliment.

His independent commands at Arroyo de Molinos and Almaraz were both brilliantly executed; both required swift forced marches with relatively few men, and carefully and precisely timed attacks followed by rapid withdrawal. His reliability was perhaps his greatest strength: 'an obedient, competent, common-sense soldier who neither panicked in the unexpected presence of the enemy nor indulged in personal embroidery of Wellington's instructions in their absence'. Another evaluation called him 'an intelligent, brave, resourceful, energetic and skilful soldier, admired by his men and foes'.[27] The French evidently held him in high respect, too.

Sir Robert Chambré Hill (1778-1860)

Sir Robert's military career is rather less well documented than that of his other military brothers. After service in the Peninsula, where he served as an ADC to his brother Rowland at Bayonne and commanded a brigade of cavalry at Vittoria, Bayonne and Toulouse, he commanded the Royal Horse Guards Blue at Waterloo, where he was wounded. He was subsequently knighted, receiving the KCB. After leaving the Army around 1821 he lived at Prees. He took an active role in county life. His three sons followed military careers: Alfred was ADC to his uncle, the Commander in Chief, and Percy attained the rank of Lieut-General. Sir Robert is credited with founding the Hawkstone pack of otter hounds.

Sir Thomas Noel Hill (1784-1832)

Thomas Noel, sometimes referred to as 'Sir Noel' by the Duke of Wellington, was the seventh son of Sir John Hill Bt. He was named Noel for his Attingham

7. Robert Chambré Hill.

cousin, the 1st Lord Berwick. He joined the Army in 1801 as a Cornet in the 10th Light Dragoons, which later became the 10th Hussars. He was a Lieutenant in 1803 and a Captain by 1805. He exchanged into the Grenadier Guards in 1806 and in February 1809 became a Major in the Portuguese Army under Marshal Beresford. He commanded his regiment at Busaco, Ciudad Rodrigo, Salamanca, Vittoria and at the siege and capture of San Sebastian. The Portuguese developed into excellent soldiers under their English officers during the Peninsular War and contributed far more than their Spanish neighbours. Thomas was knighted on 28 July 1814. He served as Assistant Adjutant General at Waterloo. In May 1824 he retired on half pay but was subsequently Deputy Adjutant General in Canada 1827-30 and then became Commandant of the Cavalry Depot at Maidstone, where he died rather young on 4 January 1832. He was a KCB and also received the Order of the Tower and Thistle from Portugal and the Order of Maximilien Joseph of Bavaria after Waterloo. In 1821 Thomas married Anna Maria Shore, daughter of Lord Teignmouth. Teignmouth was a seriously religious man and a great friend of the Hill family. Thomas Noel and Anna Maria had six children.[28]

Sir Francis Brian Hill (1779-1842)

Educated, as was Robert, at Rugby, Francis entered the Diplomatic Service. His career is difficult to follow as the Foreign Office has only sketchy records of the period but he is listed as having served as Chargé d'Affaires and Secretary of Legation at Bayreuth in 1801 in the absence of one Drake (possibly the same man with whom Rowland had travelled in his early career). He then accompanied the Court to Munich via Ratisbon. He stayed in Munich until September. He received his letter of credence as Chargé d'Affaires in Copenhagen in March 1802 and remained there until July of the following year. He then proceeded to Stockholm where he stayed until March 1804 when he returned to Copenhagen until April 1805. He married firstly a Danish wife who died shortly afterwards, leaving one son, then Emily Powys, by whom he had two more children. Apparently he also served in 'The Brazils' and attended the Congress of Vienna, but the Foreign Office has no precise records. He was knighted. The son of his first marriage, Francis Jean, was ordained.

Major General Clement Delves Hill (1781-1845)

Clement seems to have been a most popular figure. During the Peninsular War he served as ADC to his brother Rowland. After Waterloo he served as Lieutenant Colonel commanding the Royal Horse Guards Blue. He was promoted Major General in 1837 before being appointed to the Madras Army in 1841. He wrote a graphic and humorous description of part of his journey to India. Before the opening of the Suez Canal in 1868 this journey necessitated either sailing round the Cape of Good Hope or crossing the Egyptian Desert. Clement chose the latter route.

The letter reproduced here was addressed to his nephew, Rowland, at Hawkstone, and is to be found in the Rev. James Hill Collection, SRO549/210. It is dated 27.10.1841:

> On board *Cleopatra*.
> The only place I can find in the ship is a very shaky one from the situation of the engine.
> I left a letter in the post office for Lord Hill [his brother] and I find the next opportunity of sending one will be from Aden where the Indian mail will arrive a few days after we are to be there and where the steamers stop to take in coals. This is becoming an interesting place as a new English Settlement but otherwise I am told [it] is not an inviting one. Part of an English regiment from India is stationed there.
> My voyage and journey have hitherto been most interesting and altogether agreeable ... some inconveniences must of course be expected and at times

feeling that of heat in no small degree—quite hot as they tell me I shall find it in India ... at all events they have more luxuries there to [illegible] it can be expected on board a crowded ship. At Suez we took in a dozen passengers—we are now 55 in one cabin or salon as it is called with the thermometer at 90 and not above half have cabins to sleep in, the others being on deck which as far as sleeping goes is the best place but dressing in the morning is not agreeable as washing decks invariably begins at daylight when everyone has to save their clothing as well as themselves from being ducked. The ladies have all cabins though some have carried their beds on deck last night—as I and others I suspect will do. The Captain kept a cabin for me and Colonel Macdonald which closes as it is a great convenience. We have the luck to be in this steamer as well as the *Liverpool* alone. They have never been so full before. Our company in general is very agreeable. A Mr and Mrs Moule who are acquainted with Mr Sidney [Sidney was Sir Rowland's domestic chaplain] came on board at Suez. He is going out as Chaplain to India. She is a very fine woman and both appear very nice people.

I have not been seasick for a moment—or the least unwell except one day from the heat and wind.

At Malta I have only had to regret the shortage of time for seeing places. I was much struck with the ... [blank left by writer] ... of Alexandria on entering which we got my only view of Pompey's Pillar. The Pasha's fleet made a fine appearance and a number of boats came alongside fighting and scrambling for passengers to take to shore ... from the camel drivers to get our baggage and the donkey boys to carry our persons. From the moment we landed at Alexandria we were under the care and also at the mercy of Mr Hill who with his partner, Mr W—gton, are the only people who undertake to convey travellers over the desert to Suez. We got to the hotel about 3 o'clock. A Captain of the Navy there lent me his horse and servant but I only had time to ride and see Cleopatra's Needle close to the town and it was impossible to go and see any ... that was the scene of the former Egyptian campaign. A 8 o'clock all the party set out, a motley group on donkies [*sic*] for the canal about 3 miles distant where we embarked in two boats each drawn by three small horses going a good pace. The canal is a splendid work more like a fine wide river with a wide variety of sailing vessels, carts drawn by horses. At daylight we had plenty of novelty to look at, particularly in the villages and their inhabitants—about 8 o'clock at ... where the canal 45 miles from Alexandria joins the Nile. I never even in Portugal saw so filthy a place tho' there seemed to be a good deal of trade going on. There was every abominable smell and the place swarmed with fleas which seemed to be devouring the poor children but they appeared not to mind them. We got a sort of breakfast at what is called an English hotel and at 12 o'clock were off on the Nile in two steamers. Mrs Hill recommending me the smaller one as likely to arrive first at Cairo, 140 miles, the other soon gave us the go-by but we continued to get on pretty well and there was much to interest and amuse while daylight lasted but particularly from the large variety of sailing vessels ... gay in appearance at a distance tho' in general there is not a more miserable race of beings on earth in their appearance and their dwellings nearly all the villages being nothing more than a few mud walls with holes for the inhabitants to creep in and out of. Most of them are nearly or quite naked from an early age, women having their bodies covered with dirty blue cloth. Their faces ... being more carefully concealed than other parts ... we stopped at one of the miserable villages for eggs and milk and found the other steamer had passed about five hours. The *Jack o'Lantern* having kept jogging on 'til about sunset when the whole country being inundated at this time (more so than has been for some years) we contrived to get aground out of the line of the river and there we stuck for about four hours 'til got off by some villagers who were luckily at hand to assist. But we had not gone far before the engine became out of order and we were detained the whole night to be devoured by millions of mosquitoes. We are off once again. Boats are frequently stopped for four or five months. The engineer tells us we shall be in Cairo in 4 hours—we knowing nothing of the distance.

We were glad to see the other steamer come to look for us into which we all got on board and landed at ... 2 miles from the town of Cairo from whence we again mounted donkeys and rode to Mrs Hill's hotel having lost about 24 hours by being in the *Jack o'Lantern*. I had only three hours to see Cairo which requires as many days. I took a ride through some of the crowded narrow streets where perhaps (is) to be seen as great a variety of people and costumes as in many parts of the world: as for the slave market which I was late in the day for; I saw quite enough to satisfy my curiosity.

The Pasha was there from Alexandria but I had no time to go and sit with him in his Palace. I had to content myself with a view of the Pyramids from 5 miles off ... our fellow travellers in advance having gone on by different modes of convey and Mr Hill undertook to forward the remaining 16 in carriages. Colonel Macdonald and I and two others got a start in the first, they are just like small covered bakers carts drawn by three small horses and are driven by a boy who took us the first 10 miles in an hour and a half at which pace we went nearly the whole way. Except having frequently to stop for water and to get out and push ... but after all we accomplished the journey of 80 miles from Cairo to Suez in 22 hours, the whole being over the Desert ... [hard to decipher] but no part of the road more than I can recollect of it between you and Acton Reynold in an English carriage with good horses will go in less time than we did ... there being 7 stations to stop at and at 3 of them may be had very tolerable refreshments of tea and considering there is not a drop of water except what is kept in tanks or brought on camel from Cairo or Suez is not now, as a few years ago, such formidable travelling in the desert. We certainly got our bones well jumbled in the drive having to make lay on the stoney and rough parts of ... I think the pleasantest way to travel is either on donkies or camels if not in a hurry both of which are extraordinary animals particularly the latter which came the whole distance with our baggage without being unloaded and only once stopping to feed and drink a little of the water they carry on their backs. They are only 12 hours longer on the journey than we were. For short distances one of them can carry half a tun weight. Patiently laying down to be loaded or unloaded. They make a melancholy noise during both operations tho' I cannot say whether it is through pleasure or pain tho' I fear the latter and from the vast number of bodies and skeletons of them lying in this Desert, numbers must die from being over-driven or from want. We actually saw 2 lying down alive left to die on the hot burning sands without a chance of getting either food or water or anyone to put them out of their misery. If there was no track on the Desert the stench of camel's bodies and bones would be sufficient. It would be a long way to send them, or I am not sure whether it might not be a good speculation to collect the latter for your Mill. Near Suez we passed an immense number of pilgrims from different countries but chiefly Turks on their way to Mecca many of the people being of rank including ladies. They had at least 400 camels besides donkies and some on foot. Suez is a considerable but a wretched place. Mr Hill's agent has ... hotels where I was expecting to get anything but a comfortable bed. However, fortunately a lady and gentleman went on board that day and gave up a room with two very dirty ones into one of which I turned soon after dark and never woke until after daylight the next morn, notwithstanding the incessant noise I was told there had been amongst the camels and drivers all night under our windows.

I had not had my clothes off or scarcely slept for 4 nights—I got up as fresh as a lark. The whole of our journey from Alexandria having put me much in mind of some of the marches or rather retreats (from the hurry we were in) with the Peninsular Army. We were all assembled on board on the evening of the 23 except Mr Carter a very fine young man who was going to his ship (the *Wellesley*) in China. He was taken ill and left at one of the stations in the Desert.

It was dark when we passed the nearest point of the straits of Suez but in the morning and all that day had a fine view of the splendid mountains on the African and Arabian shores distinctly seeing Mount Horeb and Mount Sinai. Today we are out of sight of land and shall be until we get near Aden touching at no other place on our way.

Our principal preoccupation has been fanning and wiping ourselves. The thermometer having risen to 101 since I began to write under an awning supposed to be the coolest place on the ship tho' much hotter I think from being over the stokers who keep up the fires in steamers in our part of the world. In these seas Africans are the only people who can at all bear the work and you cannot imagine anything more wretched than those poor creatures coming on deck through a hole like those used to put down coal in London. They are almost entirely naked and when they get on deck they look as if they were at their last gasp but soon recover and the Captain says they are never ill being perhaps better off than many of their countrymen. We have a fine ... lusty set of English sailors on board. The rest of the crew and servants being of all stations and colours.

We shall not be in Aden for some days. I will leave my letter open tho' it is not probable that I shall have anything more to add. This is near the end of the month, the time that I hope some one may be writing to me tho' I must not expect the pleasure of getting letters in less than 6 weeks.

Love to all
CH

30 Oct
The weather continued uncomfortably hot 'til yesterday when it has become cooler but with a strong northerly wind frequently met with in this sea and being right in our teeth I hear we shall be a day or two longer getting to Aden tho' Captain expects we should be there tonight. We have seen no land for three days except some curious looking volcanic islands ... We are now in sight of both coasts have passed Mecca—not visible. If we pass Alocho in day light we shall have a good view of it. Before we took possession of Aden the steamers stopped there for coal.

As you are a British bird fancier [Sir Rowland had a large collection at Hawkstone] you may be interested to know that several have come on board during our passage in this sea (namely swallows, flycatchers, water wagtails, land rails, hawks, many of which might have been caught). A sailor secured a hawk, the skin of which I am getting preserved for you. If I succeed it may be curious to see if you have the same species in your collection. The wagtails were quite familiar, picking up ants living on flies— if they preferred ants and cockroaches we have them in abundance. Rats are about the deck and cabins all the day and night. We have no mosquitoes or other vermin of that description. The rats sometimes attack the feet of the poor negroes when they are asleep but I have not heard of any ladies or gentlemen being attacked by them on deck where almost all the passengers have carried their beds this hot weather. I am told by all Indians on board that the heat is never so oppressive in that country so I am getting a good seasoning on the way. I understand the Red Sea is always hotter than any other accounted for by the wind blowing over the hot Desert ... which no doubt is the case as we already feel it so much cooler. There have been a few outlandish birds on board to roost; last evening a lot of 'Paroqueets'.

Sunday 31
We passed very near Mecca before sunset yesterday a ... looking town at a distance. About midnight we passed through the straits and hope to anchor at Aden about six o'clock this evening which is ...

He took up his appointment in November 1841. In the Madras Almanac for 1842, 1843, 1844 and 1845 he appears as Major General Clement Hill, Mysore Division. In fact we read more of him in his death than ever was recorded during his life. He contracted a fever in the middle of the jungle in an area that had once belonged to Tippu Sultan, at the Falls of Gairsoppa on the northern side of a large inlet where the Gairsoppa river flows into the sea, located about eighteen miles east of Honore (Honowar). Captain H. Cust, Clement Hill's ADC, wrote to the General's nephew Rowland, now the 2nd Viscount Hill:

8. Clement Delves Hill.

> I have lost my poor General—he died at the Falls of Gairsoppa in Canara on the 20th after 6 days' illness ... we did not like to bury him by the Falls of Gairsoppa in the jungle, far away from the haunts of Europeans, so we waited about five hours (in this fearful climate haste is necessary) and hurried him in his pulonkeen to Honore (Honowar) 45 miles. Here we consigned him to the earth at 8 in the morning of the 22nd by four other European tombs. My occupation is gone. I wind up the General's affairs and return at once to England.[29]

In the same collection is a letter from Lieutenant Colonel Muller Scott, King's Own Hussars, also to Lord Hill, the 2nd Viscount. He advises Lord Hill of the death of his uncle and says that since the ADC has gone home overland they will probably have heard the news before receiving this letter. A letter from Edward Price, Household Brigade Artillery, concerns the memorial that was to be erected in Hadnall church with money raised by fellow officers and friends.

There is a very handsome memorial in Trinity Church, Bangalore. It was erected by subscriptions from brother officers and comrades in the Madras Presidency in testimony for their love for his personal character. Modest and unassuming in mind and deportment and utterly careless to advance himself in serving his country, his friends and every good cause, he was full of zeal and perseverance. In the campaigns of the Peninsula, whilst fighting under the command of his brother Lord Hill, he was amply satisfied with contributing to his glory, without seeking although deserving his share in his honours.

This quotation was sent to the author by Tony McClenaghan, who found it in a 'List of Inscriptions on Tombs or Monuments in Madras', p. 379, published by the Government Press Madras in 1905. The memorial has subsequently been photographed for me by a neighbour in the south-west of France, Kim Richards.

Edward Hill (1786-1821)

There is nothing on record of the 16th child of Sir John except that he, too, served at least briefly as a soldier in the Royal Horse Guards Blue and was also at Waterloo. He seems to have subsequently gone abroad and died unmarried at quite a young age.

CHAPTER SIX

After Waterloo
The Final Generations

WITH THE SUCCESSION of Rowland (8) as 4th Baronet in 1824 on the death of his grandfather, Sir John, Hawkstone probably reached its apogee as far as the house itself, the gardens and the Park were concerned. Rowland was young—only 24—and rather spoiled by his soldier uncles and his elderly grandfather, Sir John. His own father had died when he was only 14. On coming of age he decided on some grandiose schemes for the further embellishment of the Hall and the gardens and these are described in the chapter on the House and the Park. Some might say that he rather 'over-egged the cake' with the work he commissioned from Lewis Wyatt on the house but we certainly owe him credit for expanding the pleasure gardens on the garden side of the house. Rowland married Ann Clegg of nearby Peplow thus bringing yet another handsome property into the family. Some sneered behind their hands at the young Baronet marrying into 'Trade', his bride being the grand-daughter of a self-made cotton lord, Arthur Clegg, who started life as a cotton spinner in Irwell in Lancashire. Arthur's son, Joseph Clegg, then bought his way into the 'Gentry' with his acquisition of a country seat. The young couple lived at Hawkstone surrounded by an extended family of cousins, brothers and other hangers on, the Hall being the central focus of family life. Many of the family were parsons with local livings and Rowland had his own domestic chaplain, the somewhat sycophantic Edwin Sidney.

Rowland succeeded (by special remainder granted by the King) his uncle, the General, to the Viscountcy in 1842.[1] He lived high on the hog, kept the North Shropshire Hounds virtually at his own expense, and no doubt paid for the costs incurred by the Hawkstone Otter Hounds, a pack founded by his uncle, Sir Robert Chambré Hill in 1808. Hawkstone is not prime shooting country but the Hills kept nine keepers and the bills for their wages, the beaters, shot, etc. amounted to around £2,000 per annum. Bags of up to 2,000 birds a day were recorded in the last years of grandeur.[2]

The house may have glowed with new gilt and rich furnishings but things were not going well with the Estate itself. When the Corn Laws were repealed in 1846 under pressure from the new manufacturing magnates, who needed freedom to sell their goods worldwide and were being affected by the protectionist laws, the price of corn plummeted. Unfortunately, many rich landowners simply did not, or could not, comprehend the idea of economy, and diversification was virtually unheard of. The story that Lord Hill merely said, 'Cancel *Punch*', on being told by his Agent his financial affairs were in a bad way at Hawkstone, is probably apocryphal, but it sums up the attitudes of many who could not see their way of life already coming to an end. It was the era when the great fortunes were being made by the factory owners.

Rowland was a dedicated naturalist and especially interested in birds. His Collection included all but four of the native British birds. One of his more famous acquisitions was a Great Auk—not native to the British Isles but interesting and rare all the same. This was bought in 1838 from a naturalist called Gould together with three eggs. It formed a centre piece in the Hawkstone Collection, which the 2nd Lord Hill housed in one of the wings, and is documented as an exceptionally fine specimen. When the Collection was sold at the time of the dispersal sales it was bought by Bevil Stanier and initially housed at Peplow. He then sold the Great Auk through the famous wildlife dealer, Rowland Ward, in 1905 and it went to the John E. Thayer Museum in Lancaster, Mass., USA. It is now in the Centre for Biodiversity, Museum of Comparative Zoology, Harvard University, catalogue no. 171764. The study and collection of ornithological specimens was perhaps one of the 2nd Viscount's less extravagant hobbies. He also purchased three elands which were evidently surplus to the requirements of the London Zoological Society and they did very well in the Park; eland meat was occasionally to be found on the dinner table at the Hall.

To celebrate the coming of age of the 2nd Viscount's elder son, another Rowland, in 1854, His Lordship had the new drive from the village of Weston under Redcastle built, complete with a tunnel blasted through Grotto Hill, and a huge ball was thrown at the Hall. Rowland (9) had been born in 1833 and he ran off with his mother's stillroom maid, Mary Madax, at the age of 22. His bride was some eight years his senior but theirs does not appear to have been a 'shotgun' wedding because the first son, Rowland (10), the hapless 4th Viscount, was not born until 1863. Mary was not recognised by the family and it seems likely that she spent little or no time at Hawkstone following the marriage. She died in Sussex in 1874. Her two sons were educated at Eton and the older went into the Army and then drifted to North America. Perhaps he did not get on with his stepmother and resented her presence where his own mother's had never been accepted. I have made great efforts to try to discover more about Mary Madax but without success. The 3rd Viscount remarried the year following her death in 1875. His second wife was Isabella Wynn, a daughter of Lord Newborough. She produced four more children. The 3rd Viscount was popular and, in his youth, a

9. 2nd Viscount Hill.

great sportsman but he suffered from ill health in his later years and died in 1895 just as the great era of Hawkstone crumbled to its final, sad end.

There were a few cousins who managed to turn their hands to successful careers in public life. Amongst these were the sons of the Rev. John Hill, great uncle of the 3rd Viscount. John Hill went into the church and married Charlotte Kenyon, daughter of Thomas Kenyon (always referred to as 'His Honour' in the neighbourhood) of Pradoe. The Rev. John lived and farmed at the Citadel and served as Perpetual Curate of Weston under Redcastle for more than 60 years. He was also the epitome of the 'hunting parson', riding to hounds for many years. His eldest son, John, had rather illustrious godparents in the form of his great uncle, General the Lord Hill, and his grandfather, Thomas Kenyon. He was a bruising rider and spent a great part of his time up at Oxford hunting and riding steeplechase, with considerable success. He became a farmer and raised pure Hereford stock, his most famous beast being the great stud bull, Merry Monarch; so fertile and successful was this animal that John even had its portrait painted. John Hill was a connoisseur of horseflesh and a noted judge of hunters, and also a pigeon fancier. He took farming pupils at Felhampton, which included Bevil Stanier, who lived at Peplow and later bought the Citadel.

No. 2 son George William (1843-1905) joined the Navy, possibly influenced by his uncle, William Kenyon. This is the first record I can find of a Hill being a sailor. He entered as a Cadet in 1857, joining the training ship HMS *Illustrious*, then passing into *Britannia*. He was Acting Sub Lieutenant in the sloop HMS *Rinaldo* in the North American Squadron and West Indies, 1864-5. Promoted Lieutenant in 1868, he was on board the newly built gunboat HMS *Dwarf* on the China station from 1868-71.[3] He then served in HMS *Narcissus*, flagship of Admiral George Randolph. George's best known posting was as Commander in HMS *Bacchante*. She was either a new or totally rebuilt 4,000 tonne corvette, fully rigged but with an auxiliary engine. The ship had been selected to take the Duke of Clarence (Prince Eddy), eldest son of the Prince of Wales, and his brother, Prince George (later to be King George V), on a world cruise.[4] Prince George was bright, well-liked and made satisfactory progress, but elder brother Eddy was backward and had little application to his studies, and his habits in a future King were already causing concern. The Rev. John Dalton had been tutor to both princes since their early schoolroom days and he considered the stimulus provided by the company of the younger brother was essential to any progress that the older one might make. When Prince George passed out of *Britannia* in 1879 the decision to send the boys on a cruise was taken. Sending the heir and the 'spare' in the same ship was a risk and there was a great deal of discussion before the Cabinet, Prime Minister Disraeli and their grandmother, Queen Victoria, agreed to let both princes sail together. Initially the ministers were totally opposed to the plan but they were eventually persuaded that it would benefit Prince Eddy and that there was no question of separating the two boys at this stage of his development.

The Wardroom selected was suitably aristocratic and all were personally approved by the old Queen. In addition to George Hill, the Captain was Lord Charles Scott, a son of the Duke of Buccleuch, John Scott was nephew of the Captain, William Peel was a great nephew of Sir Robert and several cadets were from other illustrious families. Despite or because of their upbringing these officers ran a happy ship.

Prior to sailing with her precious cargo *Bacchante* was sent off with instructions to her Captain to go and find a storm, as there appeared to be some question as to the ship's stability. Eventually she sailed from Spithead on 17 September 1879

10. HMS *Bacchante*, 1878. The Prince of Wales (later Edward VII) is seated with Prince George (later George V) on the stairway. Commander George W. Hill is facing the camera, standing third from left in the third row back.

with the two young princes and the devoted but rather reluctant Mr Dalton. *Bacchante* would be the princes' home for the next three years.

This was to be the first of three cruises and visited the Balearics, Madeira, Barbados, Martinique and Bermuda before returning to Spithead in May 1880. The second cruise was only to Spain and Ireland but the third, which began in September 1880, took the *Bacchante* virtually round the world and she only returned home in August 1882. The ship now formed part of Admiral Lord Clanwilliam's detached Squadron. The Squadron was off the coast of Argentina in January 1881, in the Falkland Islands, when the Admiral received word to sail with all speed to the Cape of Good Hope; there was trouble in the Transvaal. The *Bacchante* arrived too late to play any part in the Boer uprising, the British being defeated at Majuba in February 1881, and the independence of the Transvaal was negotiated by Gladstone with Paul Kruger, that most famous of early South Africans. Prince George probably regretted that he did not see any action but the ship's officers and Mr Dalton must have been relieved that the most exciting event during their stay at the Cape was probably a visit to an ostrich farm!

Bacchante sailed from the Cape in April en route for Australia. The ship was hit by a severe storm some 400 miles off the Australian coast and suffered severe damage. The sails were ripped, the rudder almost torn off and a lifeboat lost. The ship drifted helplessly for three days and nights while emergency repairs were effected. The English press reported the ship as 'missing', which must have stirred things at Court. She finally reached Australia where the Squadron as a whole lost 108 men to desertion but only one came from *Bacchante*, which was evidently a happy ship under Commander George Hill.

George Hill was posted Captain in 1887 and commanded HMS *Marathon* and then *Mersey* during the Jubilee Celebrations before retiring on 3 August 1897; he was promoted Rear Admiral on 15 June 1901 and Vice Admiral on 21 July 1905. This sort of post-retirement promotion could not happen today, when you retire definitively at your last active rank. George died on 25 September 1905 aged only 63 at Stoney Stretton Hall after a long illness.

The third son of John and Charlotte was to have the most interesting career of the four boys. Clement Lloyd (named Lloyd for his Kenyon uncle who died very young after a stormy youth) was born in 1845 and sent off to prep school with older brother George and then to Marlborough with younger brother Brian. On leaving school and in order to prepare him for the Foreign Office exams he went to Germany and then to France to polish up his languages. While studying abroad he developed a lasting passion for the mountains and his letters home are good accounts of that period. He also wrote that he had visited a champagne estate where he had drunk champagne vastly superior to anything he had ever had in England.

He obtained the nomination of a Clerkship through Lord R— and entered the Foreign Office in 1867. One of his earliest recorded posts was as a Secretary to Sir Bartle Frere on his missions to Zanzibar in 1872 and 1873. The July 1873 *Journal of the Royal Geographical Society* published a paper that had been presented by Clement describing 'A Boat Journey up the Wami River'. He was a member of a party exploring the river following publication of Stanley's *How I Found Livingstone*, which expressed the opinion that the river could be used as one of the great roadways into 'central Africa for commerce and civilization'. Sir Bartle and his staff had been on board HMS *Briton* under Captain Malcolm in Zanzibar. It was a very small expedition but Clem's description is interesting, especially as its members were apparently the first white men ever seen there. The mouth of

11. Sir Clement Lloyd Hill (1845-1913).

the Wami lies opposite the island of Zanzibar between the towns of Saadani, to the north, and Windi, to the south. The little expedition entered by one of the river's two mouths, the northern Furanhanga, which was well concealed from the sea by mangrove swamps and rendered dangerous except at the top of the tide by shifting sandbars. The river was shallow and there was no sign of human habitation except for a few deserted huts until two small villages some 12 miles inland were reached. The wildlife was plentiful, with numerous crocodiles and hippos. Clement refers to the dangers of the latter and says that 'doubtless these animals will soon be killed and the hippopotami should be capable of being used in some way—as glue, leather or tallow for instance'! When they did manage to talk through an interpreter to some of the native people they were told that no slave dealers came so far up river, that the area was ruled on behalf of the Sultan of Zanzibar and that the people were Moslem. This Sultan was to become a good friend to Clement Hill, and was to confer on him the Most Brilliant Star of Zanzibar. Hill's conclusion, supported by his naval companions, on the possibility of this river being a commercial gateway to central Africawas that navigation was not viable unless by steam-powered vessel. Although the land seemed fertile it was so thinly populated that any successful form of trade seemed unlikely. They navigated some 23 miles up river before shortage of time forced their return to their ship.

When the Sultan paid a visit to London in 1875 Clement was attached to his suite, and he corresponded with him on a personal basis for years. The Sultan wrote expressing great sorrow on the deaths of both Queen Victoria and Edward VII. He also sent Clem a necklace for his 'lady' and was upset to find that it arrived after Clement's first wife had died. He suggested that it be kept for her daughter, Charlotte, but she died aged only one year. The Sultan was also godfather to Sir Clement's son from his second marriage, to Muriel Campbell, another Clement. One rather charming memento is a telegram to Sir Clement saying just 'Happy Christmas' and signed 'Sultan'.

In 1876 Clement was in Munich as Charge d'Affaires and in 1882 found himself sitting on the Commission for the Revision of Slave Trade Instructions; he subsequently served as Secretary to the Under Secretary of State to the Foreign Secretary, Lord Connemara. He visited Haiti as member of a Commission in 1886/7 and subsequently sat as a member of an impressive committee chaired by Sir Percy Anderson to sort out the administration of East and Central Africa. Its report was published in April 1894. He was then appointed Head of the African Department and seems to have entered something of a wasps' nest. Slavery was still an emotive subject, and, although Clem had served on the Commission some ten years earlier, his knowledge of practical administration was not deep. He spent a great deal of time in consultation with other departments and it is possible that, as had been the case with the General fifty or sixty years earlier, Clem was a little loth to take too much personal responsibility. The first two Commissioners following Britain's taking this area over from the old Imperial East Africa Company were based in Zanzibar as Consul General and only acted secondarily as Commissioner on the mainland. Hill got on well with Sir Arthur Hardinge, who had proclaimed the Protectorate in 1895, but not so well with Sir Charles Eliot, Hardinge's successor. Eliot, for example, supported the idea of encouraging white settlers who would, of course, be allowed the best land, whereas Clem Hill was more in favour of Indian immigration. They also fell out over Eliot's wish to move his headquarters to Nairobi whereas Lord Lansdowne and Hill insisted he remain based in Mombasa since this was the centre for

12. Sir Clement Lloyd Hill with Ugandan natives, 1890.

commerce and maritime trade. Eliot hated the Masai, despising their tribal customs and traditions which he considered archaic; one of the many problems with colonialism, even amongst the intelligent, was this failure to accept and acknowledge differences in culture.

Hill was much involved in the construction of the Ugandan Railway, visiting Lake Victoria several times, and he became Superintendent of the African Protectorates in 1900. His colonial career was commemorated in at least two different memorials: a street in Mombasa and a large lake steamer on Lake Victoria were named after him. He supported the ceding of the eastern part of Uganda to the East African Protectorate because he felt, probably wisely, that the railway should come under a single administration. Control of the tribes, such as the Nandi, was difficult but eventually a sort of peace was cobbled together and the railway reached the Lake in December 1901, although Clem's plan for a Lake

Province was scuppered by Eliot. He held his position at a fascinating moment in the development of central and eastern Africa.

Clem was created KCMG in 1897, and KCB in 1905 on his retirement from the Colonial Office. He was a member, and frequently President too, of several Shropshire societies and was President of the African Society at the time of his death. Following his retirement, it was not long before he found himself nominated, somewhat at the last moment, as Conservative and Unionist candidate for Shrewsbury in the 1906 Election. Although this election saw the incumbent government of Unionists suffer a crushing defeat, Clem Hill won a substantial majority largely thanks to his recognised integrity and the good name of Hill, although by this time Hawkstone had just been sold. The election also saw the first 50 Labour members take their seats; life had indeed changed. Clement was returned at two further elections before his sudden death in 1913. He was a great sportsman, being a passionate Alpine hiker, first-class shot, talented fly fisherman and bruising rider to hounds; he also successfully rode steeplechases and there is a photograph taken on the occasion of the Empress Elisabeth's (Sissi) visit to hunt at Hawkstone, showing Clem with the Empress' devoted escort, Bay Middleton, together with Count Kinsky and Lord Combermere. Clem Hill is buried in the grounds of the Abbey church in Shrewsbury.[5]

Brian was the youngest of the four boys. He went with Clement to Marlborough and then to Oxford. He was also an enthusiastic rider to hounds and of steeplechases. He bred prize Shorthorns and Herefords at The Hendre, Monmouth for Lord Llangattock and died in a hunting accident with the Albrighton.

Sir Baldwin Leighton's Loton Park Diaries (published in the TSAS) give us some rather scathing descriptions of other members of the family at this period.[6] In November 1865 they note that Godfrey Hill (son of Clement Delves Hill, a nephew—not the brother—of the General, who had married Harriet Mytton, eldest daughter of 'Mad' Jack Mytton) had 'left his ship and was dismissed'. One assumes this meant that he had more or less deserted. He then joined the Merchant Navy and 'knocked around the world for several years' before marrying a barmaid from Whitchurch and, having 'bought a share in a ship', sailed off to Australia apparently a 'source of sorrow and vexation to his parents'.

Sir Baldwin also recorded several other marriages which it has to be admitted were not very 'top drawer'. Of the Noel-Hills he wrote that young Dick Hill (nephew of the 6th Baron Berwick and the eventual 7th himself) had at the age of 22 married a 'woman of the town' called Mrs Norton who was said to be over thirty years old and was 'although at one time handsome yet now passé'. In fact, the gossipy old diarist was guilty of recording snippets that often proved untrue, although the gossip is often fruitier than the truth, and such was the event in this case. Dick Noel-Hill had in fact married a perfectly respectable Swedish woman, Ellen Nystrom from Malmo, but he had probably had a 'walk out' with the barmaid.

Leighton also comments on Algernon Hill. It would appear that the 3rd Lord Berwick, William Noel-Hill, had had a long-standing affair with an Italian woman at the Court of Savoy and at least two children whom he acknowledged. On his death these offspring appear to have received nothing in their father's will and Algy Hill was described as being in a very poor way.[7]

There were many other descendants but, with the Estate of Hawkstone becoming only a memory, they were widely scattered, many going to live in the new 'Empire'. As the First World War loomed on the horizon, the family focus was gone, the furniture sold, an invaluable archive dispersed[8] and a way of life quite over.

CHAPTER SEVEN

Hills in Shropshire Politics
The Election Scandal of 1796

'Honour and Honesty', 'John Hill for Ever', 'Prosperity to the House of Hawkstone' ... it all rings a bit thin today but that was the type of election slogan on the jugs made to commemorate some of the many Hills who were successful at the hustings. In fact there only appears to have been a single failure, the notorious affair of 1796, and even then one Hill was elected and at least three different jugs made for the loser. The election caused a scandal that is recorded in parliamentary history.

Reading the best sources for MPs and their dates, such as 'Memoirs' in the *Transactions of the Shropshire Archaeological Society*, S. Bindoff, R. Thorne and, later, Romney and Sedgewick's *The House of Commons*, plus the invaluable *Victoria County History* (Shropshire), we find Hills thick on the ground from the early 18th century up until just before the First World War. They were one of the most influential county families, along with the Kenyons of Pradoe, Bridgemans (Newport), Myttons of Halston, Corbets of Acton Burnell and Sundorne, Kynastons, Leightons of Loton, Clives, etc. These families shared the official positions amongst themselves and became increasingly unpopular with successful middle-class merchants and professionals trying to break into public life but they persisted until the First World War changed the old order.

The Borough of Shrewsbury has had more than its fair share of bribery and corruption during 700-odd years. The first recorded case of corruption (there may have been other earlier ones) was in 1708 when two well-known county families, Kynaston and Mytton, were challenged by Sir Edward Leighton.[1] Witnesses, members of the Shoemakers Guild, attested that they had been commissioned to make 200 pairs of shoes (a very large order) in return for voting for the sitting members. At least one man was promised a horse and another £25. In 1713 Kynaston attacked the successful candidate for 'notorious bribery'.[2] It appears that 41 people had been lavishly wined and dined at the *Three Tuns Inn* in the presence of the candidate and his agents.

The first Hill to attend a Parliament may have been William de la Hulle who is recorded as Member for Bridgnorth between 1327-9, but the 'Lord Mayor', Sir

Rowland, is the first for whom we have any details. He seems to have represented several different 'constituencies': Shropshire from 1543-4, Middlesex from 1547-54 and finally Surrey from 1557 until his death. The last was by dint of his having been a Lord Mayor of London, which apparently gave this right. How he represented Shropshire and Middlesex at the same time is hard to understand but Parliament did not sit very often and was also convened wherever the Monarch happened to be. On one occasion when the King was in Shrewsbury and held a Parliament, he transferred the sitting a few miles down the road to Acton Burnell, a Corbet property.

There then follows a long gap until the 'Great' Hill decided that his nephew, Samuel Barbour Hill, should enter public life. It is easy to see that the Great Hill pulled the strings and called the shots where his nephews were concerned; these lucky young men probably had little complaint about that. Samuel was returned for Lichfield as a Tory (he lived at Shenstone Park, Staffs) but evidently he found parliamentary life 'not agreeable to his natural temper which could not away with ['conform to'] the manner of speaking and transacting business in that Honourable House'.[3] His two cousins, Sir Rowland of Hawkstone (Shrewsbury), and Thomas of Attingham (also Shrewsbury but a Whig in theory if not in practice), both followed him into the House. Neither made much of a mark and Thomas gave up his seat for his son, Noel, in 1768. Noel was only twenty-two.

Noel Hill was a Whig in some people's eye but a rather independent one; he was Member for the Borough of Shrewsbury from 1768-74 and then for the County of Shropshire in two Parliaments between 1774-84. On Lord Clive's suicide (he had an Irish peerage, which enabled him to sit as a Member of the English Parliament) in 1774, and Noel Hill's decision to stand for the County, the 'old enemy' William Pulteney managed to dislodge Charlton Leighton from the Borough. Pulteney had been defeated at the Polls, polling eight fewer votes than Leighton, but had successfully petitioned the Courts. He was born William Johnstone and had married Frances Pulteney, a considerable heiress from the well-known Bath family, and changed his name. He was a clever lawyer and now had his wife's large fortune behind him. The town of Shrewsbury was not very happy; it felt it had been manipulated and lost control. Despite being under the influence of a few families, it was a real and thriving place and there was no question of two members being returned for an extinct—or 'decayed'—borough, which was the real evil.

Noel Hill started life as a Whig (all Hawkstone Hills were Tory) and remained as such until the coalition of 1783, when he was persuaded to support Pitt over the passage of some unpopular Bills such as the India Act. The 'turncoat' was then rewarded with a Barony and took the title of Lord Berwick, which was entirely undeserved. There is no record of him ever having spoken! Sir Richard

Hill of Hawkstone sat as an Independent Conservative. He was it seems truly 'independent', and although a friend and admirer of the much younger Pitt he was not always a Pitt supporter. He remained a Member of Parliament from 1780-1806, which meant that the two cousins sat together for the County in the Parliament of 1780-4. Sir Richard was much incensed by Noel's elevation to the peerage but in a letter replying to one from William Hill said he felt that to grasp at worldly honours at his time of life would only look ridiculous.[4] This was one of his better decisions. Sir Richard spoke frequently and often to the point but sometimes rendered himself an object of ridicule.

The bitterly contested 1796 Election for the two seats of the Borough of Shrewsbury seems to have been one of the nastiest battles in all electoral history and took place between two cousins! County MPs' seats do not appear to have been contested nearly as often as those of the Borough. One seat was held by a Whig, William, later Sir William, Pulteney, and was pretty safe in his hands. Pulteney sat in five successive Parliaments (1774-1805) and was known for the great wealth that enabled him to insert his 'men' into seats not only in Shropshire; he was often referred to as the richest commoner in England. The other seat had been filled by John Hill, brother to Sir Richard, since 1784. But this seems to have cut little ice with his cousin, Thomas, the 2nd Lord Berwick, who wished to put his brother, William, in in order, he said, to maintain the Attingham connection. William was just 23. Lord Berwick afterwards alleged that there had been an agreement between the two Hill families, in the persons of his father and Sir Richard, that John Hill would vacate his seat for someone from Attingham, but in 1796 the latter obviously had no intention of being pushed out by this young whippersnapper of a cousin. A family conference was held at Attingham in November 1795 but this failed to resolve the question; warfare was about to break out.

A month later, in December 1795, John Hill issued an election address.[5] According to the 'MPs' Memoirs', 'Both parties put forth their utmost powers and incurred a lavish expenditure in bringing voters to the Poll, quite regardless of whether they had legal qualifications or not ... some of the publications imputed the grossest corruption to the parties and were such as would cause the greatest amazement in the present day. It is said that the excitement of the contest spread to all classes and led practically to the suspension of business for weeks.'[6]

There is no doubt that the election began in earnest with the publication of John Hill's address and continued until polling six long months later. Why did it all matter so much? Was it just a question of pride that prevented either side from withdrawing. It certainly cost them a staggering amount of money which, despite outward appearances, neither party could afford. Both families were rich on paper, were big landowners, with Hawkstone consisting of more than

16,000 acres and Attingham of just under 4,000, but it was not to be long before the cracks began to show and in both cases wanton extravagance coupled with mismanagement were mainly to blame. The *Victoria County History* tells us that one of the Attingham expenses for this particular contest was £6,384, which went to 36 different innkeepers for food and lodging; another £2,382 was spent in hiring lodgings for the burgesses. Because the date of the election was uncertain these lodgings had to be hired for a year, which also permitted bogus 'burgesses' to try to satisfy a residential requirement. To judge by the number of votes that would be disallowed when voting finally came to pass, many were unsuccessful. Indeed, many more votes were eventually to be disallowed than were admitted. Again, according to *VCH*, 'Between December 1795 and May 1796, 1,659 new burgesses were traced and sworn.'[7] The Heber letters quoted by *VCH* mention 'non resident collected from all quarters tag, rag and bobtail fresh imported on this occasion, far fetched, and dear bought indeed if they turn out mere ciphers'. And mere ciphers many were to prove—especially for the unsuccessful John Hill.

Polling finally got under way in June and lasted eight days, a very long period when you consider how few votes were cast! John did, in fact, poll more votes than William but more of his (854) than of his cousin (721) were rejected by the Mayor. Pulteney held the other seat despite having 1,514 votes disallowed. It appears that the younger Hill, the Attingham Lad, had the support of the Town Corporation. But why did they withdraw their support for John? Perhaps he had been a poor member. Another theory is that Attingham was much nearer to Shrewsbury, being virtually in the suburbs, and the town felt he might do more for them, although he is unlikely to have done much since he was abroad almost the whole of the time he held the seat.

The Hawkstone family was furious. John Hill appealed and his petition dragged on for a year after which it seems to have been allowed to lapse through inaction, which indicates that some sort of accommodation had been arrived at. It was agreed that John Hill would not be opposed by an Attingham candidate when the next vacancy occurred. Thus it was that he returned to the House of Commons in the by-election of 1805 on the death of Pulteney. However, for some reason we do not know, he did not contest the seat in the General Election of 1806. Perhaps he had his eye on his brother Richard's County seat, Sir Richard retiring from politics in 1806. In any event, John did not again seek election.

Interesting 'souvenirs' of this contest are the election jugs commissioned, somewhat prematurely, by the eventual loser. An article in *The Antique Collector* of July 1974 by Michael Messenger entitled 'The Shrewsbury Election Saga' discusses these jugs, which are also of great interest to ceramic collectors.[8] There were three different forms of jug made for John Hill: two are very similar and bear identical inscriptions, but one is considerably more finely potted than the other; the third

HILLS IN SHROPSHIRE POLITICS: THE ELECTION SCANDAL OF 1796

13. Election jugs for John Hill, 1796 (above) and William Hill, 1802 (below). Note how John Hill's differ in shape.

is quite different and only one example is known. Perhaps it was a sample. The style of the jugs induced Messenger to place their manufacture in Shropshire. This means that they were made either at Caughley or at Coalport and as one Edward Blakeway, financial partner of John Rose at Coalport, voted for William Hill, it appears much more likely that they were made at Caughley. Messenger concludes that because the election saga dragged on so long two different lots of jugs were made for John and the second lot was slightly different to the original. The origins of the third are at the moment unknown. There was also a jug made for the victorious William—presumably at Coalport—but nobody seems to know where his 1797 jugs have gone, although I imagine there must be one or two still in the county and one was certainly in the possession of former Shropshire MP, Sir John Langford Holt, in the late 20th century. In 1898 an exhibition of Shropshire antiquities was held in Shrewsbury and listed an 'Election jug, 1797. The Honourable William Hill for ever.' 'Success to the House of Attingham'. In 1802 a model was made inscribed 'The Corporation and William Hill'.

When John Hill quit his seat in 1806 it was thought his eldest son, 'Colonel John', might stand for either the Borough or the County, but it appears that his uncle, Sir Richard, had agreed with Lord Newport to pledge his support elsewhere, for Thomas Jones, and another dirty contest ensued. It was a 'violent and expensive' campaign,[9] and the town was 'soon in a very unpleasant state of heat and confusion' according to a letter written by Thomas Eyton—he whose debts some ten years later caused such problems for the Hills of Hawkstone.[10] Despite the support being given him, Jones does not appear to have felt very beholden to Sir Richard; in his final speech before polling he attacked 'a most monstrous coalition' between William Hill (now a Tory) and Bennett (Whig). On this occasion each candidate was estimated to have spent at least £100 per day during the 12 days of voting, 'exclusive of a little bribery'. So fierce was the fight that Lord Bradford, Colonel of the Militia on exercise in Essex, was asked to permit the men to return to vote.[11] Since the Hon. William Hill (or more likely his brother, Lord Berwick) was probably in a better position to make this request to Bradford and more likely than Jones to benefit from it, it was indeed another case of maximising advantages. After all these efforts Hill topped the poll with Bennett second, but the latter was subsequently disqualified; apparently he had not correctly qualified himself. A new election was held in 1807 and in this contest Bennett was said to have spent £20,000 to £30,000. He lost to Jones and then complained loudly that the rules had been changed by the Mayor, whom he accused of ignoring a recent Commons ruling in the way he accepted or rejected votes.

There was never much doubt that the General, the highly popular son of Shropshire, would be elected even though, or perhaps mainly because, he was far away in the Peninsula. Ironically, in view of recent history, he filled his cousin William's seat and his campaign was run by his father, now Sir John. The General never sat, first because he was abroad at the time of the election, and secondly because he was elevated to the Upper House before he could ever take his seat in the Lower. William, who had gone on to 'represent' Marlborough (1814-18), was also seldom in England since he was serving as Envoy to a succession of different courts: Ratisbon, Turin, Naples, Palermo and Sardinia.

There were no Hills sitting for either the Borough or the County between 1814 and 1821. In 1821 John Cotes died and Rowland Hill, grandson of Sir John, was proposed for the County at the age of 21. He had just come down from Oriel College, Oxford and was serving alongside several other Hills in the Royal Horse Guards Blue. He resigned from the Army in 1824 on the death of his grandfather, Sir John, who had reached the grand old age, for those days, of 84. Rowland was to sit for 21 years through seven Parliaments and probably might have continued but for the death of his uncle and his own succession to 'the other place' as a peer in 1842. He was seldom opposed.

The elections of 1831 were held at the height of the furore over reform. The Tory old guard, headed by the Duke of Wellington, was much opposed to this and Shropshire was, itself, very divided on the subject with the new industrial towns being pro and the old county squires being anti. Lord Hill, now General Commanding in Chief at Horse Guards, was certainly against the Bill and refused to be persuaded by King William to vote for it. For the first time, the sitting members were challenged by Lloyd (Whig) and the notorious Jack Mytton of Halston.

The Myttons had been prominent in Shropshire for some five hundred years; in the famous skullduggery of 1708 one of his ancestors, Richard Mytton, had been found guilty of bribery and his election declared void. Jack Mytton was a wild and undisciplined man who seems to have inspired affection in many despite his terrible behaviour and cruel practical jokes. He was undoubtedly guilty of mistreating his rather delicate first wife, Harriet Tyrwhitt-Jones, who died only a year after giving birth to their daughter, Harriet. This girl would end up marrying Clement Delves Hill, son of Richard Hill, brother of the 2nd Viscount. Mytton's second wife was Caroline Giffard and for a short time everyone thought he had reformed; alas, no. He had five further children including an eldest son whom he insisted on calling 'John Fox Mytton' and a younger boy burdened with the name of his father's most successful racehorse, Euphrates. Eventually Mytton was forced to flee abroad, so great were his debts. The principal contents of Halston were sold and Jack Mytton ended up dying as an alcoholic in the King's Bench Prison having been brought back from France in irons. He was a famous sportsman whose exploits in the hunting field have been recorded in many publications, principally by C. Apperley 'Nimrod'.

Rowland was duly elected, with John Cressett Pelham in the second seat. Both Hill and Pelham chose to stand for the Borough in 1832 which left the County seats up for grabs; the contest for the Borough was again very bitter. 'The Irishman', William Ormsby-Gore, who had estates in both Ireland and in Wales, came forward. He called himself a Tory but three years later, in 1835, described himself as 'Independent' in his Electoral Address. Ormsby-Gore was defeated on this occasion by John Cotes, son of the John Cotes whose death in 1821 had given Rowland his first electoral success. Cotes was described as being 'backed by secret service money and the wild cry of Reform'. According to the *Victoria County History* he was the only Whig ever returned for this Shropshire division.

More election jugs were made in the 1830s and there may have been some in the intervening years. Those of 1835 and 1841 are both handsome commemorative models listing much information.[12] The 1835 jug had the name of the politically influential Lord Lieutenant, the Earl of Powys aged 82, around the top; then, in a curved band, came the 'The Rt Honble Lord Hill of (Hardwick Grange) Commander in Chief' and below this inscription:

1835
In Commemoration of the
Twelve Conservatives of
Shropshire
Representatives of a free and
An intelligent People

Sir R. Hill	Earl Darlington
The Hon R. Clive	W. Ormsby-Gore
Lord Clive	E. Charlton
Sir John Hanmer, Bart	J.C. Pelham
The Hon G. Forester	J. McCaskell
T.C. Whitmore	R. Pigot

On the other side was written 'When bad men conspire, the good must unite', and around the very foot 'The Shropshire Journal, Corn Market' which, one imagines, indicates that the newspaper commissioned the production. Under the bottom of the handle is 'J. Wildig, Shrewsbury', presumably the retailer as his name also appears on the 1841 jug. Below the spout is painted:

Church, King
And
Constitution.

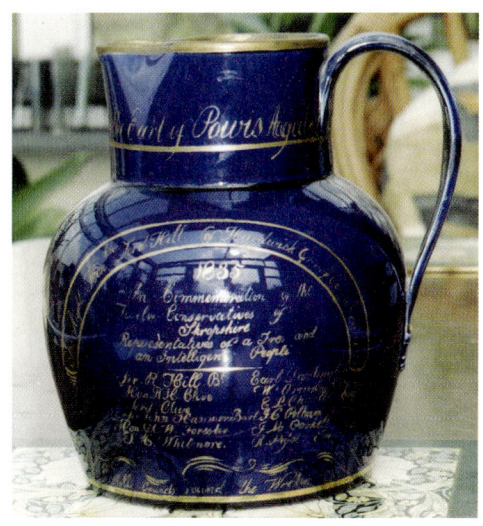

HILLS IN SHROPSHIRE POLITICS: THE ELECTION SCANDAL OF 1796

14. Election jugs from 1835 (above) and 1841 (below).

The 1841 version saw this changed, of course, to 'Church, Queen and Constitution' following the accession of Queen Victoria. This jug is quite large. It is a handsome piece also potted in dark blue and gold ... Conservative colours?

It again commemorates the election of twelve Conservative members for the County. The name of Lord Hill, Commander in Chief, is repeated on one side and that of Admiral Sir E.W.C.R. Owen, Admiral of the White, on the other. The members' names, Hill, Ormsby-Gore, Darlington, Clive, Tomline, Botfield, Ackers, Gaskell, Pigot, Forester and Disraeli, tell us that not much has changed although the inclusion of Disraeli is a little more surprising! A letter from Disraeli to his sister following his election describes the ceremony of 'chairing' in which the elected members were carried through the Borough in elaborate chairs accompanied by bands and crowds. The jug also records the name of the Hon. Thomas Kenyon, Chairman of the Quarter Sessions, and that of the Mayor, John Loxdale. It was once again sold by J. Wildig of Shrewsbury.

When the 2nd Viscount married heiress Anne Clegg in 1831 the family tacked the rather undistinguished 'Clegg' on to a not entirely distinguished 'Hill' to make a double-barrelled name that may have been considered smart by Anne's father. (The names continued to crop up in Parliamentary and County Affairs— a fact often animadverted on by Sir Baldwin Leighton of Loton Hall, whose diaries are a fascinating rag bag of jottings concerning people and events in the county.[13] Why he complained so bitterly is a little hard to discern, since his was an old Shropshire family of considerable influence, but at this point in the 19th century those with less influence were still powerless to do much to break the stranglehold of the principal county families.) Their son, yet another Rowland, was the next member of the family to go to Westminster.

Rowland Clegg-Hill was only 24 when he took his seat in Parliament alongside John Whitehall Dod. He was nominated for the Northern Division of the County in 1857 by Robert Burton and seconded by C. Spenser Lloyd on the resignation of John Ormsby-Gore. The Lloyd family was another which had been eminent in Salopian politics over the past fifty years. In his acceptance speech Rowland declared that he had been amazed, first of all, to be asked to stand and then by the number of signatures on a 'requisition' he had received the previous week. He continued by saying that his principles were very much those of 'one whose name I bear', i.e. his father: '... loyalty to our Sovereign, sincere attachment to the institutions of our country, and an undeviating support of our Protestant faith'.[14] He did not compete with his father's record for length of service and left the House in 1865. Unfortunately his deeds do not seem to have lived up to the high ideals he expressed on his first election.

In Sir Baldwin's diaries there are some fascinating comments, always jealously critical, on the Hill family and, with the benefit of hindsight, it is easy to see that many of the younger members of the family in the second half of the 19th century were a fairly hopeless bunch. Sir Baldwin wrote in 1865 that he had met with Lord Hill in the Carlton and Hill was annoyed that he 'had to retire his son from the representation of the county'. '[Lord Hill] appears to forget that Rowland was a useless member seldom attending the House and never taking any part. It is these sort of members who in my opinion are a great injury to the landed interest and we have too many of the class on both sides of the House.'[15] He was, sadly, perfectly right.

Useless he may have been as a Member of Parliament, but before illness overtook him the 3rd Viscount was a great sportsman and twice served as Master of the Shropshire Hunt. He was also an enthusiastic otter hunter. He had a strange life, it eventually emerged, with a virtually secret first marriage to his mother's stillroom maid, serious illness and inheritance of a mortgaged estate. His obituary in the *Shrewbury Chronicle* refers to 'serious family troubles the nature of which we need not allude to but which awakened many expressions of deepest sympathy with the late Viscount when they were made known'. The bankruptcy had just become public knowledge. The senior branch of the family had been crumbling but had somehow maintained a clear front to the outside world until the collapse of 1895.

There was only one more Member of Parliament—from a junior branch, those who had to earn their living proving more effective in the 'modern' world than their spoilt cousins. The last Hill to go to Westminster was the third son of the Rev. John Hill and Charlotte Kenyon, Clement Lloyd Hill. Sir Clement Hill, KCMG, KCB had had a highly successful career in the Diplomatic Service ending up as Superintendent of the African Protectorates (Head of the African Department of the Foreign Office). As a Unionist (Conservative), he was returned three times for Shrewsbury. In 1906 he had just retired from his role as Superintendent of the African Protectorates, the election was only a few weeks away and the Unionist Party had no candidate. The Liberals, 'led by an aspirant for Parliamentary honours who had conducted for some time a tearing campaign, were confident of victory'.[16] Sir Clement stepped forward and the whole picture changed. It was said that his victory was personal, 'the reward of service to his country, a recognition of his integrity and the real significance of the motto under which he fought'—Honour and Honesty.[17] Perhaps Sir Clement was more deserving of this than most of his predecessors. It was evidently yet another bitterly fought contest but one in which Clem Hill maintained his 'straightforwardness and gentlemanliness'. The election saw the country throw out the long established Conservative and Unionist Party government, which only retained 150 seats. But, against the national swing, Sir Clement was elected by a majority of 440. This was increased at the election of 1910; he was also returned in 1911. He died in 1913.

CHAPTER EIGHT

Hawkstone Hall
The Park · The Citadel

The Hall

Hawkstone Hall is a Grade I listed house which was the home of the Hill family for almost 350 years. Since 1926 it has been in the ownership of the Redemptorist Order and is now used as a Pastoral Study Centre.

Hawkstone lies on the great plain that includes south Cheshire and north Shropshire, just where a sudden and unexpected outcrop of rugged sandstone abruptly changes the landscape, rising and 'evoking romantic impressions redolent of Arthurian legend'. Hawkstone Hall stands poised on a slope between the two, with extensive views north and west towards the Welsh hills, and with its famous romantic Park lying out of sight over the brow of the hill to the south.

The Hill family's first connection with Hawkstone (many previous spellings are to be found, such as Hauckston) came with the purchase of property in the parishes of Wem and Hodnet by Sir Rowland Hill, Knight. He was born in the parish of Hodnet where his father, Thomas, had some property, and in 1556 he purchased, for the sum of £700, land at Hawkstone together with the Manor of Soulton, near Wem. Hawkstone remained in the possession of the Hill family until 1906.

Sir Rowland planned to leave this estate—very much smaller than it was later to become—to his cousin Humphrey, son of his uncle Ralph. However, Humphrey predeceased his own son, who was fortunate enough to inherit and become the first Rowland (2) to make his home on the property. Rowland's date of birth is not recorded in the family pedigree but he died in 1619. His son (Rowland 3) was born in 1594 and was succeeded, in turn, by his son (Rowland 4) born in 1623. None of these men left much of a mark on history although the last is said to have been a Royalist supporter imprisoned by Cromwellian troops in the Red Castle (on a rock above what is now the Hawkstone Park golf course) who, on escaping, hid in a cave nearby. In the 1780s the 2nd Baronet, Sir Richard, placed an urn in the Park to commemorate the event, for which there is, in truth, no concrete evidence, although it is certainly a possibility given that the local town of Wem was garrisoned by the Parliamentarians early in the Civil War,

15. George Hill with otter hounds.

and raiding parties were sent into the local villages. The commemorative urn, bearing a long inscription typical of Sir Richard, vanished but was discovered in undergrowth during the restoration of the Park in the early 1990s and has been reinstated on its original site. Rowlands 2 and 3 seem to have lived quiet lives but Rowland 4 probably added a little land to the estate. There may have been a few minor alterations to the house before his death in 1700, but if there were it could be that they were done with his son Richard's money as Rowland's Will does not indicate any degree of affluence.

Richard, the 'Great' Hill, was born in 1654, and, having an older brother—yet, another Rowland—who died in his early 20s, he travelled to London to make his fortune, and succeeded on a grand scale. He inherited the Hawkstone estate in 1700. By the time he began major work at Hawkstone, around 1719, the Great Hill had lived and travelled extensively on the Continent, where he had educated his eye and taste in common with many of his peers. He was interested in architecture and design and set about turning Hawkstone into a 'gentleman's' residence. Although he is recorded as having retired from active government service in around 1708, he does not appear to have begun work on the house and grounds until ten years later.[1] He had long been buying property not only in Shropshire but also in Staffordshire and Cheshire, using several different agents.[2]

16. Pleasure gardens, Hawkstone.

These included his brother John, his nephew Thomas Harwood Hill and Francis Chambré, a local lawyer who was to marry his niece.

A significant purchase was that of Hardwick Grange. In a letter dated 2 December 1721, John Dicken, his steward and agent, wrote to Richard Hill informing him that this property, together with another in the village of Hadnall, was for sale.[3] Hardwick was the estate that the 2nd Baronet, Sir Richard, was to leave to his nephew, the General, on his death in 1808. It was also one of the first properties to be sold when money got tight in the 19th century.

The Chambré family lived at Petton and was said to be descended from Johan de la Chaumbre, 'a Nobelle Norman' who entered England in 'ye train of King Willaume ye Conqueraure'. One of the family married Mary, daughter of Humphrey Hill, Lord of the Manor of Hill (Court of Hull). Francis Chambré, the lawyer, became closely connected with the family at Hawkstone when he married Richard Hill's niece, Elizabeth, daughter of Richard's younger brother, Robert Hill. Their grand-daughter, Mary Chambré, married back into the Hill family when she wedded John (later 3rd Baronet) in 1768, and she gave birth, amongst many other children (16 in all), to the famous 'brave soldier sons' of Peninsular and Waterloo fame.[4]

Much has been made of the fact that there is no record of Richard Hill's visiting Hawkstone during the entire rebuilding programme, but since he had presumably been brought up there he must have held a picture of the site in

17. A pond in the restored gardens of the Hall

his head. He certainly seems to have had a clear idea as to what he wanted in his house, and drawings of 'portiques', pilasters and their capitals went back and forth for his approval.

Inner and outer forecourts were constructed outside the west entrance. Both of these were subsequently removed.[5] There is a description of an inner walled courtyard with handsome gates supplied by Robert Davies of Wrexham. In an aquatint by W. Williams dated 1789 the gates so described are possibly visible, but standing to the north of the house. There is no sign in the picture of any sort of closed inner courtyard, just a gravel sweep in front of the main west entrance. Another picture (formerly in the Courtauld Collection) by John Russell, dated 1785, also shows that the inner courtyard had been removed, leaving a simple carriageway leading up to a flight of shallow steps. It is possible that the outer court was still there but outside the field of view of this particular painting. At the top of the steps is shown another, narrower, pathway and then the steps leading up under the portico to the main entrance. This front entrance looks different today, with plinths surmounted by sphinxes flanking the steps.

Richard Hill also sent detailed instructions concerning the design of the immediate pleasure grounds or gardens: formal walkways and parterres; orchards of grafted apples, pears and walnuts; plantations of trees including elm and Scots pines, the latter being 7ft high so as to give them a good start. The walkways required an enormous quantity of pebbles—some 100 tons—when they were laid out in 1721. There were ponds, some of which were stocked with carp, a horse-wash, a home farm and, of course, the stable block. The man responsible for the gardens and immediate grounds was gardener Joseph Holcroft. When he became too ill to work in 1725/6, Francis Chambré and Mrs Hill, widow of brother John who had died in 1713, took on the supervision of the outside work. Sarah Hill, together with her children, apparently lived in the house throughout the period of rebuilding, which must have been uncomfortable, but probably gave young Rowland (5), the eventual heir, a love of and feeling for the property. A new lane or drive was made connecting the Hall with the village of Marchamley, which lies to the north-east, and today it provides the only access to the house. The work on this drive employed 30 men and was guaranteed for seven years.

An amusing anecdote concerned John Dicken, who wrote to ask the Great Hill for a recommendation to Lord Derby for his brother, Thomas Dicken, who wished to become a Yeoman of the Guard.[6] Unfortunately this young man had been rejected as being 'too low', but John Dicken was sure that if Richard Hill were to write on Thomas' behalf the half inch lacking might be overlooked!

William Price was the mason in charge of the stone work, carried out principally in Grinshill stone and with local stone from the river Dunge on the west front. Price was also responsible for the construction of the family vault in Hodnet church.

The north and south porticos which were added at this time, after much debate, were subsequently removed but the one over the west entrance remains. In 1854 a drive from the village of Weston-under-Redcastle was created by the 2nd Viscount to commemorate the coming of age of his son, Rowland Clegg-Hill. This drive gave an excellent first view of the house as you emerged from the dark of the tunnel under Grotto Hill and saw the house at a little distance. Unfortunately, with the separation of the Hall from the Park, the drive, although still passable, is closed.

Building was not completed during Richard Hill's lifetime and so it was that his fortunate young nephew and heir, Rowland (5), aged only 22, came into both a great estate and the beginnings of a handsome 'seat'. He also found himself a baronet. His uncle had refused this honour for himself but managed to procure it for his heir. Had Richard accepted it, the title being a first generation creation would have died with him.

Superficial study might lead one to think that the most imaginative and outlandish parts and buildings of the Park were the work of Rowland's eccentric son, Sir Richard. But deeper investigation shows that Sir Rowland himself was responsible for much of the work, and especially the use of the natural landscape. Whether he continued to develop his uncle's ideas for the house and immediate grounds or whether his remodelling and embellishments were entirely his own, the results were on the whole very successful.[7] He was responsible for the two

18. Plan of Hawkstone Park.

19. Hawkstone Hall.

original wings—two pavilions on the west side connected with the central block by curved quadrants—which seem to have been built around 1750. One of the pavilions housed the library that had come to Hawkstone following the death of the Great Hill. Rowland also added another storey to the main house with pyramidal 'pepper pot' towers at each corner. His other major work consisted in extending the east front by about nine feet to create the great Saloon. The creation of this room also entailed reducing the length of the entrance hall by seven feet. An impressive piece, the Saloon is two storeys in height and was created around 1740. Sir Rowland appears to have had good taste—probably schooled by his uncle—and employed a follower of Kent, Henry Flitcroft, to create the Saloon. When Lewis Wyatt carried out the last major alterations to the house in the 1830s it became the dining room. Flitcroft is usually credited with a lighter touch in his plasterwork designs than his mentor, and for Hawkstone he created a handsome coved ceiling decorated in grisaille on a gold ground. The flat rectangular central portion of the ceiling is embellished with cherubs riding on clouds done in stucco, and the frieze below the cornice contains profile medallions of Roman emperors. Full-length portraits of Queen Mary II and King William III together with a large painting of the Siege of Namur, 1695, showing the Great Hill together with King William, the Elector of Bavaria and John, Duke of Marlborough, adorn the north and east walls, set in delicately stuccoed frames. In a Kentian overmantel above the handsome marble chimney piece on the south wall a portrait of Richard Hill has pride of place.[8]

In addition to his work on the house Sir Rowland purchased more land, including the medieval Red Castle which he incorporated into the Park as a genuine ruin among the many 'follies'.

Sir Rowland died in 1783 and his eldest son and heir, Richard, was a man of very different temperament. His father had been a Member of Parliament and Sheriff of the County, but during his long tenure as a Knight of the Shire, Sir Richard was to become best known for his probity, his independence, his undoubted eccentricity, his wit, his conversion to Methodism and, above all, more than two hundred years later, for the romantic park of Hawkstone. His alterations to the house itself were not so happy but, fortunately, far less enduring. He incorporated a chapel into the south wing, extending both wings westwards with canted bays at ground floor level. An etching dated 1827 shows the changes, which did not survive the attentions of Sir Rowland, 4th Baronet, and Lewis Wyatt in the 1830s. (Lewis Wyatt was the son of Benjamin Wyatt, agent to Lord Penrhyn of Penrhyn near Bangor. His work at Hawkstone followed commissions involving remodelling at both Hackwood Park in Hampshire and Lyme Park in Cheshire.) Between 1832 and 1834 Wyatt removed Sir Richard's single-storey bays, added a parapet to the upper floor to give the pavilions a height more in proportion with the main block of the house and rounded off the west ends up to their full height. The wings have been tampered with throughout the life of the house—even Lord Marchamley could not resist changing them, and destroying their symmetry, when he bought the Hall from the Hills in 1906.

When Rowland, 4th Baronet (Rowland 7), first called on Wyatt, the architect immediately proposed pulling down the entire house and re-siting it a short distance away in what he considered to be a more favourable situation. He graciously allowed that any of the original building that was salvageable could be reused. His patron thankfully retained a vestige of sanity and did not accept this extravagant proposition; had he done so, the bankruptcy would certainly have arrived some years earlier than 1894! Under Wyatt's alterations the library was moved to the central block, the old library becoming a billiard room. The southern quadrant became a winter garden containing the 4th Baronet's impressive collection of English birds and their eggs.

Other family trophies displayed in the bird gallery included a uniform given to Sir Thomas Noel Hill by George III, the banner Lord Hill carried at the King's funeral, and the two helmets of Lord Hill which saved his life in Egypt and in the Peninsula.

Lewis Wyatt's best known work in the house is the new ballroom/drawing room which he added in the south-east corner. By 1830 any lingering French Empire influence was being discarded in favour of the heavier, sumptuous decoration in the *Louis Quatorze* style. This was not out of keeping with the date of the house as inherited by the Great Hill, when Louis had been the feared enemy. Wyatt treated the room in opulent fashion, with lavish gilding of the rich plasterwork to walls and ceiling, handsome doorways, large gilt mirrors and walls hung with French silk damask. The curtains were of crimson and white damask and the suite of Louis XIV seating furniture was covered in the same crimson fabric. The rest of the furniture consisted of 'ancient' pieces and the ensemble was estimated to have cost £2,400.

By the time Rowland, 4th Baronet and 2nd Viscount died in 1875, all these and many other extravagances had caught up with him and it was only after the sale of the house in 1906 that any more changes were made. One may regret the loss of the great entrance hall, but this change took place as early as the 1740s, when it was reduced to accommodate the Saloon. This work also required the reversing of the staircase, which is now approached by an arch from the hall. The staircase was constructed in the early 18th century and is a three-light, rectangular-well cantilevered staircase. It has barleytwist balusters, two to each tread, with four balusters forming newel posts and a ramped moulded handrail.[9] The two-storeyed hall, typical of the 1720s, was reduced in height by the insertion of an extra room at first floor level.

For nearly fifty years after its purchase by the Redemptorist Order in 1926 the house was a seminary for young priests. During that time the Hall, buried in the depths of rural Shropshire, was almost forgotten. Since 1973 it has been used as a Pastoral Study Centre and for three months at a time offers a haven of rest and renewal to priests and religious who have been working in Catholic missions throughout the world. Works of restoration are ongoing, notably in the Saloon, and the beauty of the House and Park is now enjoyed and appreciated by the hundreds of people of all nationalities who arrive each year to stay there.

The style and grandeur maintained at Hawkstone in former times proclaimed the importance of the Hills as a great landowning family carrying out the public duties expected of their class. If some generations lavished too much money on embellishment, we must acknowledge that they left an important legacy for posterity, and thanks to its purchase by the Redemptorists the beauty they created has been preserved.

The gardens around the Hall itself have been restored. Work began in 1988. A feasibility study was carried out by Walding Associates of Newport (who also did the study for the park) and the work of restoration and replanting was skilfully carried out by David and Monica Weller. Some original features remain, such as the Temple Walk which ran for 300 metres between two 'temple rotundas'. Only one of these rotundas now stands. Constructed in grey sandstone, they were built in the early days of the 2nd Baronet, c.1784. One of them collapsed in 1957. The remaining rotunda is Grade II listed. A number of the great trees such as the huge Irish yews could have well been planted in the time of the Great Hill. The old 'stewpond' is possibly the one supplied with a 'parcel of carp' sent from London in 1725. It is some 190 metres long and Richard Hill may well have been influenced by a similar use of water in Holland and possibly Italy. Unfortunately, this one no longer holds water and merely forms a depression in the ground.

The extravagant 4th Baronet also carried out extensive work around the time of his marriage in 1832, when he employed the landscape architect, William Sawrey Gilpin. Some of the restored garden is almost certainly Gilpin's—for example, the part of the flower garden with gravelled paths in the shape of a starfish, the pergolas and the rockery. The English Heritage listing suggests a date of 1900 for more of the pleasure gardens but the 4th Viscount was certainly in no position to pay for any such luxury by that date and it is more likely that Lord Marchamley did a little work after he bought the house in 1906. One of the interesting facts about the flower gardens is that, in common with the Park, they are mainly invisible from the house itself. From the east front the ground rises gently, shallow steps leading past the Orangery of the 1830s up to the Temple Walk, which forms a central axial path. The gardens lie to the north across lawns, partially concealed by shrubberies.

20. 'Old Jones' at the Grotto, Hawkstone Park.

The Park

'Eccentric, breathtaking and fun' is how Hawkstone's romantic landscape park was described by James Stevenson in a small book published locally; and Arthur Oswald's article on the park (*Country Life*, 7 July 1958) is captioned 'Beauties and Wonders of Hawkstone; Nature and Artifice in a Shropshire Park'.

Widely known and much visited in the last quarter of the 18th century, the Park at Hawkstone became a forgotten gem as the fortunes of the Hills declined one hundred years later. The estate having been split up in the early decades of the 20th century, much of the park became a golf course in 1935, a development which probably helped prevent its final ruin. Pevsner (*Buildings of England: Shropshire*, 1958) wrote, 'Hawkstone is not as well known as it ought to be ... neither the remarkable house nor the even more remarkable Park.' Another admirer, Richard Haslam (*Country Life*, 9 May 1985), described it as 'one of the most extraordinary places in the country'. By that time the Park was in overgrown and ruinous condition, and urgent discussions were taking place as to how to restore it. Today, 20 years later, this work has been most successfully—and generously—carried out by the brothers, Sir David and Sir Frederick Barclay, acting on the detailed plans for restoration drawn up by Walding Associates of Newport, Shropshire. Some of the original buildings/follies have vanished and the shells and fossils in the Grotto are, sadly, just a memory, but a great tourist attraction of the 1780s has become, once again, a visitor attraction in the 21st century.

21. View from Red Castle.

The *Hawkstone Inn* was built in 1790 to accommodate the increasing number of visitors to the park. T. Rodenhurst in his invaluable guide *Description of Hawkstone* described it as 'genteely fitted up for the reception of company' and suggested that parties travelling to Wales or Buxton—no doubt to take the waters—would find in it 'the most comfortable accommodations, both for themselves, their servants and their horses'. Today, it serves as a clubhouse for the three championship golf courses.

It is possible, although probably a contentious statement, that the rampant, uncontrolled spread of rhododendrons in the middle years of the 20th century actually helped preserve some of the follies from vandalism. The plants were more than content in the Shropshire soil and multiplied rapidly, covering many of the follies from view and obscuring the rocks which contribute so much to the character of the park and which so excited the imagination of our 18th-century forebears.

Evidence that Sir Rowland, 1st Baronet did carry out a good deal of work landscaping the Park, such as the creation of the drive along the Terrace, is confirmed by several different sources. As early as 1748 Philip Yorke wrote, 'The place has great rude beauties and the owner is constantly improving it.' Even Dr Johnson, visiting the Park on his way to North Wales in 1774, was impressed: 'He that mounts the precipices at Hawkstone wonders how he shall return'—portly Johnson was more accustomed to the flat pavements of London than the low hills of Shropshire. 'The Ideas which it forces upon the mind are the sublime, the dreadful and the vast.' The most 'awesome' feature amongst the ten miles of paths, steps and bridges was the Grotto Hill. Dr Johnson was accompanied on his visit by Mr and Mrs Thrale. Hester Thrale was obviously equally impressed because she made a second visit 26 years later when she brought her second husband, Gabriel Piozzi, in 1800. Another well-recorded visit was made by General Pascal Paoli, the Corsican patriot, in 1792. Rodenhurst records in his guide that Paoli was much struck by the view under the Grotto Hill where 'the Red Castle breaks upon you'. The spot was forthwith named 'Paoli's Point'.

In 1786 Sir Joshua Reynolds addressed the question of whether places such as Hawkstone Park and its follies could be classified as gardens: 'gardening as far as gardening is an Art, or entitled to that appellation, is a deviation from Nature, for if the true taste consists, as many hold, in banishing every appearance of Art or any traces of the footsteps of man, it would then no longer be a garden'.[10]

Two men were principally responsible for creating this early example of a romantic park: Sir Rowland Hill and his son Sir Richard. They made maximum use of the natural situation with its hills, craggy rocks, water and, of course, the genuine medieval ruins of the Red Castle, ancient stronghold of the Audley family. They were fortunate in being able to employ a large workforce. Sir Richard was a considerable philanthropist in his day and certainly kept bread on the tables of many houses on his estate and beyond. As to which of the two men did what, we know that many of the follies were already *in situ* by 1787 because they are marked on a Survey of that time, and it is unlikely that Sir Richard could have achieved so much in the four years since his father's death, although it is possible that the younger man may have initiated some of the work in his father's lifetime. The fantasy and whimsy of some of the features seem typical of his character, but we cannot discount ideas produced by his mother, Jane (*née* Broughton, first wife of Sir Rowland), or his sister Jane. One thing is certain, we can credit Richard—with possible help from his sister Jane and younger brother Brian—with the moral and religious verses which abound:

> O may the Hills for ever live
> Around this pleasant shore
> Till rocks shall crumble into dust
> And time shall be no more

is one typical example. Sir Richard could not avoid bringing his religion into every part of his life. His humour and wit are also equally and amply demonstrated in the follies of Hawkstone. The sentiments expressed in the inscriptions reflect the spirit of the age, and there is a marked similarity between some of his compositions in the Park and those of the family friend Reginald Heber, Rector of Hodnet and later Bishop of Calcutta and author of many familiar hymns.

22. Grotto Hill.

Rodenhurst's *Description of Hawkstone* provides rich material on the Park. There is no known copy of the first edition (1783?), which was only available locally. Probably only a few copies were printed and these would have been principally for distribution to visitors to the Hall. The second edition was printed in 1784 and was also available in London. The ninth edition, published in 1807, is valuable because this updated version appeared at the very end of Sir Richard's life, when all the 'natural and artificial beauties' had been introduced. Sir Richard's heir, his brother John, did not concern himself with work on House or Park. This may well have been because he inherited rather late in life, but most probably he had little interest in such matters, being more of a sporting fellow.

The landscape architect, William Emes, who had worked on schemes for several families in the county, including the Corbets, was employed also at Hawkstone. His greatest project was undoubtedly the creation of the Hawk Lake, two miles in length. This work took nearly four years to complete and involved, apart from the necessary excavation, the construction of several dams. It was a rich source of employment locally. The lake gave a lot of scope to Sir Richard and his fertile imagination but many of the original attractions are now gone, such as a large figure of the god Neptune holding an urn from which water spilled to be caught and thrown back by nereids. A cottage nearby was built in the Dutch style and there was a windmill on the opposite bank of the lake. This was ornamental, but served also a practical purpose since it was used to extract oil for cattle cake. According to Roy Gregory's *The Industrial Windmill in Britain*, 'the Hawkstone mill is the only surviving example of an English wind-powered oil mill'. Although in a somewhat ruined state, it retains its windshaft and some of its gearing. A modern cap has been installed to offer some protection until such time as the mill can be restored.

Another body of water was formed between Red Castle Hill and Grotto Hill; this is clearly shown in one of Emes's aquatints but it seems to have disappeared quite quickly, a letter from Emes to Sir Richard dated 1786 indicating that there were problems keeping water in it. Emes was also responsible for the Menagerie Pool (currently very overgrown) near to the Citadel on the Hodnet/Weston-under-Redcastle road. The Menagerie itself contained a varied collection of animals and birds.[11] At one time there were monkeys, which did not survive long, parrots, an eagle and a macaw. Apparently there were also stuffed birds—possibly part of, or the original basis for, the collection formed by the 2nd Viscount, which he subsequently displayed in the winter garden in the house itself.

There were other delights: a Lion's Den, which disappointingly contained only a stone lion; the Ravens' Shelf, on which ravens perched and nested for many years; the Fox's Knob, a rock from which a fox leapt to its death pursued by hounds, several of which, according to Rodenhurst, followed the poor beast over the edge in the heat of the chase. There was also the Vineyard, which must have been one of Sir Rowland's ideas, since it is mentioned as far back as 1748. It was not a successful enterprise; despite every effort to cultivate vines, the climate of Shropshire at that time proved unsuitable to ripening grapes.

Like the pleasure gardens, the ten miles of pathways and steps leading to the delights of grottoes, eye-catchers, 'awful precipices' and romantic buildings are hidden from the Hall itself and reveal themselves only gradually as the visitor proceeds. They are, in fact, part of a mystery tour, providing the excitement of a sudden narrow bridge, a precipice, a deep ravine or an enthralling vista through a faux antique arch, with the eye being drawn to carefully sited follies such as the early 19th-century White Tower, a Gothic, turreted building intended to be seen from a distance.[12] Gingerbread Hall, originally called the Temple of Patience, not mentioned in Rodenhurst's guide but now restored from almost total ruin, was where exhausted tourists were revived with ... gingerbread!

The Grotto is splendid even in its vandalised state. Reached by a small path that appears to end in solid rock, it is a labyrinth of natural and man-made passages with a chamber reached after a dark corridor some 50 metres in length. There is a second chamber and a long gallery. It is altogether quite a complex and a portion of it may have been part of a mine. The visitor is frequently lured into 'false' exits and must often stoop and grope along the walls to find the

The GROTTO HILL and RED CASTLE in HAWKSTONE PARK, the SEAT of Sr RICHARD HILL BART

The RED CASTLE and WHITE TOWER in HAWKSTONE PARK

23. Aquatints of Hawkstone Park. Top left: the Grotto Hill and Red Castle; bottom left: the Red Castle and White Tower; above: the Red Castle; below: the House and lawn at Hawkstone 1789 (W. Williams).

24. Faux arch.

25. Grotto.

way. It is very advisable to be armed with a flashlight. The openings in the sandy rock walls were once filled with coloured glass; some of the walls were painted black, others green; all was designed to make it dark, exciting and exotic and to give a *frisson* of fear to the visitor. The shells and coral that once decorated the walls—the handiwork of Richard Hill's sisters and nieces—are long gone, with only traces of their fossilised shapes remaining. A few could still be seen in the 1950s but most vanished when many of the Park's buildings were vandalised in the Second World War. A cliff-hanging terrace outside the Grotto gives a wonderful view across to the Red Castle.

The whole Park was truly a fairyland at its completion and included a Fairy Glen, an Elysian Hill and a Hermitage. This last was a great feature for many years and, although it became ruined, it too has been restored in the 1990s. There may once have been a permanent hermit, but more often the role of 'resident' hermit (known as 'Father Francis') was played by one of the men of the family when showing their guests around, or by a guide when paying visitors were conducted round the Park. (Members of a local family, the Joneses, were guides at Hawkstone for at least four generations.) The 'live' hermit was eventually replaced by a rather unreliable automaton and, ultimately, by a barely visible stuffed figure.

26. The 'Obelisk'.

In 1795 Sir Richard erected the Monument. Known inaccurately as the 'Obelisk', it is in fact a column of the Tuscan order, built to commemorate his great ancestor Sir Rowland Hill, Knight, Lord Mayor in 1549 and purchaser of the Hawkstone estate in 1556. His statue was carved by John Nelson but fell from its 28m. high plinth in a storm in the 1930s, leaving only the feet. In August 1992 a new statue carved by Guy Portelli was unveiled and Jack Jones (fourth generation of guides) was present at the ceremony held to mark the occasion. Unfortunately the day was cold, damp and foggy and there was no view to reward the effort involved in climbing the internal spiral staircase. The view on a clear day is inexpressibly beautiful, the green pastures of England and Wales stretching for miles in every direction, ringed by distant 'blue-remembered hills'. The sight helps us appreciate the excitement of those who saw the great beacons lit to celebrate the triumphant news of the victories of Trafalgar and Waterloo. As the flames leapt high above the Hawkstone hills they were seen in 'twelve' counties.

The Citadel

The Citadel, even its earliest form, seems to have been a folly, a romantic-looking 'Gothick Revival' building. A relatively small two-turreted house was first built for Sir Richard's inefficient steward, George Downward. In 1789 this servant was reprimanded but not, unfortunately, dismissed. Downward survived to preside over further extravagant expenditure by his master, and it was he who occupied the house which Rodenhurst referred to in the ninth edition of his Guide (1807) as an 'object to be remarked among the late additions'.

In 1824 the Citadel was rebuilt as a dower house by the 4th Baronet. It was among the first of his extravagances and is a splendid monument to early 19th-century taste. The design is taken from the family coat of arms, which shows a triple-towered castle; whereas the original Citadel had only two towers the new house, designed by Thomas Harrison of Chester, has three. A castellated building also forms the family crest. Harrison had been responsible for the work carried out on Hardwick Grange for Lord Hill of Almaraz and Hawkstone between 1822-4. If he had been a little disappointed by the simplicity of Lord Hill's renovations at Hardwick, Harrison must have felt he had more scope for his talents at the Citadel which, despite its relatively small scale, is a highly original construction. The house of red sandstone stands on a large and unusual 'platform' of cobbled paving and the three castellated towers have decorative arrow slits to add to the conceit of an impregnable fortress. It commands wide-ranging and impressive views: north-east to the Grotto Hill, Red Castle Hill and the Terrace; south to Shropshire's very own 'mountain', the Wrekin. The rooms are delightful, with large windows to embrace the views, and many of them are circular, contributing to their unique charm. There is some elegant plasterwork in the ground floor rooms, both on the ceilings with plaster rib and foliated bosses and on the decorated dados. The dining room ceiling is coffered and has more elaborate plasterwork and wainscotting. The open stairwell rises from the hall, top lit by a lantern, with a simple but pretty Gothic balustrade.

Sir John, 3rd Baronet, died in 1824 and was succeeded by his grandson, Rowland, 4th Baronet. By the time of his death in 1875 this young man would

27. The Citadel.

have effected the financial ruin of his family. Now, in 1824, it was decided that young Rowland's mother, Mrs John Hill, who had been widowed in 1814, would move into the renovated Citadel together with her sister-in-law, the formidable sounding Miss Jane Hill. A few years later Mrs Hill's second son, another John, moved in on his marriage to Charlotte Kenyon. This John Hill took Holy Orders and was perpetual curate of Weston-under-Redcastle and sometime Rector of Bolas. The little church in Weston was built by Sir Richard in 1791, although parish registers are in existence showing a chapel on the site as early as 1565. John Hill's tenure of the living at Weston lasted for 60 years, from 1825 to 1886. Following his death his four sons (John, George, Clement and Brian) commissioned the East Window representing Holman Hunt's *Light of the World* in memory of their remarkable parents.

The Rev. John Hill farmed the Citadel Farm and was evidently renowned for his exemplary methods. He died in 1891 at the age of 89 just before the estate went bankrupt. The Citadel was eventually sold in 1916, when it was bought by Sir Bevil Stanier. The contents were sold in 1898 following the death from sunstroke of Isabella, Dowager Viscountess Hill, who had lived there for some years. It was a five-day sale by local auctioneers Barber of Wellington, Hodnet and Market Drayton. The 'contents' included the farm stock of cows, harness, carriages, ducks, turkeys and prize-bred Andalusian chickens.

Constance, Lady Stanier lived in the house until after the Second World War, and it was later sold and used for a while for the storage of grain. It was subsequently owned by Sir Alexander Stanier. In recent years extensive restoration has been carried out and the house is delightfully decorated and the garden well maintained. The present owners welcome guests on a definitely 'upmarket' B&B basis, and the spirit of comfortable hospitality lives on.

THE NOEL-HILLS OF ATTINGHAM

ROWLAND HILL of Hawkstone = Margaret Whitehall
(d. 1700) m. 1653

- Rowland Hill (d. 1663)
- Rev. RICHARD HILL (1654–1727) builder of Tern Hall
- Elizabeth Hill = Samuel Barbour
- MARGARET HILL (d. 1734) = Thomas Harwood (1661–1738)
- John Hill = Sarah Stubbs m. 1699

Children:

- Samuel (assumed surname of Hill) (d. 1758) = Elizabeth dau. of Earl of Chesterfield m. 1722
- Elizabeth = John Egerton (1679–1724)
- THOMAS HARWOOD (assumed surname of Hill) (1693–1782) = (1) Anne Powys (d. 1739) m. 1723 = (2) Susanna Maria Noel (d. 1760) dau. of Sir William Noel m. 1740
- Sir Rowland Hill (d. 1783) = Jane Broughton m. 1732 — 5 daus
  Hills of Hawkstone

Next generation:

- Richard (1723–34)
- Anne (1726–71) = Robert Burton of Longner
- Margaret (1729–67) = Earl of Harborough
- Susanna (1741–61)
- Maria (1742–1813) = (1) Sir Brian Broughton-Delves (d. 1766) = (2) Henry Errington
- Samuel (1743–66)
- NOEL HILL (1745–89) created 1st BARON BERWICK 1784 builder of Attingham Park = Anne Vernon (1744–97) m. 1768

Next generation:

- Henrietta Maria (1769–1831) = Charles, Marquess of Ailesbury m. 1793
- THOMAS NOEL HILL 2nd BARON (1770–1832) creator of the Picture Gallery = Sophia Dubouchet (d. 1875) m. 1812
- Anne (1772–1837)
- WILLIAM NOEL-HILL 3rd BARON (1773–1842) (took Noel as additional surname)
- Rev. RICHARD NOEL-HILL 4th BARON (1774–1848) (took Noel as additional surname) = Frances Maria Mostyn-Owen (d. 1840) m. 1800
- Amelia (1776–1850)

Next generation:

- RICHARD NOEL-HILL 5th BARON (1800–61)
- Col. WILLIAM NOEL-HILL 6th BARON (1802–82)
- Rev. Thomas Henry Noel-Hill (1804–70) = Harriet Rebecca Humffreys m. 1845
- Charles Arthur Wentworth Noel-Hill (1811–53) = Catherine Mary Adams (d. 1894) m. 1845 — 4 daus

Next generation:

- RICHARD HENRY NOEL-HILL 7th BARON (1847–97) = Ellen Nystrom of Malmö (d. 1934) m. 1869
- Rev. Thomas Noel-Hill (1847–88) = Frederica Sarah Morrice (d. 1883) m. 1874
- Kate Maria Louisa Ada Noel-Hill (1847–1921)
- Rev. Charles Noel-Hill (1848–1911) = Edith Mary Benson m. 1891

Next generation:

- Mary Selina Noel-Hill (1875–1950)
- THOMAS HENRY NOEL-HILL 8th BARON (1877–1947) = Teresa Hulton (1890–1972) m. 1919
- Charles Michael Wentworth Noel-Hill 9th BARON (1897–1953) = Gwen Guest m. 1947 — 2 daus

Owners of Attingham in CAPITALS

28. Noel-Hill family tree.

CHAPTER NINE

The Noel-Hills (Berwicks) of Attingham Park

'Qui uti scit, ei bona'

The somewhat ironic motto of the Hills of Attingham could be applied equally to the Hills of Hawkstone. Noel's old Cambridge tutor, writing to congratulate him on his peerage in 1784, had quoted the following passage from Terence: 'Atque hac perinde sunt, ut illius est Animus, qui ea possidet; Qui uti scit, ei bona; illi, qui non utitur recta, mala' (which loosely translates 'Wealth is a blessing to those who use it wisely, but a curse to those who do not'). Noel Hill, 1st Lord Berwick, liked this and chose the phrase as his motto. It was more appropriate than he realised at the time.

The branch of the family which had the fortune to inherit the Attingham Estate was no better with their finances than the cousins at Hawkstone. They started with the right money and, for the most part, excellent taste but delusions of grandeur eventually brought the Noel-Hills to extinction and early bankruptcy; fortunately the 3rd Lord Berwick (1773-1842) had more sense than his older brother and managed to retrieve some of the family fortunes following the great house contents sale in 1827 which lasted for 16 days. The 'Great' Hill, creator of the fortune which enabled both nephews Rowland at Hawkstone and Thomas at Tern/Atcham (Attingham) to found noble dynasties, must have spun in his grand vault under Hodnet church as the estates were milked of all cash and finally had to be abandoned. We are more fortunate with Attingham in that, having been given to the National Trust by the 8th Lord Berwick in 1947, it is at least open to the public.

Thomas (Harwood) Hill (1693-1782)

Richard Hill gave Tern Hall, on which he had started work in 1701, to his sister Margaret with remainder to her elder son, Thomas. Margaret's second husband was Thomas Harwood, described as a 'grocer' (sometimes referred to as a draper but probably just a member of the Drapers Guild) of Shrewsbury, and the couple lived for much of their married life at Tern. Richard Hill undertook to supervise the education, which he almost certainly also paid for, of Thomas, who went to

Eton before being dispatched to the Continent to learn German and French and about financial affairs. He started in Germany and then moved to the banking house of Clifford in Amsterdam. He also fell in love with the French way of life and tried to introduce certain aspects of it in later years at Tern (Attingham.) He appears to have studied well because he was soon successfully wheeling and dealing both on his own account and on behalf of others. His principal hobby in life was the study of grammar. Although Thomas was successful, he did not hanker after grandeur and appears to have been content to live between his uncle's house in Cleveland Court, St James when in London and in the country house, Tern, which remained much as it had been when he was a child. Younger brother Rowland went into the Church—of course! Thomas' first wife, Anne Powys, died in 1739 leaving him with two surviving daughters, Anne and Margaret; several sons had died in infancy and one, Richard, at the age of ten.

One of the more interesting items that has emerged during research is the fact that Thomas also had a sister Anne. Perhaps the family was ashamed of her Jacobite activities because there is no mention of her in the family pedigree! She married a local man, John Kynaston of Horley, as his second wife in 1708. Kynaston also came from an old Shropshire family and possibly had Jacobite leanings himself. He was a fervent Tory and was elected to Parliament in 1695, sitting in six consecutive Parliaments. What is certain is that his oldest son by his first marriage, Corbet Kynaston, was a fervent and active supporter of the 'King over the Water'. He cannot have been much younger than stepmother, Anne, and it seems clear that it was he that involved her in the Cause. Corbet Kynaston was one of several men who had warrants issued for their arrest at the time of the first attempted invasion by the Old Pretender in 1715. He escaped capture and went into hiding for several months. He gave himself up in January 1716 and was soon released. Corbet Kynaston died in June 1740 and his friend Thomas Carte wrote, 'the Pretender hath had a great loss in the death of Corbet Kynaston who would have ventured his life and future for him in any circumstance whatever'. Perhaps his father was unhappy about his son and his wife being so involved in the Jacobite cause, because he disinherited Corbet of all but the entailed estates and left everything to his son Edward.

We also know that in November 1752 one Thomas Andersen was tried and condemned in Worcester as a Jacobite supporter and brought to Shrewsbury to be hanged. On the day of his execution he sent a letter to the Sheriff in which he said 'the whole town and you with Lady Kynaston have the assurance of my sincere thanks'. Anne certainly carried funds to the Continent for the Court in Exile at St Germains on many occasions.

A year after his first wife's death, Thomas Hill married 'advantageously' Susanna Noel, a daughter of Sir William Noel, MP for Stamford and a Judge of the Court of Common Pleas. Thomas and Susanna were to have four more children, two girls, which came as a grave blow to Thomas, and then two sons, Samuel and Noel. Samuel was named for the cousin, Samuel Barbour Hill, whose death, childless, in 1758 brought Shenstone in Staffordshire to Thomas. Noel was, of course, named for his mother's family. His second son was to tack the Noel onto the Hill. Thomas was a shrewd and successful businessman, an investor in the East India Company and even holder of some French stocks. He was elected MP for Shrewsbury in 1749; although Lord Powys (Lord Lieutenant in the County) considered him a Whig, he always took care to remain 'easy' with both sides and was probably virtually a Tory by 1753. He is not on record as having spoken once during his 18 years in the House and stood down on the grounds of age and infirmity in 1768. He was to work hard that year for the election of his son Noel in a bitter contest.

So what did this first Hill of Attingham achieve? He made a great deal of money for his son and grandson to dissipate and he fathered 13 children of whom only three survived past the age of 23, which was a poor statistic even for the 18th century. He would be succeeded by the 13th child! Perhaps one of his principal, if unexpected, successes was bringing John Fletcher into his household. This Swiss-born man (his original name was Jean Guillaume de la Fléchère) came to tutor Sam and Noel because their parents, and especially their mother, did not wish to send them off to school too young. This decision may have been a fatal error in the case of Sam; eventually dispatched to Cambridge at the early age of 16—Noel went with him and was only 14—the boy 'went to the bad' in a big way and was dead at the age of 23 from the effects of his dissipation. He almost certainly died of syphilis.

When cousin Samuel died in 1759 Thomas asked Susanna if she would like to move to Shenstone, but she elected to stay at Tern and to start making 'improvements'. She was happy to spend her husband's hard-earned money, in contrast to his rather austere style of life, and set about turning the house into a real 'gentleman's residence'; son Noel was to turn it into a nobleman's 'seat'. Even Thomas's agent, Bonnell, thought his master lived rather simply for a man in his position. The Hills employed a local man, Thomas Pritchard, to enlarge the house by building on a series of rooms in front of the old house. These were to be the new reception rooms and best bedrooms. Work dragged on for some years and was still not finished on Susanna's death in 1760 or by the time Thomas moved out in 1768.

The boys had gone to St John's, Cambridge in April 1759. They were to study law but it seems that Samuel, revelling in his new freedom from the controls of his elderly father and Fletcher, the strict and religious tutor, did little work. Thomas wrote to the boys saying that he hoped they would speak French together; it seems unlikely. Sam's university career was catastrophic, huge bills being run up for drink, and he quit in June 1760 leaving behind him a string of debts. He was sent abroad, his father recalling his own profitable years on the Continent as a young man and hoping the experience would do the same for his beloved son and heir. He seems to have been entirely blind to his favourite's excesses and markedly preferred Samuel to the younger Noel. Back in Shropshire the boy's drunken behaviour at the notorious Shawbury Wakes could not have left him in much doubt of the true situation, although the formation of the new Shropshire Militia gave him hope that Sam's energies could be channelled in that direction. Unfortunately Sam fell in with bad company. In February 1766 he was at home, with his father away in London, when he went on the week-long 'binge' which led to his death in March.

Noel Hill (1795-89)

Meanwhile Noel had taken his degree at Cambridge and been admitted to the Inner Temple. He, too, went on a continental tour but his father, not approving of frivolity, sent him on a strictly planned journey that did not cover the Grand Tour's usual cultural sites at Florence, Venice and Rome. Instead, he was made to concentrate on fortifications, agriculture, a subject that could be considered to have some merit for a landowner, and, for some reason, the police. This was many years before police forces as such were formed and may have been applied to a sort of local militia.

In March 1768 Noel was elected at the young age of only 23 to one of the Shrewsbury parliamentary seats.[1] It was quite a fierce battle but he easily topped the poll ahead of Lord Clive, with whom he collaborated, and William Pulteney, who was contesting his first Shropshire seat. Pulteney would eventually be elected in 1774 and remain in Parliament for 30 years. Noel Hill was to sit for the Borough until 1774 and for the 'Shire' between 1774-84, when he was created Lord Berwick and kicked 'upstairs'. He was always independent—except when there was a peerage at stake—in his allegiance, but considered 'a Tory in principle who professes himself an independent man' by Robinson. This is hard to check as Hill is often described as a Whig. He frequently voted with the Opposition but elected to support Lord Shelburne's American peace preliminaries; he is on record as having voted against Fox's East India Bill (which brought/bought him his enoblement!) and on the whole supported the Prime Minister, Pitt. There is even a portrait of Pitt at Attingham. It is not easy to see how he deserved his peerage; his father, Thomas, never spoke in 18 years and neither did Noel during 16 years in the House of Commons.

The second event of 1768 was his marriage to Anne Vernon of Hilton Park, Staffordshire, which lies near Shenstone so the families had obviously known each other for a long time. It seems to have been a love-match and the Hill side were not overly enthusiastic. The couple married in November in London and then went to Tern for their honeymoon. They were to have six children, three girls, three boys. All three of the boys would succeed to Attingham and the title. Noel and Anne divided their time between Tern, as it still was, and London. Home in London to begin with remained the Great Hill's house in Cleveland Row, which Thomas had made over to his son on his marriage, but eventually the young couple moved to Sackville Street off Piccadilly. A few years later, when Noel got his teeth into building, he bought a fine house in Portman Square and called in George Steuart to renovate it. All this was unquestionably expensive and Noel was constantly asking his father for more money. Thomas did not approve of Noel's extravagances and especially frowned on the pack of hounds that he kept together with his racehorses.

There was something of a family scandal in 1769. This was to worry old Thomas who was strait-laced and not *au fait* with the lax behaviour of some of the upper crust. Anne's sister, Henrietta—known in the family as Harriet—was married to Richard Grosvenor, a fast-living, womanising, racing enthusiast. He was also a good friend of Noel. Unfortunately, Harriet attracted the attention of the Duke of Cumberland, an unsavoury and drink-sodden brother of King George. She was a pretty young woman with little, according to Walpole, between the ears, and she was probably flattered by having a royal lover. Scandal broke out and Thomas told Anne that she must not be seen with her sister, his middle-class morals fearing his family might be tainted by the connection. In fact they managed to help her in private, and when the Grosvenors were finally separated Richard Grosvenor settled £1,200 a year on his wife. In her turn, Harriet was to be a support to Anne after Noel's early death.

Noel now had great plans for Tern. First of all he called on a fashionable London architect called Robert Mylne, who paid several visits to the house and submitted some drawings, but there is no record that any of these plans were executed. William Emes, a landscape designer who also worked at Hawkstone on the Hawk Lake, did some work on the grounds in the mid-1770s, as did Thomas Legett who was responsible for planting many of the trees and changing the slope of the land running down to the river. It was to be Humphry Repton, however, called in in the time of Noel's son, who can be credited with the major improvements to the grounds, especially the exploitation of the river Tern.

In 1782 Noel commissioned George Steuart, the Scottish architect, to work on the 'new' house. Steuart had worked for Adam in the past and the great designer's influence is especially apparent in the interiors. He cannot be credited with much in the way of domestic architecture, but worked at Baron's Court in Northern Ireland, the home of the Dukes of Abercorn (now much altered), and the new St Chad's Church in Shrewsbury. This church replaced the original, which fell down in 1788, and the new building is an elegant and original neo-

Classical building much admired then and now. Unfortunately most of George Steuart's other houses have vanished but Michael Rix's article in *Country Life* notes that several buildings in the Isle of Man have been identified as being by Steuart, who died there in 1806.[2]

Construction began in early 1783 with yet another new building incorporating the original house. The existing Tern House was intended to be used for servants' quarters. Work had only recently been completed on this portion of the building, which suggests a heavy financial outlay and not much regard for any form of economy. The new stable yard at the rear of the house was built to take 56 horses and the yard is entered through a handsome neo-Classical archway.

The main block of the house is flanked by two pavilions linked to the central portion by colonnades. Noel Hill had his quarters in the west wing and the drawing room and Lady Berwick's boudoir was in the east, thereby, according to Michael Rix, mimicking the masculine and feminine quarters extant at Versailles. Steuart's handling of the façade is rather ponderous; it is massive and severe with an overall length of approximately 400ft. The columns supporting the portico appear rather thin and flimsy for the overall structure and are very tall. The whole façade is of the local grey Grinshill stone, the colour of which does tend to exaggerate the rather dour appearance of the exterior.

Inside all was very different. The interiors were magnificently done and, despite definite evidence of Adam's influence on Steuart, there is a pervasive French feeling. This is especially evident in the Boudoir, the prettiest room at Attingham. It is not possible to be certain who was responsible for the charming arabesque decoration on the walls but it has a definite French flavour. Various names have been suggested as the painter, Boileau, Rigaud or Bonomi amongst them, but the Attingham Guide suggests Louis Andre Delabriere, who worked at Carlton House for the Prince Regent. Whoever the painter was, the room is a delight, a circular chamber with four doors divided by painted Corinthian columns and topped by a domed ceiling. Whether this was a current fashion, or whether Noel Hill had a taste for French furnishings, is hard to establish now, but the treatment was very successful.

It is a matter of great regret that almost all the original furnishings and many of the paintings that were collected by Noel Hill and his equally extravagant heir, Thomas, were sold in 1827. On the other hand, it was fortunate that Thomas' next brother, William, 3rd Lord Berwick, amassed such a wonderful collection of Italian and Empire furniture during his diplomatic career in Sardinia, Naples and Palermo. He is also reported to have purchased several items at the bankruptcy sale. Happily, the family portraits had not been included in that auction. William's Italian acquisitions sit very happily in the great rooms of Georgian Attingham.

Noel was elected Mayor of Shrewsbury in 1778. Later he was Mayor of

29. Attingham Park.

30. Picture Gallery, Attingham Park.

Oswestry. Richard Hill of Hawkstone and Noel of Attingham occupied seats for the Shire in the Parliament of 1780.

Noel was also serving as Lieutenant Colonel in the Shropshire Militia.[3] With the war in America a worry to everyone, and the French having thrown their lot in with England's former colonies, these county regiments were on pretty much full-time service for a few years. When the Shropshire Militia marched off to Kent Anne joined her husband. Noel appears to have rather enjoyed his military life, the social side including parties, troop reviews and sporting events. With the bulk of the Army in America, the Militia had a very real role, England finding herself somewhat isolated. The Militia was also employed in putting down the Gordon Riots in 1780. Noel moved to Devon with the regiment in 1781 but still had enough time to take care of estate business on visits back to Tern. After Devon the regiment was moved to Gravesend

Noel moved into his 'new' house in October 1785. He would only enjoy it for four years, dying in 1789 at the young age of forty-four. Whatever his faults, which mainly lay in his extravagancies, the 1st Lord Berwick must be credited with the building of Attingham and the exterior we see today. He had style and taste and has left a handsome memorial. The bitchy comments made by the Hon. John Byng in his Torrington Diaries of 1793—'pass'd by Lord B's great tasteless seat, a thing like the Mansion House, but I visit not such houses; all around is in most deplorable taste ... He does right to begin building a wall'—are entirely undeserved although it should be admitted that it was not easy creating a setting worthy of the mansion on the low-lying and flat terrain which it would occupy.

Anne's brother Henry Vernon was another victim of extravagance. He was a great sportsman, in common with his brothers-in-law Hill and Grosvenor, and also expended a vast amount of money on the grounds at Hilton. He fell out with his mother, who cut him out of her will, then spent more money contesting this although Noel Hill, with his legal education, told him he was wasting his time. Noel seems to have helped Henry financially, and is on record as having lent him one sum, at least, of £8,000, but Vernon had to flee abroad for a while to escape his creditors. Noel was obviously a generous character; having been financially improvident himself, he would lend a friendly ear to people who applied for help, even though he really did not have any spare cash. Henry Vernon was to be fortunate, inheriting a large estate from his uncle, Lord Strafford, in 1791 which presumably helped him to recover.

Noel Hill had long suffered from some sort of stomach problem—often described as 'being bilious' in those days—and had been to try the waters at Cheltenham more than once. In January 1789 he died at Attingham. A kind and generous man, he unquestionably lived beyond his means and set a bad example to his heir, Thomas.

Thomas Noel Hill (1770-1832)

Thomas was 19 and at Cambridge when his father died; the two younger boys, William and Richard, were at Rugby. At the age of 22 Thomas set off for Italy; he would be away for two years. He went in company with Edward Clarke, a university contemporary who always claimed that it was he who formed Thomas's taste and urged him into his purchases. Clarke was a geologist so a certain amount of their journey was devoted to that subject and Thomas brought some samples back to Attingham. Clarke and Thomas left Attingham in July and finally reached Turin in October. Their journey was made difficult by the upheavals in France, the Revolution being in full swing. From Turin they journeyed south to Rome where they arrived in December. In Rome Clarke introduced Thomas to Angelica Kauffmann.[4] Kauffmann had lived and worked in England in the 1770s (it is possible to detect her influence in some of the decoration at Attingham) but on her marriage to the Venetian painter, Zucchi, she returned to Italy and finally ended up working in Rome. The young Lord Berwick sat to Kauffmann for his portrait in 1793. He also bought some other pictures by her. The portrait now hangs over the fireplace (by John Deval) in the drawing room. Thomas is portrayed wearing fancy dress. In Tipping's *Country Life* article the portrait is shown hanging to the left of the fireplace in the dining room and it can also can be seen there in the watercolour dated 1840 by Lady Hester Leeke reproduced in the Attingham Park Guide. At the time brother William hung to the right.[5]

Thomas had expected to buy a number of antiquities in Rome—they were very fashionable at that time amongst the English—but the Hill party was put off by the tales of counterfeits and fakes. They did, notwithstanding, eventually make some purchases and Tipping's article of 1921 describes Edward Clarke as having also bought a quantity of Etruscan pottery. We know, too, that Thomas bought some Etruscan pieces because he housed them in his 'museum' in the old room at Attingham.

Thomas really was the collector *par excellence*; he was to admit to brother William some years later that he could not abstain from buying paintings. The current guide to Attingham Park says that he was also busy buying books and early manuscripts. His purchases were so numerous that the volumes overflowed the existing library, and in 1810 he took over the original breakfast parlour as the 'Inner Library'. This is the room at the north end of the West Wing. A large part of the library was sold in the 1827 sale. The last Lord Berwick (the 8th) to live at Attingham was also a book addict but he sold all the early manuscripts, probably to pay for much needed repairs and redecoration to the House.

Thomas and Clarke eventually reached Naples where they were to join up with Thomas's mother, Anne, Lady Berwick, and his three sisters. Social life in Naples was brilliant. The English contingent was led by Sir William Hamilton and his wife, Emma Hamilton. The Hill family was rapidly absorbed into this circle and very soon the eldest daughter, Henrietta (Harriet) met, fell in love and married young Charles Bruce, son of the Earl of Ailesbury. Bruce was under age and doing his Grand Tour with the Rev. Thomas Brand. Brand approved of Henrietta, writing to the Earl that she was of 'amiable disposition and sensible and conversible to a degree, which surprises me considering the shyness and timidity of the rest of the Family'. Why was the family considered so timid? It is hard to picture Thomas thus and Anne, his mother, was certainly a woman of Society. Having received his father's blessing, Charles Bruce and Henrietta were married in Florence in May 1793. Thomas was annoyed that he had not been present at the marriage although he had been given adequate notice. Evidently *his* permission was not required.

Henrietta gave birth to twin daughters a year later; sadly, one of them died. The young Bruces eventually left Italy and the following year had another daughter, Augusta, in Germany. Henrietta's mother and sisters came to join her for the birth. It would be the last time they saw each other. Lady Berwick, together with younger daughters Anne and Amelia, became a homeless wanderer. She enjoyed a longish a stay in Venice before returning eventually to Naples. The Naples she found was greatly changed, with most of her former friends long gone for fear of being cut off from England by the advances of Napoleon. Anne had left it too late. She tried to return to England in 1797 by the 'Adriatic' route but fell ill and died in Apulia. She was 53. It seems sad that for lack of sufficient money to live in England she had adopted this rootless life and never returned home or saw her other two sons again. Her second son, William, was to spend the greater part of his career as a diplomat in Italy and even in Naples.

Thomas sounds as if he was a selfish fellow, inheriting too young and not concerning himself with his mother or unmarried sisters. He was too preoccupied with his acquisitions and the further building projects at Attingham that he undertook in order to house his purchases. A good steward should surely have known what the rental income could support and the agent at the time was Francis Walford, who was lucky enough to live at Cronkhill, but the Estate was around 6,000 acres, which could not have possibly supported Thomas's rate of expenditure. His inability to curtail a passion for 'shopping' brought on the bankruptcy but, on the credit side, we must admire and be grateful for the work that he commissioned from John Nash and Humphry Repton.

In 1801 Edward Burton wrote to Lord Berwick, who must presumably have been abroad again, about the possibility of an election if George III died. He urged Thomas to tell William he must return home immediately and enclosed an 'advertisement' he had prepared. King George survived this crisis but there was still an election in 1801 and William continued in his seat until 1812, when he switched to Marlborough, a noted 'rotten borough'. He probably made the change because he had a house not far off in Hampshire, but there is a theory that Thomas told him he could not afford another expensive campaign. This seems unlikely as William must have had money of his own; he could not have purchased all the furniture and pictures that now fill Attingham if he were reliant solely on a diplomatic stipend.

Repton began his work on the grounds in 1797. His Red Book is full of charming watercolour sketches illustrating his proposals. One of these, the most important, is the alteration he made to the course of the river Tern to provide a broader stretch of water. Unfortunately, due to silting up, the effect of this is now largely lost. He changed the drive so that it curved around a clump of trees to give the visitor a sudden, unexpected view of the big house. He also brought the parkland right up to the house. This was a fashion at the time which had been first advocated by 'Capability' Brown.

The great Picture Gallery at Attingham is a triumph; the ironwork involved in the glass panels of the ceiling was unique at the time and the notion of top-lighting was also highly innovative.[6] The gallery was constructed in 1805 and the space Nash needed for it meant that three existing but rather unimportant staircases had to be removed. The room rises for one and a half storeys. The decoration is showy, with scagliola pillars at either end and the walls coloured in the deep red which was very fashionable at that time, the strong colour also serving to set off the gilt-framed pictures. A few of the paintings remain from those collected by Thomas on his Grand Tour but the majority were purchased by his brother, William, 3rd Lord Berwick. The new principal staircase, although somewhat impractical in that it only rises to the first floor, is also very handsome. It was completed around 1810.

In 1812 Thomas married for the first time at the age of 42. I suppose he did not feel any pressure to provide an heir since he had two brothers and, in any event, it was fast becoming a question as to what might remain for his eventual heir to succeed to. As it was, he could not have chosen a more unsuitable wife. Sophie Dubouchet was 17 years old.[7] She was the daughter of a Swiss clockmaker and together with her sisters had become part of a group of ladies of shady reputation on the fringe of the court of the Prince Regent. Sophie's more famous older sister, Harriette Wilson, has left us her *Memoirs*. She was the mistress of Society figures such as the Marquis of Worcester (heir to the Duke of Beaufort), the Duke of Argyle, the Duke of Wellington and the Duke of Leinster. Sophie, in turn, began her 'career' at the age of thirteen. She appears to have been a less interesting and extrovert character but she soon attracted the attention of Thomas, Lord Berwick. Berwick was many years her senior and Harriette's Memoirs tell us that Sophie detested him for a long time despite his best efforts to win her as his mistress. Berwick was plainly infatuated and spent vast sums trying to please her. He eventually offered marriage but probably lived to regret it; she was both enormously extravagant and socially quite unacceptable as the wife of Lord Berwick; she did not even produce an heir.

We have only a few details of the life that Thomas led between his marriage and the bankruptcy in 1827. The Sale of Contents did not pay off all his debts; the big house was leased to brother William and Thomas went off to live in Italy. He died in Naples in 1832 but his widow lived until 1875 and died in Leamington Spa. One interesting comment in the *Memoirs* is on Thomas's strange manner of speaking. We know from remarks made by Lady Bessborough that next brother William also spoke in a peculiar lisping manner and third brother, Richard, had a stammer, a serious handicap for a parson.

William Noel-Hill (1773-1842)

Brother William was also a strange character. Educated at Rugby and Jesus, Cambridge, he entered the Diplomatic Service. Following his father's death in 1789 and his mother's departure to live abroad with his sisters, William and his younger brother Richard were left behind in England. Richard (known as Dick) took Holy Orders and is memorable principally for the quantity of wine that he could consume. He did, at least, produce an heir; William's children were all illegitimate. The first mention of William as an adult is for his standing in the election of 1796. He must have been of some intelligence and ability to achieve his diplomatic appointments and he early developed a fondness for Italy. In common with his father and his elder brother he had good taste, but whereas they simply spent money on *objets d'art* and building, William seems to have had a rather more responsible attitude and he did his best to preserve Attingham following the bankruptcy sale of 1827. He had been left some money by his grandfather, old Thomas, and may also have received some from the estate of Lord Strafford, his great uncle after his mother's death.

His first listed appointment is to Franconia in 1805. William had become a close friend of Lady Hester Stanhope, niece to the Prime Minister, William Pitt. Hester acted as her uncle's hostess at this time and his early death no doubt left her lacking a *raison d'etre*; she did not get on with her father. In 1806 Lady Bessborough, writing to Lord Granville Leveson Gower, 'told me yesterday as *certain* that Hetty's marriage with Mr Hill is *declared a*nd to take place immediately; can this be so? If it is, il est tres bon.' Unfortunately it was not. Lady Hester, an eccentric, spent the second half of her life roaming the desert sands of the Middle East, and her former 'suitor' was evidently regarded by some as a trifle peculiar too. In 1807 he was sent to Cagliari in Sardinia which Lady Bessborough suspected, again probably erroneously, was due to Lady Hester's influence; she described it as a 'little bit of a job' but in fact there was plenty for William to do, what with the large number of English visitors (including Lord Byron, en route for Greece, who apparently approved of WH); he was a social fellow and enjoyed entertaining the swarm of visitors. The poor King, Victor Emanuel, had Napoleon in his capital of Turin, in Savoy, but still ruled over his island kingdom for the present; like his wily ancestor in the days of the Great Hill, he was still deciding which horse to back, remaining neutral whilst (what a familiar tale!) demanding arms and money from the Allies. The poor Protestant Vaudois were again complaining of their treatment in Savoy.

It was evidently not too tough a posting for William, who probably began his long love affair with Italy, and evidently with at least one Italian lady, at that time. On the fall of Napoleon, Savoy was restored to Victor Emanuel and William moved to Turin. Here he ran up against Lady Bessborough again. She described him 'as being very attentive to us and makes us almost live with him and is very amusing in his odd way ... You know it, his lisping, mumbling manner of speaking which often gives the appearance of more humour to what he says than it deserves'. The lisping could have been some sort of hereditary speech problem which was far worse in his younger brother.

It was a very unstable period in 'Italian' history with clamours for a constitution which Victor Emanuel was initially completely opposed to. Ultimately he was forced into abdication in 1821 after revolution in Piedmont/Savoy, and the Prince Carignan was put in his place. He did not last long either.

In 1824 William was created a Privy Councillor, formally added his middle name 'Noel' to the Hill of his surname, and was sent to Naples where he was undoubtedly very content. He began to indulge his apparently inherited passion for collecting furniture and paintings but in a considerably more sensible fashion than that employed by his elder brother. He rented the Palazzo Belvedere, which had belonged to Caroline (Bonaparte) Murat, Queen of Naples, and lived in truly ambassadorial style. Caroline had virtually ruled Naples while her husband Joachim Murat, one of Napoleon's most faithful and successful Marshals, had been away fighting. After the fall of Napoleon and the return of the Bourbons to Naples (King Ferdinand), Murat had been captured and shot.

According to the Attingham handbook, William had put his entertainment allowance for the purchase of silver plate to good account and ordered a handsome dinner service from one of the best known silversmiths in London, Rundell and Bridge. This, together with other magnificent pieces, he cleverly managed to hang on to when leaving his post. There is an impressive French ormolu set of table decorations by Tompire which closely resembles the suite that belonged to Pauline (Bonaparte) Borghese, Princess of Italy, and now graces the table of the British Embassy in Paris.

It seems likely that William bought the furnishings of the Palazzo Belvedere but he also evidently acquired other furniture of the Empire era. It is from the peak of the Napoleonic period although with a decidedly Italianate flavour. Whereas, so often, 18th-century Italian furniture seems to exaggerate in an uncomfortable manner compared to French pieces of the same date, this furniture, while certainly highly ornate, is very beautiful.

The 4th, 5th, 6th, 7th and 8th Barons
William, 3rd Lord Berwick died in 1842 and was succeeded by his brother, Richard, Rector of Berrington, a village on the Estate.[8] He had married a wife from a neighbouring family, Frances Mostyn-Owen, and produced eight children. His son, the 5th Lord seems to have been a more conscientious 'housekeeper' where the great house was concerned and managed to carry out some pressing repairs to the fabric. His 'extravagance' lay not in the purchase of works of art but in the breeding of prize Hereford cattle and American trotters which he imported from the US. He was another noble Lord Berwick who did not marry.

He was succeeded by his brother, another William, who was a reasonably successful soldier. He had no children either and was succeeded by his nephew, another Richard, who married a Swedish woman from Malmo and spent a lot of time on his yacht. Again, no children. The last Lord Berwick to live at Attingham was his nephew, Thomas. Their parents having died when they were very small, Thomas and his sister, Mary Selina, lived with their aunt at Cronkhill, which had previously been occupied by the Estate's Agent. The holders of senior positions on these great estates were frequently very well housed: at Hawkstone the 'Rangers Lodge' is a delightful small square Regency house, probably a little later than Cronkhill, sitting under the hill off the back drive to Marchamley; and prior to its rebuilding in the early 19th century, the Hawkstone Agent lived and farmed at the Citadel.

Cronkhill was designed by John Nash in 1802.[9] It sits rather incongruously in the Shropshire countryside, an Italianate villa, one of the earliest to be built in England, with a round tower and a square one together with a colonnade. The rather plain interiors presumably reflect the fact that it was for the use of the steward and not the family. Part of the Attingham estate, it now belongs to the National Trust.

If the 8th Baron did not totally escape the family's former vice, the purchase of works of art, he was at least more responsible. A diplomat, he fell in love with things French during service in the British Embassy in Paris and made a number of purchases of furniture and objects; he also collected books. The big house was let for a period but eventually Thomas and his wife Teresa, *née* Hulton, moved in. Teresa had spent her life in Italy where her English father, a painter, and her Italian mother lived.

These two were a couple with taste and energy. They tried hard to make the house viable and to repair and restore what they could; with insufficient land

31. Cronkhill, Attingham, built for the steward by John Nash, *c*.1802.

to support such a house it was probably always a losing battle, and the Second World War finally put an end to any chance they might have had of holding on to it. Their decision to give it to the National Trust was probably not too difficult; it has certainly been a happy thing for the house. Lord Berwick died in 1947 and Teresa, Lady Berwick continued to live in a part of the house until her death in 1972 in a car accident almost outside the Park gates. She was a charming and elegant woman who gave enjoyable summer parties in the Picture Gallery. The couple had no children.

The last (9th) Lord Berwick was a second cousin who never lived at Attingham. He had no children either and the title became extinct.

Not an especially extraordinary building externally, Attingham is most handsomely and imaginatively decorated, with interesting furnishings and a splendid gallery; it is sad to consider that the house was enjoyed in the manner for which it was built during a period of just some 25 years.

CHAPTER TEN

The Bankruptcy
The Dispersal Sales · The Lawsuits

ON THE DEATH of his father in January 1875, Rowland, 3rd Viscount was to find his inheritance was impossibly encumbered with a large number of mortgages outstanding on most of the Estate, settled or unsettled. His representative at the bankruptcy hearing stated that on his accession Lord Hill did not know exactly what his liabilities were but thought they amounted to around £215,000. In fact the sum was greater. His knowledge did not stop him from falling further into debt and nor did it prevent the affair of Vere Somerset. It seems a strange idea to permit your niece's (Annette's) future husband to invest his marriage settlements in such an encumbered estate but this gesture would trigger the final disaster. Of course, the bankruptcy would have come shortly in any event, as there was no way the 3rd Viscount could have begun to pay off the debts. In any event, the wretched man had to borrow to service the extant mortgages; it was Catch-22. Hawkstone was only one of many great estates that vanished under mountains of debt, victims of indifferent management and gross extravagances. The state of 19th-century agriculture in England also played a part in the collapse.

In Sir Baldwin Leighton's Loton Park Diaries it is interesting to read that Leighton had learned in 1869, in the course of conversation with Mr Dod of Cloverley, who had previously had the patronage of Lord Hill, that 'although Lord Hill was supposed by many to have a large income, he should be sorry to change places with him'. At the time the Hawkstone Estate had an income of more than £21,000 per annum but, known only to a few, the mortgages were beginning to bite. Already some property had been sold off, and this by a man who had not only inherited a vast estate but also married an heiress. He had led a life of extravagance that would have had one or two of his ancestors spinning in their graves. Despite the mishandling of his 'patrimony', he seems to have been well-liked, and a generous and kind employer.

In 1868 the Hardwick property was sold, followed in 1873 by Peplow, which was sold to Francis Stanier. More farms were sold in 1891 and 1892 but it was too late. When Vere Somerset sued his trustees, Earl Poulett, Lord Dorchester, Sir Thomas Meyrick (married to Annette's sister, Selina) and Granville Somerset (his father) for improper investment, and the case came to the Chancery Division in 1891/2, the collapse gathered speed and ended in financial ruin.

The Affair Somerset

The background to this case is interesting and the learned Mr Justice Kekewich described it as unique in his experience. In 1875 Vere Somerset had married Annette Catherine Hill, a niece of Lord Hill. The Headnote in Somerset, Somerset v Earl Poulett (1892) Court of Chancery, reads, 'In August 1878, the trustees of a settlement committed an innocent breach of trust by investing trust money [the marriage settlements] upon mortgage property of insufficient value'. The mortgagor (Lord Hill) paid the interest on the money advanced direct to the tenant for life (Somerset) until 1890. By this time Annette Hill Somerset had died leaving five children; these infants were, of course, joined with their father in the case. Her father-in-law, Granville Somerset, a QC who should have known better and could be largely held responsible for allowing this debâcle, had also died. The Headnote goes on to say that although the case fell outside the period of the Statute of Limitations of six years from the date that the investment was made, and the tenant for life (Somerset and his children) had both suggested and approved of the investment, he had left it to his trustees to determine it was right and proper for the moneys proposed to be advanced to Lord Hill. The funds comprised in the settlement of 1876 were Russian and Brazilian bonds and that year Vere and Annette (Hill) Somerset asked for the bonds to be liquidated and the proceeds invested in Hawkstone at 4 per cent. The term 'Hawkstone Estate' is used frequently throughout the legal proceedings, but in fact the property concerned was only some 720 acres of the whole 16,500 acre Hawkstone Estate; it included two or three farms which produced rents that were intended to cover the mortgage interest. It seems apparent that the rents being realised were far too low—another sign of overall mismanagement. The only trustees with any knowledge of Hawkstone were Granville Somerset, who was said to have large experience of landed estates, and, presumably, Thomas Meyrick; Vere Somerset himself was familiar with the property as, of course, was his father-in-law, Colonel Richard Hill who was a trustee of Hawkstone. Surely Lord Hill knew how badly situated he was; I think he chose to involve his family to try and save his skin. At the time everything seems to have been arranged rather cosily amongst the family, Lord Hill's agent, Edward Haste, and the family solicitors.

A valuation was undertaken by Sir John Ellis of Farebrother & Co. on the instructions of the solicitors, Messrs Wilde Berger & Co., who acted for both sides in the interests of economy. Three of the trustees (including, it would appear, Meyrick) of the Somersets obviously did not involve themselves sufficiently, relying on co-trustee Granville Somerset and the local solicitors. It was an omission that would cost everyone. Lord Hill had needed to raise at least £35,000, and when the case came to court this sum was considered to have been far too high given the actual property involved. Sir John's valuation suggested only £30,000 but Lord Hill pushed for the higher figure and, it would seem, Sir John concurred with it. All continued well as long as Lord Hill paid the interest to Vere Somerset, which he did directly. But from 1890 the payments ceased; there simply was not the money to meet them. It was this that brought the matter to court; things were not made easier by the fact that the agent who had been closely involved in the arrangements for the mortgage, Mr Haste, had died some years before. The first court action was in May 1891 when the trustees sued Lord Hill for the sum of the mortgage of £34,612 plus interest, with foreclosure in default of payment. On 29 January 1892 an order was made in chambers for the sale of the mortgaged property. In November Lord Hill did pay the sum of £1,106 18s. 3d. in interest but the machinery was now rolling and after he was declared bankrupt in 1894, his Estate was in the hands of the Official Receiver. It then appeared that a large part, if not all, of the Estate was mortgaged. A letter to Hill's agent, Ponting Cox, dated 20 September 1894, demands repayment of a loan made on Prees Manor (long time home to various members of the family including Sir John and his son, Sir Robert Chambré, and the birthplace of 'The General') by Colonel A. Greville, William Cavendish Bentinck and G.H. Bailey. But it was all too late.

The Bankruptcy

The first meeting of the creditors of the 3rd Viscount was held at the end of August 1894. Lord Hill did not attend, already being in very poor health. The Debtor's Statement of Affairs (as quoted in the *Shrewsbury Chronicle* on 31 August 1894) reported unsecured creditors of around £24,000 with fully secured creditors of £243,000. Realisable assets amounted to about £9,500 including the contents of the Hall, which were valued at the tiny sum of only £5,362; contents of the Citadel were assessed at £411 pounds; stables, horses, carriages £403; live and dead stock together with 'implements' were appraised at £2,315; the herd of eland deer in the Park at £300. At this point the diamonds were claimed as heirlooms by the trustees of the settled estates.

Lord Hill said that in a forced sale he doubted if even the sums quoted would be realised. He blamed the situation on the sale at rock-bottom prices of mortgaged properties. The principal secured creditors were first, the trustees of the late Lord Penrhyn holding £71,400 on the settled portion of Hawkstone of approximately 5,395 acres producing an annual income of £4,200 on the let portion. The non-let portion was the Hall itself, the gardens and the Park, the farm lands and the woods of 2,333 acres producing around £1,463 p.a. The second large secured creditor was the trustees of the Duke of Portland who held a mortgage for over £90,000. The 2nd Viscount had raised a first mortgage in 1872 of £70,000, increased it in 1874 to £85,000 and then the present Lord Hill had increased it again in 1880 and 1884. Numerous other pieces and properties of the Estate were mortgaged. There were monies arranged with Lord Hill's brother, Major Richard Hill (father of the Annette who married Vere Somerset), and with his second wife, Isabelle, Viscountess Hill. Mr Edward Bygott, solicitor of Wem, representing the Somerset trustees, gave as his opinion that full repayment of 20s. in the pound could be made but that this would take time; his clients would not wait. This is what ultimately was to cause a family tragedy; it is almost certainly true that with some judicious sales and trimming of the Estate at a more favourable time full payment would have been possible. At the end of this first hearing Mr W. Hall was appointed special manager of the estates at a salary of £8 a week and the official receiver, Mr Bullock, announced that he had been giving Lord Hill an allowance of £10 a week which he intended, with the agreement of those present, to continue for a further month; Mr Bygott, who seems to have been very much on the side of the Hills despite his position in the hearing, commented that it was a very small sum!

The public examination took place the following Wednesday at Hawkstone because of the state of Lord Hill's health. He disclosed more money he had pledged to various family members, including three small annuities. He had 'inherited' an obligation to pay these to the three surviving children of Sir Thomas Noel Hill, General Charles Hill and his sisters, Mrs Allgood and Mrs Trevenon, from the days of his great uncle, the 1st Viscount. Evidently the capital sum set aside to meet these payments by the 1st Viscount had proved insufficient but since he had left the Estate of Hardwick and most of his money back to his nephew, it seemed only correct that these annuities should continue to be paid out. It was also disclosed that Lord Hill had 'rented' the Citadel to Lady Hill the previous year at a rent of £180 per annum.

The *Shrewsbury Chronicle* devoted its leader on 24 September 1894 to the Hill bankruptcy. Entitled 'A Sad Reverse of Fortune', it was a sympathetic piece exonerating poor Lord Hill from blame and citing 'ancestral extravagance'. It said it was

> painful to dwell upon the circumstances which have overwhelmed a noble house whose very name was dear to 'all around the Wrekin' ... and the changing of hands of so noble an estate will naturally cause a pang of grief to those who know the real causes which have brought about a disastrous termination to the residence amongst us of a family whose ancestral claims to distinction are heirlooms to future generations.

The editor also included a reference to the infamous Jack Mytton, saying that at least the family had the consolation of knowing the collapse was not due to the depravity or vice which had brought Mytton with an annual income of £80,000—staggering in those days—to death in a debtors' prison.

Lord Hill died a few months later in April 1895. The family belief that there was a dispute over the succession is, I think, just a family 'myth' and quite untrue; Hill certainly had two sons by Mary Madax and this marriage was kept secret for some years, but it is virtually impossible to know how much time she spent at Hawkstone after the marriage. We know she died in Sussex. We know that Rowland was only 22 when he married Mary, aged 28, in 1855, but their first son, the 4th Viscount, was not born until 1863, after they had been married some eight years, and so it would seem that this was not a 'shot gun' wedding. Francis William (known in the family as Frank) was born three years later. Perhaps 'Dad' disapproved so strongly that it was some years before he could accept his grandsons as legitimate

In 1887 the 3rd Viscount and this eldest son by the first marriage had executed a 'disentailing' deed, barring a settlement made in 1855 between the 2nd Viscount and himself, and by an agreement dated 16 June 1887 they conveyed the 'said mansion house and estates to the use of a mortgagee in fee for 70,000 pounds'. On 30 January 1894 this mortgage was transferred to Lord Penrhyn, with some others, as mortgagees in fee. It is obvious, therefore, that Rowland Richard Clegg-Hill was well-known as heir apparent to his father the 3rd Viscount at least by the date of 1887 and probably long before. As he was only 11 when his mother died in 1874 it is impossible that his stepmother did not know of his existence or that of his younger brother. He served in the Royal Warwickshire Regiment but then, evidently, went abroad. He returned on his father's death and so it is possible, even likely, that he did not get on with his stepmother and chose to live away from Hawkstone. He is described as having been living in the United States until he had married someone of Irish descent, in Canada, in 1890. The fact that he was given the family names of Rowland Richard, would seem additional, if not legal, proof of his legitimacy. The 3rd Viscount remarried a year after the death of Mary in 1874 and had four more children. None of these sons did anything to retrieve or further the fortunes of the family—in fact they merely seem to have dissipated the little which remained, much of it on ridiculous legal actions. The behaviour of Isabella, the Dowager Viscountess in contesting the case of the diamonds is one possible indication that, somehow, she really had expected her own eldest son to succeed his father in 1895, but the appearance of an older, legitimate half-brother could not have come as such a shock.

Isabella died of sunstroke at the Citadel in 1898.

Break up and Dispersal

The next court case was brought by the 4th Viscount, who sued his stepmother, Isabella, Dowager Viscountess Hill for the return of the family diamonds. The jewellery consisted of a tiara, necklace, pendant earrings, two miniatures of Sir Richard Hill (2nd Bt) and 'Miss Hill' (either Sir Richard's sister, Jane, or Mrs John Hill) mounted in velvet as bracelets, and a small ring set with rubies 'which was given by the Pretender to Sir Richard Hill'. It appears that the bulk of these pieces had been given by Sir Richard (who never married) to Elizabeth Cornish, the wife of his nephew John, at the time of their marriage in 1795. She in turn gave them to the bride (Anne Clegg) of her son Rowland at the time of their marriage in 1831 when it appears likely that more jewellery was included. Elizabeth Hill apparently told her daughter-in-law at the time of the gift that Sir Richard had given the pieces to her without restriction but she asked Anne Hill to treat them as 'heirlooms' and pass them on at her death to her eldest son. Shortly before she died Anne made a new Will, dated 25 May 1891, in which she bequeathed the diamonds to her eldest son until he should die and 'after his death to each and every of the persons for the time being entitled to the said title and dignity of Viscount Hill'.

The Dowager Viscountess Anne died in October 1891. The case was first heard in the Queen's Bench Division, where the Dowager Viscountess Isabella (widow of the 3rd Viscount) was victorious on the basis that the diamonds had become her husband's absolute property. Her stepson appealed. A great deal seemed to hinge on what was intended by 'heirlooms' and whether or not a precatory trust had been created. Another important factor in the final judgment was the fact that the plaintiff, the 4th Viscount, had been born in the lifetime of Anne, his grandmother. He was deemed to be absolutely entitled to the jewellery.

In March 1902 the family was back in court. Rowland, 4th Viscount Hill was the plaintiff; his brother and heir presumptive, Francis, was defendant. The plaintiff was asking for a definitive judgment as to whether he was entitled absolutely or for life only to the diamonds. Judgment was given in his favour, the Lords Justice being unanimous that he was absolutely entitled and that there was no 'shifting clause' in favour of the next successor to the title. Frank must have been as enraged as his stepmother had been. One rather assumes that the jewellery was immediately sold, which is probably exactly what the Hon. Francis would have done if he had got his hands on it!

But they had not finished in Court ... there were the stuffed birds! By the time this case came to court, in 1897, almost everything in the Hall had been sold and the Trustee in Bankruptcy (Mr Bullock) and Lord Hill were wrangling over fixtures and fittings, i.e. what was part and parcel of the building and what could be deemed personal chattels.

The birds and their settings were installed in wooden trays which were in turn fitted into glass-fronted cases. The cases had been especially constructed to fit the curved wall of the gallery and the dispute was twofold: were the cases part of the house or were they moveable chattels; if they were part of the house, then were the stuffed birds an integral part of the decoration of the house too, or were they moveable chattels? Naturally, the Trustee in Bankruptcy insisted that both cases and birds were moveable chattels and as such belonged to him as Trustee in Bankruptcy of the late tenant (3rd Viscount) for life. The 4th Viscount, clutching at any straw, claimed they were annexed to the freehold. In the Court of Chancery Justice Kekewich pronounced that the birds were chattels. Lord Hill appealed and the Appeal Court heard the case in July 1897. It was dismissed.

The birds were obviously of considerable interest to some: Bevil Stanier obtained the collection for the Shropshire Archaeological Society and installed it at Peplow, which he had bought through the bankruptcy. He reported on the subject at meetings of the Society saying how important it was that the collection should not be broken up for lack of a home and recounting that there were approximately 1,000 examples of bird species plus some Bronze- and Stone-Age objects which were believed to have been picked up by the 2nd Viscount in the area of the Red Castle in the Park. Bevil Stanier had added some objects of his own.

The Sad Disposal/Dispersal

The first sale took place in November 1894 before the 3rd Viscount's death. The auctioneers, Messrs William Hall, Wateridge & Owen, in announcing the forthcoming sales in the *Shrewsbury Chronicle*, said that 'the sales are of such importance that comments are needless ...' The first sales were of stock and agricultural machinery, equipment, grain, etc. from the Abbey Farm, Woods Farm and the Citadel Farm. These were the home farms 'in hand'. The disposal of these effects took three days and included over 150 crossbred shorthorn cattle (famous for the Hawkstone cheeses), almost 100 pedigree Berkshire pigs, '8 fancy Spanish sheep' from Woods Farm and another 12 Spanish sheep from Home Farm, possibly descendants of the Spanish sheep sent home by the General and his brother, Clement, from the Peninsula. There were 34 draught horses, seven carriage horses, other ponies and cobs, 10 London built carriages, 10 hunting saddles, endless other pieces of tack, more than 20 rugs in beige and blue, and so on. There were quantities of oats, barley, clover, hay; the furniture of Abbey Farmhouse, the dairy equipment, agricultural implements and the equipment of the 'gasworks'.

The same firm of auctioneers were commissioned to sell the contents of the Hall but this did not take place until the following year, after the death of Rowland, 3rd Viscount. The disposal took 11 days and began on Tuesday 17 September with the pictures being sold in the Shrewsbury Music Hall. The Hall was packed out for the occasion and Mr Wateridge opened proceedings by saying that everyone was aware of the sad reasons for the sale and that right up until the last moment some accommodation had been sought to 'arrange matters' and render the sale unnecessary; unfortunately (fortunately for him!) a solution had not been worked out.

Apart from the curious, there were many picture dealers present, including at least two names that are still dealing in London: Colnaghi and Tooth. Most of the paintings were family portraits (Keeling being an artist favoured by the family at the end of the 18th and early 19th centuries) and some were bought by members of the Hill family. The day's total was about £2,000.

The next day's sale saw the disposal of furniture from the principal rooms, including the large suite of Louis XIV furniture that had been bought when Lewis Wyatt created the new drawing room in the early 1830s; it fetched 130 guineas. There were buhl tables, commodes, clocks and firescreens—including the one worked by Queen Anne for the Great Hill. Following the furniture came the sale of the porcelain. Special mention was made of two large Sevres dessert services. In its detailed report of the sale, the *Shrewsbury Chronicle* mentioned some of the Election Jugs, that made for John Hill's 'victory' in 1796, and those of 1835 and 1841. The latter two were bought by a Shropshire MP, H.D. Greene, QC.

Next up was the impressive collection of silver, silver gilt, Sheffield plate, etc. The total weight came to over 10,000 ounces. There were many presentation pieces, such as the Ascot Gold Vase which had been won in 1845 by Sweetmeat owned by A.W. Hill, son by his second marriage, to Emily Powys, of Sir Francis Brian Hill, the diplomat brother of the General. The huge trophy in silver and gilt made £86 12s. 6d. There was much interest in the commemorative pieces, with Mr Wells, dealer of Shrewsbury, and a Mr Jones of London both buying many lots, often on commission for family members. Another notable piece was the candelabrum presented to Major General Clement Delves Hill in 1837 by the officers of the Royal Horse Guards Blue, of which regiment he was the Colonel. There were the usual tureens, epergnes and entree dishes but the biggest money spinner was a large silver dinner service weighing a hefty 3,647 ounces, which realised £1,083. Many items, including ceremonial swords, had been presented to the General by Kings (George III, George IV, William IV), Queens (Adelaide and Victoria) and City Corporations such as Birmingham, Shrewsbury, Plymouth and the City of London. It must have been very painful to watch for those members of the family who braved the Sale Rooms. There were also at least two Freedom boxes, one from the Guilds of Shrewsbury and the other from the City of Plymouth.

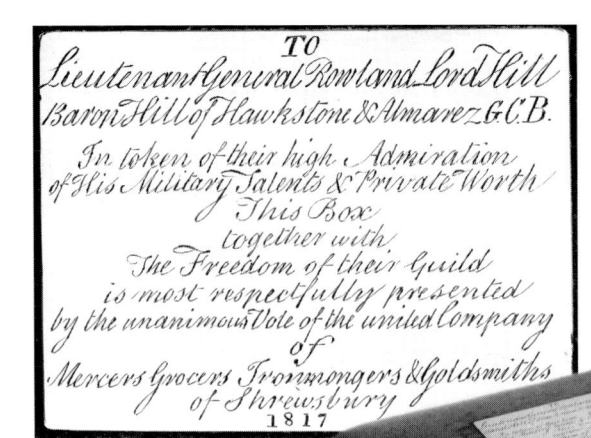

TO
Lieutenant General Rowland, Lord Hill
Baron Hill of Hawkstone & Almarez, G.C.B.
In token of their high Admiration
of His Military Talents & Private Worth
This Box
together with
The Freedom of their Guild
is most respectfully presented
by the unanimous Vote of the united Company
of
Mercers Grocers Ironmongers & Goldsmiths
of Shrewsbury
1817

32. Various pieces from the Hill collection: Freedom boxes from Shrewsbury (above) and Plymouth (left); Sir Robert Chambré Hill's helmet worn through the Peninsula Wars and at Waterloo; a French Cuirassier's breastplate picked up on the battlefield of Waterloo.

Two pieces now in the Victoria and Albert Museum may well have come from this sale. One is a handsome black and yellow lacquer chest on stand that had belonged to Sir Richard, 2nd Baronet, the other a large gilt ewer by David Willaume, 1700, which had belonged to the Great Hill.

Thursday 26 September saw great excitement when General the 1st Viscount Hill's medals and decorations came up for sale. Any relic connected with the Battle of Waterloo was much sought after. John Hill bought two brass and steel cuirasses inscribed 'Battle of Waterloo June 18th, 1815' and a helmet owned by Sir Robert Chambré Hill inscribed 'Waterloo' and 'Peninsula'; the enormous sum of £100 was paid for the helmet worn by General Lord Hill at the Battle of Aboukir, where he commanded the 90th Regt and was wounded, his life probably being saved by the headgear. Another fiercely contested trophy was 'Brown George's hoof'; this rather macabre object heavily mounted in silver bore the following lengthy inscription on the silver lid, 'The hoof of Brown George, a favourite charger and hunter, ridden by Sir Rowland Hill and his brother Clement Hill esq. In the Royal Regiment of Horse Guards for fifteen years, who died at the Regents Park Barracks in October 1833 aged 23 years'. Arthur Hill paid 39 guineas for the lot. This young man bought several items including signet rings that had belonged to his famous uncle.

Dealers Spink and Phillips from London were major purchasers in the sale of Lord Hill's decorations and orders. The star lot was the Gold Cross for Peninsular with six clasps. The newspaper reported that only three were made. This one was in the form of a Maltese Cross with the name of a battle in each division of the cross: Pyrenees, Nivelle; Corunna, Talavera; Orthes and Nive. It had the original riband of crimson with blue edges and with it came an original autograph letter from Frederick, Duke of York, Commander in Chief dated 1 July 1815. It was bought by the dealer Spink on behalf of the Hon. Francis Hill. This news apparently produced cheers and applause in the Sale Room. The price was 1,030 guineas. It is therefore a little confusing to find Lord Hill's medals and decorations being sold by auction at Sothebys on 19 April 1910; 28 items included item no. 3 'General Officer's Peninsular Gold Cross for Roleia, Vimiera, Corunna, Talavera, with clasps for Pyrenees, Nivelle, Corunna, Talavera, Orthes, Nive', which was described as 'fine and extremely rare'. There was no mention of the Duke of York's letter being included. This time the collection was sold as a single lot for £1,010. If it was intended to keep the pieces together the scheme succeeded, but it could hardly be foreseen that it would end up in India. Against the first item in the Sotheby's catalogue is written 'Messrs J. Spink', who were presumably acting for the Maharajah of Patiala; the collection remains in India in the Sheesh Mahal Museum in Patiala in the Punjab where it can be seen to this day. Francis Hill had acquired a number of items of both historical and financial value at the dispersal sale and after his death his widow, Caroline (Corbett), presented what had not already been sold to the Imperial War Museum. In 1904 Sothebys sold a quantity of autograph material including Clement's diary from the Peninsular Campaign and his service in India.

The 4th Viscount died in 1923 and Francis, who succeeded him, in the following year. Neither had any children. The 6th Viscount was their half-brother, Charles, the eldest son of the 3rd Viscount and Isabella Wynn. There was precious little for him to succeed to.

Rowland had continued to scrap over crumbs with the Official Receiver and in 1906, after standing empty for several years, the Hall was sold. It was bought by George Whitely, to be created Baron Marchamley. This couple made some alterations to the entrance and also to the wings but Lady Marchamley died only a few years later and the house was again sold, to William Grey. It was sold again in 1926 and purchased by the present owners, the Catholic Order of the Redemptorists. It was then called St Joseph's. At this time the remaining land was divided, the Park being separated from the Hall which only retained a small acreage around the house.

Epilogue

THE FOLLOWING description of the work of the Redemptorists at Hawkstone is taken, at his suggestion, from Father Denis McBride's brochure *A History of Hawkstone*:

'Hawkstone Hall is now an established pastoral centre which serves the universal Church in its work for religious education and spiritual renewal. The Redemptorist community collaborates with other religious and lay people to make Hawkstone a resource for the wider Christian community. The pastoral centre has two principal objectives: to meet the personal and spiritual needs of women and men who have served the Church for some time; to enable people to face the new challenges put before them by the Church and the world.

'Three courses are offered during the year, each normally lasting three months. The courses provide a setting in which participants from different nationalities and from various cultures share a community life in a spirit of Christian hospitality. Aware of the changing patterns of ministry in the Church, the staff at Hawkstone now welcome other Christian denominations and lay people working in collaborative ministry.

'The atmosphere in Hawkstone is welcoming and attentive. Throughout the house there is a spirit of freedom and respect, and ample opportunity for sharing with others. The breadth of background and experience of those who attend the courses makes for true catholic community and witnesses to the enduring power of the gospel.'

Attingham, today, is open to the public. It was given to the National Trust by the 8th Baron. The rear section of the house contains the regional offices of the Trust. In the main portion, repair/restoration work continues and it is fortunate that sandstone has been available from the Grinshill quarry that supplied the original stone to Noel Hill, the 1st Lord Berwick, in 1782.

Cronkhill also belongs to the Trust. It is privately tenanted and, therefore, not open to the public.

Pedigree of the Hill Family

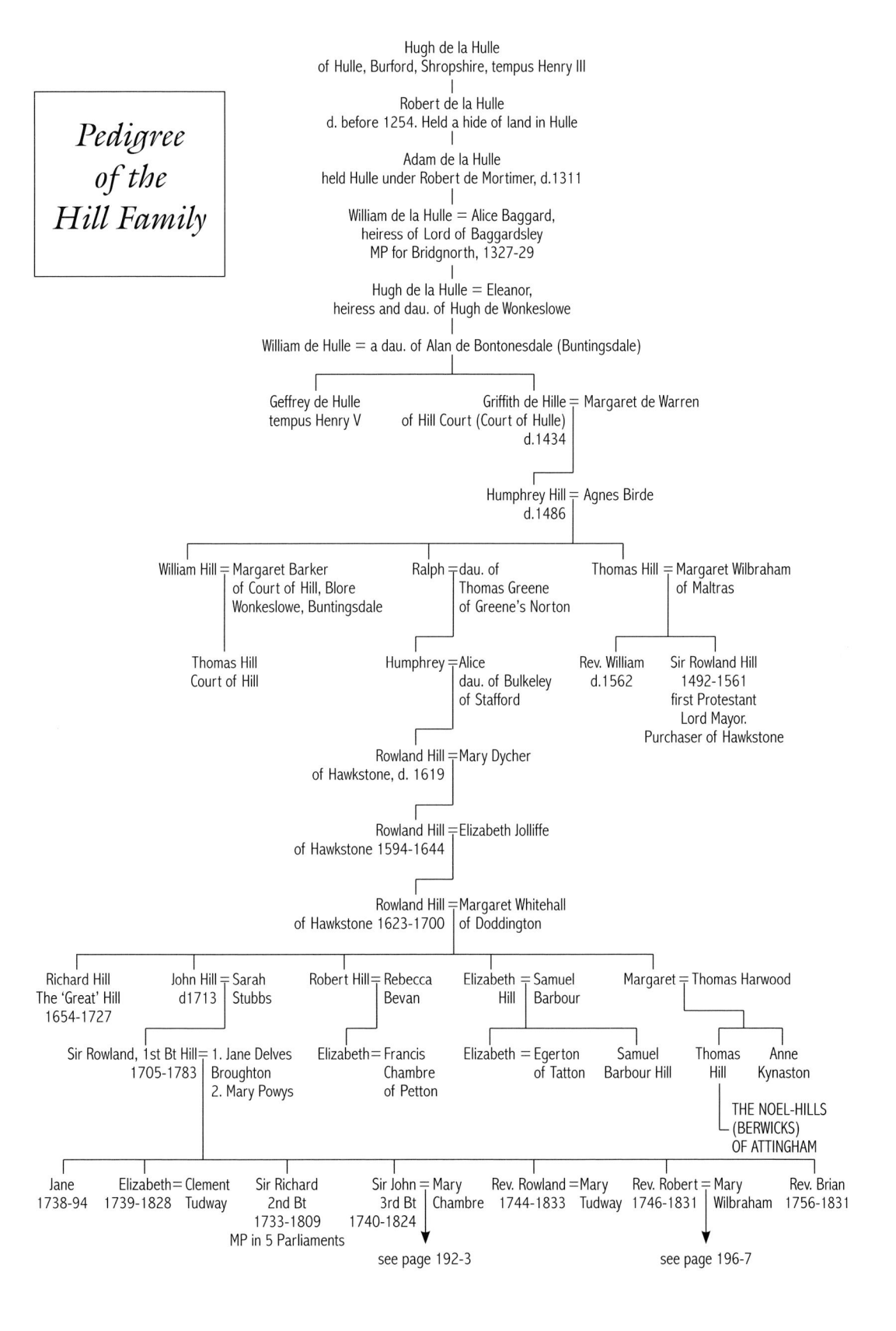

Hugh de la Hulle
of Hulle, Burford, Shropshire, tempus Henry III
│
Robert de la Hulle
d. before 1254. Held a hide of land in Hulle
│
Adam de la Hulle
held Hulle under Robert de Mortimer, d.1311
│
William de la Hulle = **Alice Baggard**,
heiress of Lord of Baggardsley
MP for Bridgnorth, 1327-29
│
Hugh de la Hulle = **Eleanor**,
heiress and dau. of Hugh de Wonkeslowe
│
William de Hulle = a dau. of Alan de Bontonesdale (Buntingsdale)
├── **Geffrey de Hulle** tempus Henry V
└── **Griffith de Hille** = **Margaret de Warren**
    of Hill Court (Court of Hulle) d.1434
    │
    Humphrey Hill = **Agnes Birde**
    d.1486
    ├── **William Hill** = **Margaret Barker**
    │   of Court of Hill, Blore, Wonkeslowe, Buntingsdale
    │   └── **Thomas Hill** Court of Hill
    ├── **Ralph** = dau. of Thomas Greene of Greene's Norton
    │   └── **Humphrey** = **Alice** dau. of Bulkeley of Stafford
    │   │
    │   **Rowland Hill** = **Mary Dycher**
    │   of Hawkstone, d. 1619
    │   │
    │   **Rowland Hill** = **Elizabeth Jolliffe**
    │   of Hawkstone 1594-1644
    │   │
    │   **Rowland Hill** = **Margaret Whitehall**
    │   of Hawkstone 1623-1700 | of Doddington
    └── **Thomas Hill** = **Margaret Wilbraham** of Maltras
        ├── **Rev. William** d.1562
        └── **Sir Rowland Hill** 1492-1561
            first Protestant Lord Mayor.
            Purchaser of Hawkstone

Children of Rowland Hill (1623-1700) and Margaret Whitehall:

- **Richard Hill** The 'Great' Hill 1654-1727
- **John Hill** d1713 = **Sarah Stubbs**
  - **Sir Rowland, 1st Bt Hill** 1705-1783 = 1. Jane Delves Broughton; 2. Mary Powys
- **Robert Hill** = **Rebecca Bevan**
  - **Elizabeth** = **Francis Chambre** of Petton
- **Elizabeth Hill** = **Samuel Barbour**
  - **Elizabeth** = **Egerton** of Tatton
  - **Samuel Barbour Hill**
- **Margaret** = **Thomas Harwood**
  - **Thomas Hill**
  - **Anne Kynaston**
  - THE NOEL-HILLS (BERWICKS) OF ATTINGHAM

Children of Sir Rowland, 1st Bt Hill:

- **Jane** 1738-94
- **Elizabeth** 1739-1828 = **Clement Tudway**
- **Sir Richard 2nd Bt** 1733-1809 MP in 5 Parliaments
- **Sir John 3rd Bt** 1740-1824 = **Mary Chambre** → see page 192-3
- **Rev. Rowland** 1744-1833 = **Mary Tudway**
- **Rev. Robert** 1746-1831 = **Mary Wilbraham** → see page 196-7
- **Rev. Brian** 1756-1831

(from page 191)
Sir John Hill, 3rd Bt

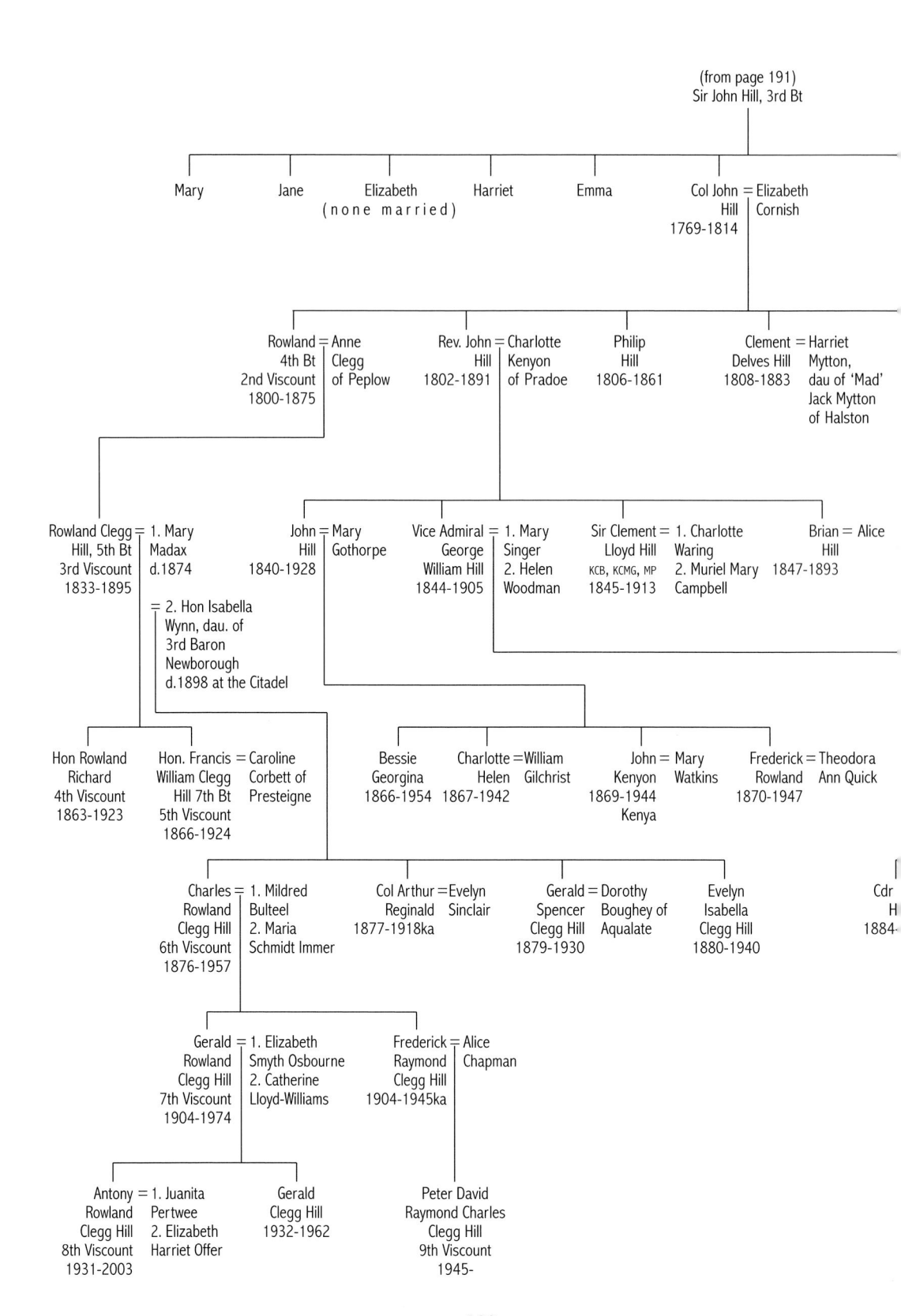

- Mary
- Jane
- Elizabeth
- Harriet
- Emma
(none married)
- Col John Hill 1769-1814 = Elizabeth Cornish

Children of Col John Hill and Elizabeth Cornish:

- Rowland, 4th Bt, 2nd Viscount, 1800-1875 = Anne Clegg of Peplow
- Rev. John Hill 1802-1891 = Charlotte Kenyon of Pradoe
- Philip Hill 1806-1861
- Clement Delves Hill 1808-1883 = Harriet Mytton, dau of 'Mad' Jack Mytton of Halston

Children of Rowland (2nd Viscount) and Anne Clegg:

- Rowland Clegg Hill, 5th Bt, 3rd Viscount, 1833-1895 = 1. Mary Madax d.1874; = 2. Hon Isabella Wynn, dau. of 3rd Baron Newborough, d.1898 at the Citadel
- John Hill 1840-1928 = Mary Gothorpe
- Vice Admiral George William Hill 1844-1905 = 1. Mary Singer; 2. Helen Woodman
- Sir Clement Lloyd Hill KCB, KCMG, MP 1845-1913 = 1. Charlotte Waring; 2. Muriel Mary Campbell
- Brian Hill 1847-1893 = Alice

Children:

- Hon Rowland Richard, 4th Viscount, 1863-1923
- Hon. Francis William Clegg Hill, 7th Bt, 5th Viscount, 1866-1924 = Caroline Corbett of Presteigne
- Bessie Georgina 1866-1954
- Charlotte Helen 1867-1942 = William Gilchrist
- John Kenyon 1869-1944 Kenya = Mary Watkins
- Frederick Rowland 1870-1947 = Theodora Ann Quick

- Charles Rowland Clegg Hill, 6th Viscount, 1876-1957 = 1. Mildred Bulteel; 2. Maria Schmidt Immer
- Col Arthur Reginald 1877-1918ka = Evelyn Sinclair
- Gerald Spencer Clegg Hill 1879-1930 = Dorothy Boughey of Aqualate
- Evelyn Isabella Clegg Hill 1880-1940
- Cdr H... 1884-

- Gerald Rowland Clegg Hill, 7th Viscount, 1904-1974 = 1. Elizabeth Smyth Osbourne; 2. Catherine Lloyd-Williams
- Frederick Raymond Clegg Hill 1904-1945ka = Alice Chapman

- Antony Rowland Clegg Hill, 8th Viscount, 1931-2003 = 1. Juanita Pertwee; 2. Elizabeth Harriet Offer
- Gerald Clegg Hill 1932-1962
- Peter David Raymond Charles Clegg Hill, 9th Viscount, 1945-

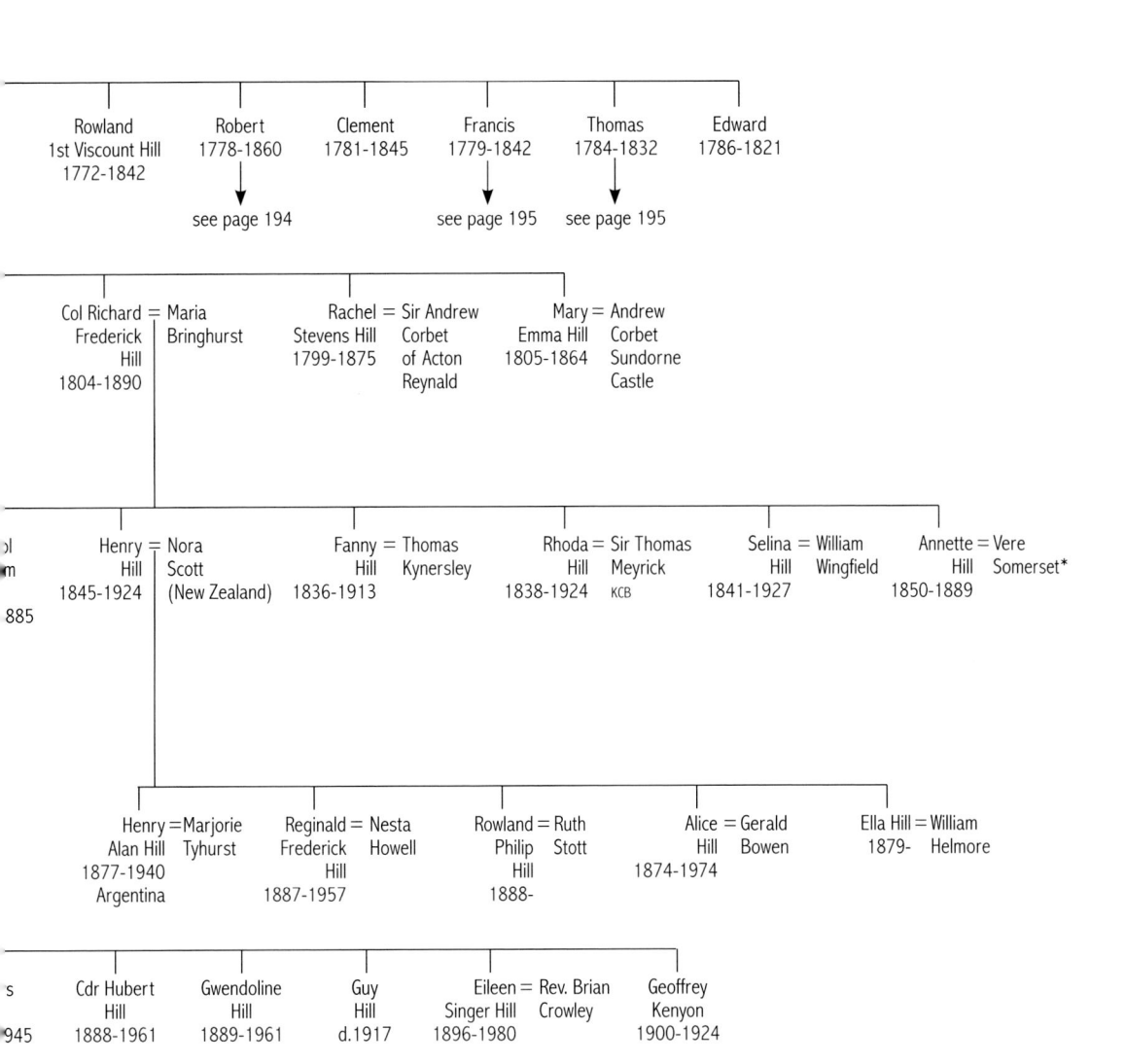

```
Rowland              Robert           Clement          Francis          Thomas           Edward
1st Viscount Hill    1778-1860        1781-1845        1779-1842        1784-1832        1786-1821
1772-1842
                     ↓                                 ↓                ↓
                     see page 194                      see page 195     see page 195
```

```
Col Richard = Maria          Rachel = Sir Andrew           Mary = Andrew
Frederick     Bringhurst     Stevens Hill  Corbet          Emma Hill  Corbet
Hill                         1799-1875     of Acton        1805-1864  Sundorne
1804-1890                                  Reynald                    Castle
```

```
  Henry = Nora         Fanny = Thomas        Rhoda = Sir Thomas    Selina = William    Annette = Vere
  Hill    Scott        Hill    Kynersley     Hill    Meyrick       Hill    Wingfield   Hill      Somerset*
  1845-1924 (New Zealand) 1836-1913          1838-1924 KCB         1841-1927           1850-1889
```

```
Henry = Marjorie    Reginald = Nesta     Rowland = Ruth     Alice = Gerald     Ella Hill = William
Alan Hill  Tyhurst  Frederick  Howell    Philip    Stott    Hill    Bowen      1879-       Helmore
1877-1940           Hill                 Hill              1874-1974
Argentina           1887-1957            1888-
```

```
Cdr Hubert    Gwendoline    Guy       Eileen = Rev. Brian    Geoffrey
Hill          Hill          Hill      Singer Hill  Crowley   Kenyon
1888-1961     1889-1961     d.1917    1896-1980              1900-1924
```

(from page 193)

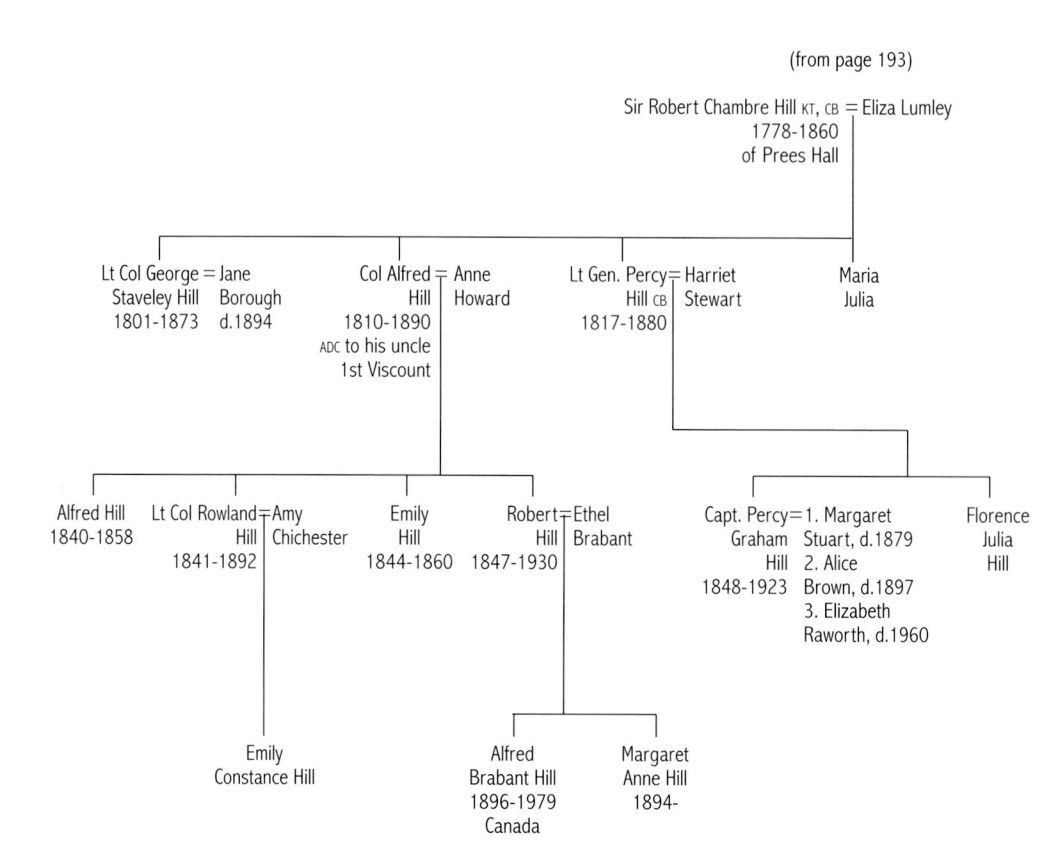

```
Sir Robert Chambre Hill KT, CB = Eliza Lumley
            1778-1860
           of Prees Hall
```

- Lt Col George Staveley Hill 1801-1873 = Jane Borough d.1894
- Col Alfred Hill 1810-1890 ADC to his uncle 1st Viscount = Anne Howard
- Lt Gen. Percy Hill CB 1817-1880 = Harriet Stewart
- Maria Julia

Children of Col Alfred Hill and Anne Howard:
- Alfred Hill 1840-1858
- Lt Col Rowland Hill 1841-1892 = Amy Chichester
- Emily Hill 1844-1860
- Robert Hill 1847-1930 = Ethel Brabant

Children of Lt Gen. Percy Hill and Harriet Stewart:
- Capt. Percy Graham Hill 1848-1923 = 1. Margaret Stuart, d.1879; 2. Alice Brown, d.1897; 3. Elizabeth Raworth, d.1960
- Florence Julia Hill

Child of Lt Col Rowland Hill and Amy Chichester:
- Emily Constance Hill

Children of Robert Hill and Ethel Brabant:
- Alfred Brabant Hill 1896-1979 Canada
- Margaret Anne Hill 1894-

(from page 193)

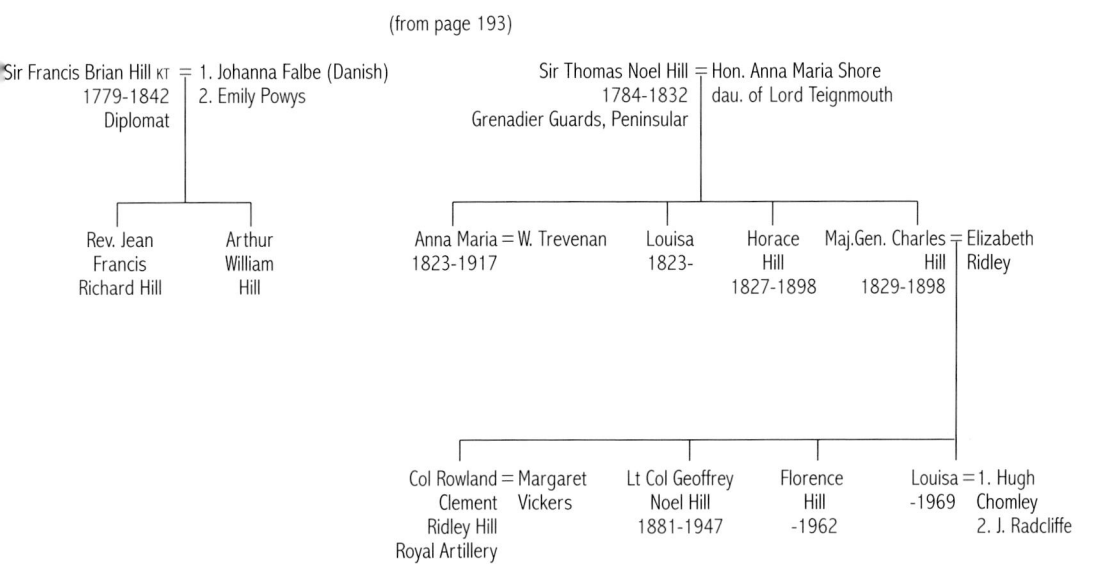

```
Sir Francis Brian Hill KT = 1. Johanna Falbe (Danish)          Sir Thomas Noel Hill = Hon. Anna Maria Shore
     1779-1842          2. Emily Powys                              1784-1832         dau. of Lord Teignmouth
     Diplomat                                                 Grenadier Guards, Peninsular
         │                                                              │
    ┌────┴────┐                              ┌──────────────┬───────────┴──┬──────────────────┐
  Rev. Jean   Arthur                    Anna Maria = W. Trevenan   Louisa    Horace    Maj.Gen. Charles = Elizabeth
  Francis     William                    1823-1917                  1823-     Hill         Hill         Ridley
  Richard Hill Hill                                                        1827-1898      1829-1898
                                                                                              │
                                           ┌──────────────────┬──────────────┬──────────────┐
                                      Col Rowland = Margaret   Lt Col Geoffrey  Florence   Louisa = 1. Hugh
                                        Clement    Vickers      Noel Hill         Hill    -1969     Chomley
                                        Ridley Hill            1881-1947         -1962            2. J. Radcliffe
                                       Royal Artillery
```

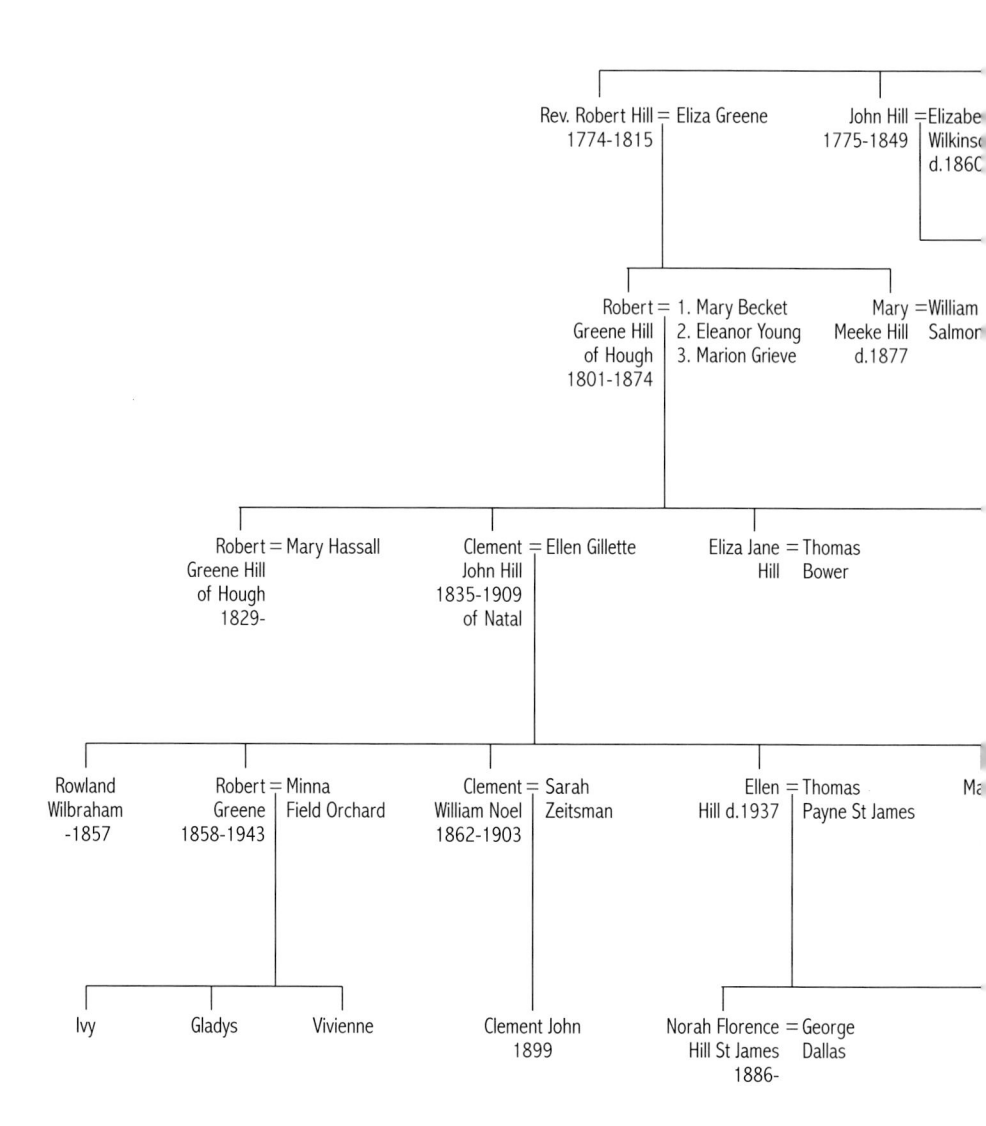

```
Rev. Robert Hill = Eliza Greene      John Hill = Elizabeth
   1774-1815                         1775-1849   Wilkinson
                                                 d.1860

   Robert    = 1. Mary Becket      Mary       = William
 Greene Hill   2. Eleanor Young   Meeke Hill    Salmon
   of Hough    3. Marion Grieve    d.1877
   1801-1874

   Robert  = Mary Hassall    Clement    = Ellen Gillette   Eliza Jane = Thomas
 Greene Hill                 John Hill                       Hill       Bower
   of Hough                  1835-1909
   1829-                     of Natal

 Rowland       Robert  = Minna        Clement   = Sarah      Ellen      = Thomas
Wilbraham      Greene   Field Orchard William Noel Zeitsman  Hill d.1937  Payne St James
  -1857        1858-1943              1862-1903

   Ivy     Gladys    Vivienne         Clement John     Norah Florence = George
                                         1899          Hill St James    Dallas
                                                           1886-
```

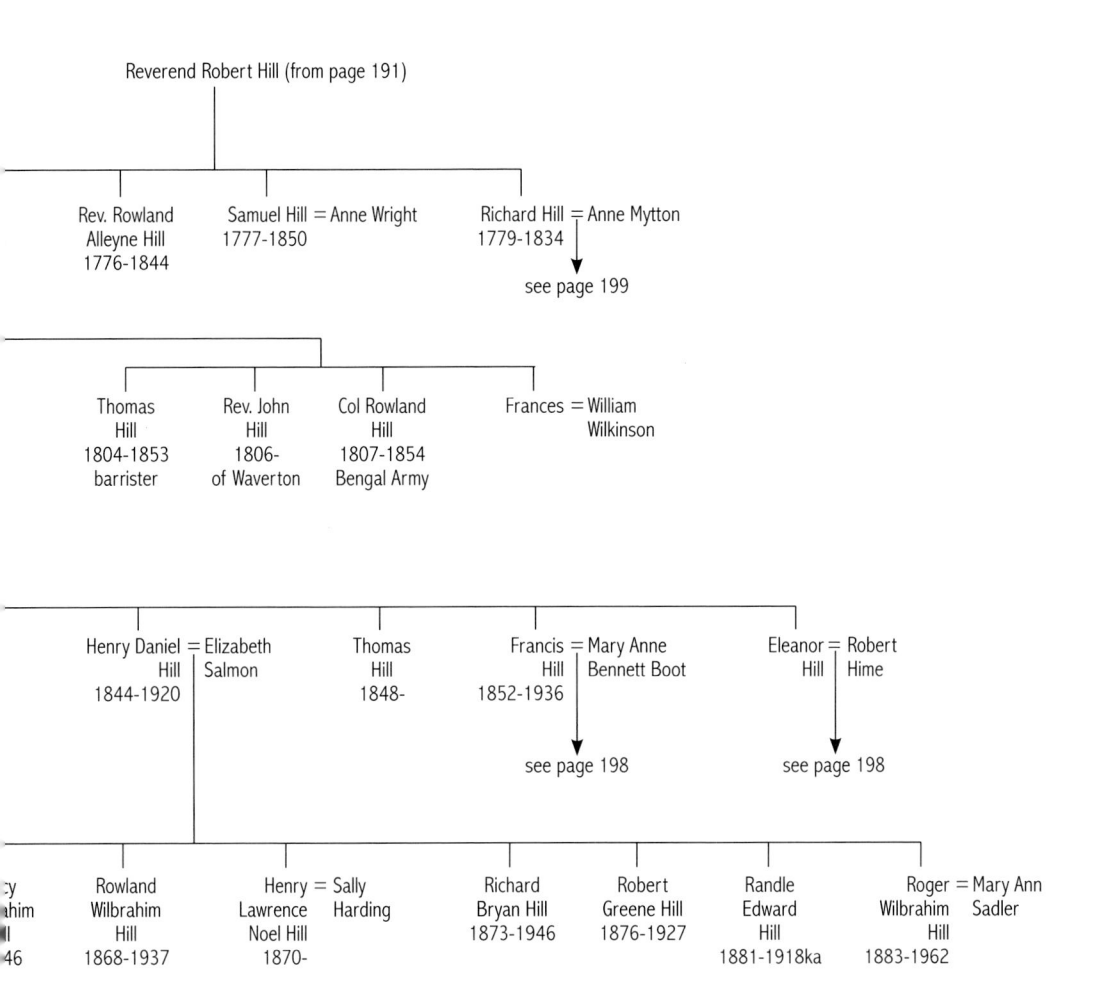

```
                    Reverend Robert Hill (from page 191)
                                  |
        ┌─────────────────────────┼─────────────────────────┐
   Rev. Rowland              Samuel Hill = Anne Wright    Richard Hill = Anne Mytton
   Alleyne Hill              1777-1850                    1779-1834
   1776-1844                                                     ↓
                                                           see page 199
```

┌──────────┬──────────┬──────────┐
Thomas   Rev. John   Col Rowland   Frances = William
Hill   Hill   Hill   Wilkinson
1804-1853 1806-   1807-1854
barrister of Waverton Bengal Army

┌──────────────┬──────────────┬──────────────┬──────────────┐
Henry Daniel = Elizabeth   Thomas   Francis = Mary Anne   Eleanor = Robert
Hill   Salmon   Hill   Hill   Bennett Boot   Hill   Hime
1844-1920   1848-   1852-1936

                                                    ↓   ↓
                                             see page 198   see page 198

┌────┬──────────┬──────────┬──────────┬──────────┬──────────┬──────────┐
y   Rowland   Henry = Sally   Richard   Robert   Randle   Roger = Mary Ann
him Wilbrahim Lawrence Harding Bryan Hill   Greene Hill   Edward   Wilbrahim Sadler
     Hill   Noel Hill   1873-1946   1876-1927   Hill   Hill
46   1868-1937 1870-   1881-1918ka   1883-1962

alie Ivy = John Francis
   James   Hill
-1968

(from page 197)

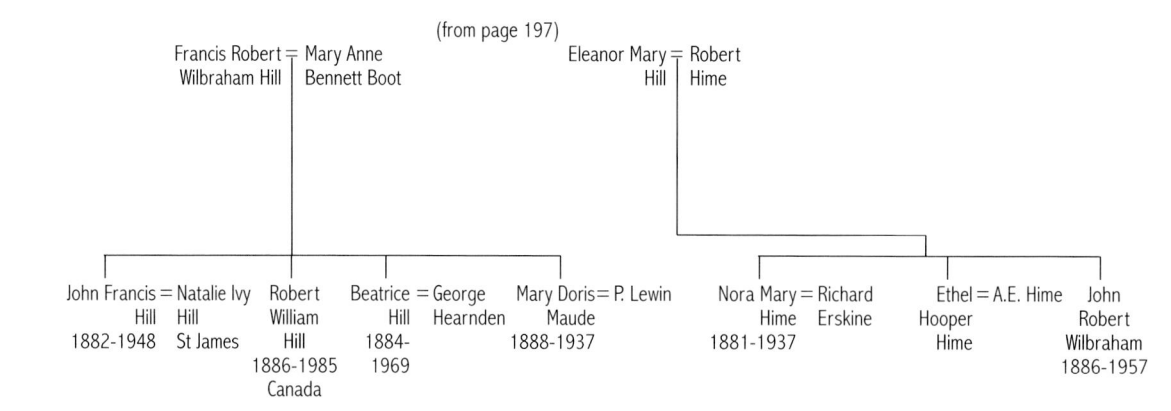

```
Francis Robert = Mary Anne                    Eleanor Mary = Robert
Wilbraham Hill   Bennett Boot                  Hill          Hime
```

John Francis = Natalie Ivy	Robert William Hill	Beatrice = George	Mary Doris = P. Lewin	Nora Mary = Richard	Ethel = A.E. Hime	John Robert
Hill	Hill		Hill Hearnden	Maude	Hime Erskine	Hooper Hime	Wilbraham
1882-1948	St James	1886-1985 Canada	1884-1969	1888-1937	1881-1937		1886-1957

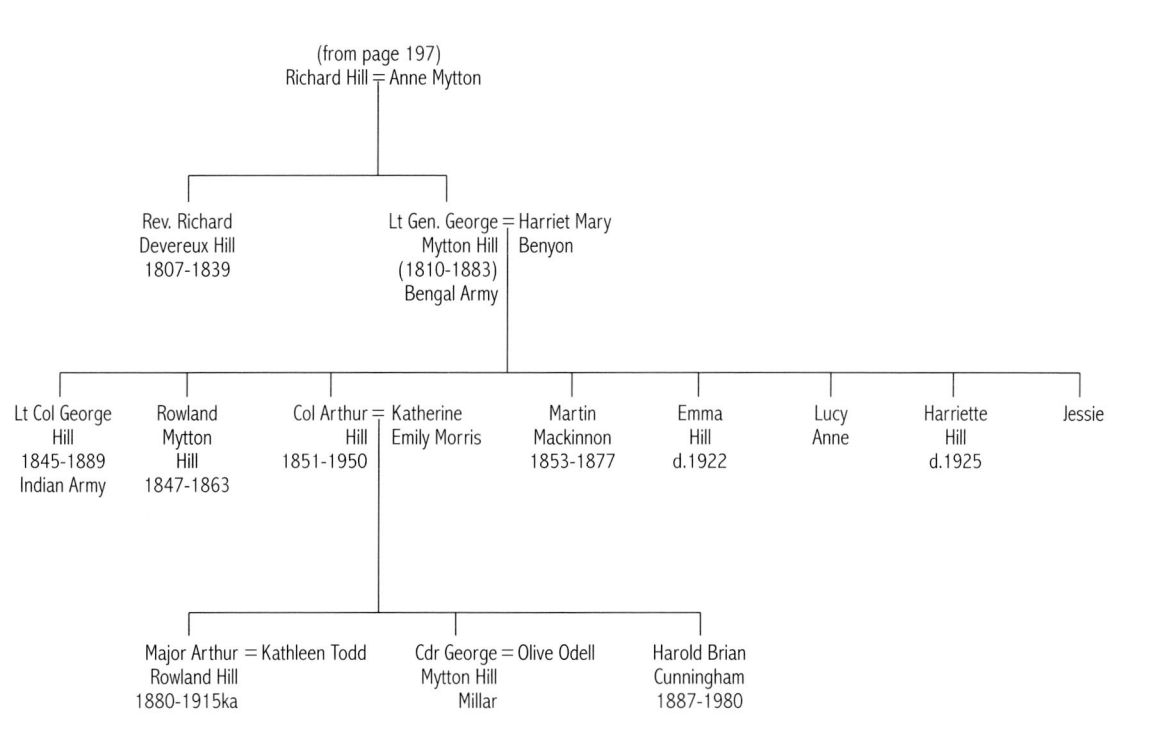

```
                         (from page 197)
                      Richard Hill = Anne Mytton
                                |
              ┌─────────────────┴─────────────────┐
         Rev. Richard                  Lt Gen. George = Harriet Mary
         Devereux Hill                  Mytton Hill     Benyon
         1807-1839                      (1810-1883)
                                        Bengal Army
                                             |
  ┌──────────┬──────────┬──────────┬──────────┼──────────┬──────────┬──────────┬──────────┐
Lt Col George Rowland   Col Arthur = Katherine  Martin    Emma      Lucy      Harriette   Jessie
Hill         Mytton     Hill        Emily Morris Mackinnon Hill     Anne      Hill
1845-1889    Hill       1851-1950               1853-1877  d.1922             d.1925
Indian Army  1847-1863
                         |
             ┌───────────┼───────────────────┐
        Major Arthur = Kathleen Todd   Cdr George = Olive Odell   Harold Brian
        Rowland Hill                   Mytton Hill                Cunningham
        1880-1915ka                    Millar                     1887-1980
```

Notes

Chapter 1: The Earliest Hills · Court of Hulle · Sir Rowland Hill, Kt

[1] Eyton's *Antiquities* mentions Court of Hulle in Overs Hundred in 1221 when William de la Hulle gave it to his son Robert de la Hulle; and Owen and Blakeway in *Sheriffs of Shropshire* (pp.142, 179) considered the William de la Hulle living in 1331 to be the founder of the Hill 'dynasty' in Shropshire.
[2] SRO 549/660.
[3] On the grounds that she had already been married to Henry's elder brother, Arthur, who died young.
[4] *Dictionary of National Biography*; he was a Freeman, then Warden and finally Master (three times) of the Worshipful Company of Mercers of the City of London.
[5] State Papers Domestic, King Henry VIII, vol.XV, p.1540.
[6] State Papers Domestic, King Edward VI.
[7] Much of the quoted information comes from the Noble Collection of Ephemera compiled by Mr L'Anson in the Corporation of London Guildhall Library, ref. C78.
[8] S. Bindoff, *History of the House of Commons 1509-1558*, p.359.
[9] *Ibid*. This is one of only two references to his being married.
[10] In the Noble Collection there are accounts by Sharpe and Wriothesley of this incident, *Wriothesley's Chronicles* vols.XI, p.135 and XX, pp.24, 25, 53.
[11] He made several wills, one of which was proved before he died; see Noble Collection and *DNB*.
[12] Probably a urinary infection.
[13] *Machyn's Diaries*, quoted in *DNB* and Noble Collection.
[14] Casseys *Parishes of Shropshire*, SRO, pp.171-6.

Chapter 2: The 'Great' Hill

[1] Harwood's *Alumni Etonenses* (1797).
[2] Owen and Blakeway's *Sheriffs of Shropshire* (1831), pp.179-82.
[3] Bishop Burnett, *History of his Own Time* (1833), iv, pp.317-18, vi, pp.77, 120.
[4] See Preface of the *Correspondence of the Rt Hon. Richard Hill* edited by the Rev. Blackley, 1842.
[5] *International Herald Tribune*, 25 February 2002.
[6] He left his silver, pictures and library to nephew Rowland with the wish that they be considered as heirlooms.
[7] See State Papers of William III.
[8] *Correspondence of Richard Hill* (ed. Blackley), Appendix D.
[9] Many of his letters are quoted in the two volumes edited by Blackley, but there are many more in SRO series 112.
[10] *Correspondence of Richard Hill*, Appendix K.
[11] *Correspondence of Richard Hill*, Appendix H, pp.799, 800.
[12] Undated account of Richard Hill's journey to Turin, pp.803-16.
[13] Letter from Queen Anne dated 9 November 1703.
[14] Copies of Stepney's correspondence are to be found in many libraries but his exchanges with Richard Hill are mainly held in the Carmarthenshire Records Office.
[15] *Correspondence of Richard Hill*, Appendix G, pp.950-7, Appendix G, 'Secret Terms'.
[16] *Correspondence of Richard Hill*, Hedges to Hill, 2 September 1703, p.25.
[17] Churchill's *Life of Marlborough* intimates that Hill and Aglionby may have been a bit indiscreet.
[18] Letter to Lord Nottingham re. journey to Turin, 13 November 1703.
[19] Letters to Nottingham of 2 and 5 November 1703.
[20] See letter from Sir George Rooke to Hill dated 12 December 1703, and Appendix B describing the 'dismal tempest'.

NOTES

21. Later on Hill was given two more ships.
22. Hill to Marlborough, 26 August 1704, from Turin, p.413.
23. Hill to Admiral Sir George Rooke, p.405.
24. *Correspondence of Richard Hill*, p.473.
25. Letters to Captain Fisher, 6 and 7 March 1705, p.502.
26. Letters to Captain Dolman and Captain Fisher of Hill's 'Navy' dated between 5-12 March 1705, *Correspondence of Richard Hill*.
27. *Correspondence of Richard Hill*, pp.506-10.
28. Cavallier was a first-class soldier who subsequently served as a Colonel in the Duke's army before going to England, where he became a General and Governor of Jersey.
29. Letter from Hill to Secretary Hedges re. Cavallier, dated 6 November 1704, pp.458, 459.
30. Flotard to Hill, 18 August 1704, p.151.
31. Hill to Hedges, p.590.
32. Hill to Marlborough, p.618.
33. Hill to the Lord Treasurer, p.617.
34. *Correspondence of Richard Hill*, pp.615-20, for Lord Treasurer's suspicions of the Duke of Savoy's real intentions.
35. *Correspondence of Richard Hill* with Secretary Hedges, pp.614, 615, 618, 620, 622.
36. Letters to agents Messrs Scudamore and Co., Geneva, and Messrs Western at Livorno (Leghorn), p.669.
37. Miss E.M. Jancey, 'The Hon. and Rev. Richard Hill; an account of his investments in North Shropshire', TSAS, vol.XV.
38. Barbara Coulton, *A Shropshire Squire*.
39. Romney and Sedgewick, *House of Commons 1715-1754*.
40. He died June 1740. His friend Thomas Carte wrote, 'The Pretender hath had a great loss in the death of Corbet Kynaston who would have ventured his life and future for him in any circumstances whatever.'
41. Owen and Blakeway's *Sheriffs of Shropshire*, p.50.

Chapter 3: The Evangelist Brothers: Sir Richard Hill, Bt, MP and the Reverend Rowland Hill, Renowned Preacher

1. Julian McQuick, 'Sir Richard Hill', TSAS, vol.LVIII, pp.167-77; *VCH*, vol.2, pp.169, 170, 176, 179-82; R.G. Thorne, *House of Commons 1790-1820*, pp.337, 338.
2. He was MP for Lichfield 1734-41 and a 'Moderate Tory', Romney and Sedgewick's *House of Commons 1715-1754*.
3. Edward Sidney, *Life of Sir Richard Hill*, pp.156-9; V. Charlesworth, *Life of the Reverend Rowland Hill*, pp.75, 76.
4. After the Bishop of Carlisle was told not to ordain him, Rowland said that 'he had run off with only one ecclesiastical boot on'.
5. Sidney, *Life of Sir Richard Hill*.
6. See James Gillray cartoon 'Dr Busby settling accounts with Master Billy', showing Pitt, Sir Richard, Edmund Burke and Richard Brinsley Sheridan, in the National Portrait Gallery.
7. Sidney, *Life of Sir Richard Hill*, pp.156-9.
8. *Ibid.*, p.76.
9. *VCH* (Shropshire), vol.3, p.130.
10. This is a well documented saga: Sir Richard published many pamphlets on the subject and also *Pietas Oxoniensis*.
11. Sidney, *Life of Sir Richard Hill*, pp.156, 157.
12. Barbara Coulton, *A Shropshire Squire*, pp.58-64.
13. Sidney, *Life of Sir Richard Hill*, pp.311.
14. *Parliamentary History* vol.XXII, p.944; TSAS, vol.LVIII, p.167.
15. Coulton, *A Shropshire Squire*; H. Avray Tipping, 'Attingham Park', *Country Life* February 1921 and Michael Rix, 'Attingham Hall', *Country Life*, October 1954.
16. Rev. J.C. Hill Collection in SRO, ref. 549, dated 12.8.1828 from Mr Smith to Elizabeth Cornish Hill, mother of 2nd Viscount.
17. T. Rodenhurst, *A Description of Hawkstone* (9th edition, 1807).
18. Sidney, *Life of Sir Richard Hill*, pp.491-3.
19. Sidney, *Life of Sir Richard Hill*, chapter XVI has an account of this journey.

20. *Ibid.*, p.433.
21. Letter re. George Downward in SRO 731 box 226.
22. Rodenhurst, *A Description of Hawkstone*.
23. Eton College Register, p.271.
24. V. Charlesworth, *Rowland Hill, His Life, Anecdotes and Pulpit Sayings* (Hodder, 1877); Wotton-under-Edge Heritage Centre contains information about the Rev. Rowland Hill, and there are almshouses there named after him.
25. Charlesworth, *The Reverend Rowland Hill*, p.15.
26. *Ibid.*, p.23.
27. *Ibid.*, p.27.
28. Cabinet Annual Registry, quoted in Charlesworth, *The Reverend Rowland Hill*, p.76.
29. Account of Jane Hill's journey on the Continent in Sidney, *Life of Sir Richard Hill*, pp.369-76.

Chapter 4: General Rowland, 1st Viscount Hill, Part 1

1. Edwin Sidney, *Life of Lord Hill*.
2. Although this painting was catalogued for sale by Bonhams as 'The General', it is, in fact, his nephew, the 2nd Viscount.
3. Sidney, *Life of Lord Hill*, p.8.
4. *Ibid.*, p.11.
5. *Ibid.*, p.18.
6. Major Arthur Griffiths, *The Wellington Memorial, Wellington, his comrades and contemporaries*, p.313; David Chandler, *Dictionary of the Napoleonic Wars*, p.175.
7. Sidney, *Life of Lord Hill*, pp.22, 23.
8. *Ibid.*, p.35.
9. *Ibid.*, pp.35, 36.
10. *Ibid.*, pp.39, 40.
11. *Ibid.*, pp.70, 71.
12. *Ibid.*, p.77.
13. Ian Robertson, *Wellington at War in the Peninsula*, pp.78, 79.
14. *Ibid.*, pp.98, 99; Sidney, *Life of Lord Hill*, p.112.
15. Letter from Wellington to Hill, 18 December 1809, quoted in Sidney, *Life of Lord Hill*, p.121.
16. Robertson, *Wellington at War in the Peninsula*, Battle of Arroyo de Molinos, p.179; Sidney, *Life of Lord Hill*, pp.167-9.
17. Chandler, *Dictionary of the Napoleonic Wars*, p.9; Robertson, *Wellington at War in the Peninsula*, pp.199, 200; Philip Haythornthwaite, *The Armies of Wellington*, p.63, 'Virtual starvation at Almaraz'.

Chapter 5: General Rowland, 1st Viscount Hill, Part 2

1. William Hill was *en poste* in Sardinia, a position said to have been engineered by Lady Hester Stanhope to whom he was thought to be getting engaged. He seems to have had considerable success with the ladies. See Heber Letters 1783-1832 and Granville Corres. 1781-1821, *Victoria County History*, vol.3, p.274.
2. Edwin Sidney, *Life of Lord Hill*, p.235
3. *Ibid.*, pp.235, 236.
4. Michel Collection, Dorset Archive Service, X1-X58.
5. Arthur Bryant, *The Great Duke*, p.30; Ian Robertson, *Wellington at War in the Peninsula*, p.249; Christopher Hibbert, *Wellington; A Personal History*, pp.134-6. The silver chamber pot is in the proud possession of the King's Own Hussars and is put to a different use these days.
6. Robertson, *Wellington at War in the Peninsula*, p.303; Philip Haythornthwaite, *The Armies of Wellington*, pp.254, 255.
7. Wellington is recorded as saying that if Hill had begun to swear they must all mind what they were about. Hill was known for never using foul language. Elizabeth Longford, *Wellington, Years of the Sword*, p.338.
8. G. Bell, *Rough Notes of an Old Soldier*, p.111.
9. Sidney, *Life of Lord Hill*, pp.269, 270.
10. *Ibid.*, letter to sister Maria, pp.286, 288, 289.
11. *Ibid.*, p.292.
12. *Ibid.*
13. Leaflet: *A Description of the Column in Shrewsbury in Honour of Lord Hill*, SRO.

NOTES

14. Ney was shot as a traitor, SRO 549/223.
15. Quoted with permission from Sir Digby in Sidney, *Life of Lord Hill*, pp.308-10.
16. *Ibid.*, p.313.
17. Ney had initially been permitted to retire in obscurity but on being recognised was returned to Paris, court martialled and condemned to death. Richard Aldington, *Wellington*, p.237.
18. Sidney, *Life of Lord Hill*, p.321.
19. Creevy Papers, vol.II, p.278.
20. *Liverpool Courier*, undated cutting c.1820.
21. Creevy Papers, vol.II, p.157.
22. Creevy Papers, vol.II, p.240.
23. Woodham Smith, *The Reason Why*, p.52; Donald Thomas, *Cardigan*, pp.40-53, 61-63.
24. On Hill's death the Queen wrote a letter of condolence to his nephew, Sir Rowland, 2nd Viscount, saying he had long been a valued member of her household; letter from Wellington to 2nd Viscount in Sidney, *Life of Lord Hill*.
25. Sidney, *Life of Lord Hill*, pp.380, 381.
26. Sale Catalogue of Sotheby's of London, 19 April 1910.
27. Biographie Nouvelle des Contemporains, *Hommes Illustres* (Paris, 1823).
28. *Gentleman's Magazine*, July 1831 and *DNB*.
29. Letter of Cust, Hill's ADC, to Lord Hill in Rev. James C. Hill Collection, in the SRO 424/20.

Chapter 6: The Final Generations after Waterloo

1. Letter from Sir Robert Peel, Prime Minister, to Lord Hill in 1842. See Sidney, *Life of Lord Hill*, p.381.
2. *Victoria County History* (Shropshire) vol.2, pp.168, 170, 185, 186.
3. Lean's Royal Navy List 1906, Admiralty Library.
4. Kenneth Rose, *King George V* (Knopf, NY, 1984), pp.9-15.
5. Much of the information on Sir Clement's career comes from *Who was Who, 1893-1916*, obits in *The Times* and other national press and the *Shrewsbury Chronicle*, April 1913; VCH, vol.3, 'Parliamentary Representation', p.353; TSAS 4th series, XII, p.267; Foreign Office Statement of Service of 1906, p.259.
6. TSAS, 4th series, LLX, 'Loton Park Diaries', p.146.
7. *Ibid.*, p.147.
8. Sothebys held a Sale of Autograph Letters and Historic Documents in 1904. It included Clement's diary of the Peninsula and India, the General's correspondence with Lord Fitzroy Somerset, Military Secretary to the Duke of Wellington, while General Commander in Chief, the letters the General wrote home from the Peninsula and many others.

Chapter 7: Hills in Shropshire Politics – The Election Scandal

1. Oldfield, *Representative History of Great Britain and Ireland*, p.378, and TSAS, 'Shrewsbury MPs' Memoirs', 4th Series, XII, p.116.
2. TSAS, 4th series, XII, p.116; Oldfield, *Representative History*, p.380.
3. Romney and Sedgewick, *House of Commons*, pp.138, 139.
4. Letter in Rev. J.C. Hill Collection, SRO 549/60.
5. 'The Free Man'. See R.G. Thorne, *House of Commons 1790-1820*, pp.337, 338.
6. 'Shrewsbury MPs' Memoirs', p.243; VCH, 'Parliamentary Representation', pp.271, 272.
7. 'Parliamentary Representation', p.272; Heber Letters 1783-1832 (edited by R.H. Cholmondeley), p.94.
8. See also Michael Messenger, *Coalport*, Antique Collectors' Club, 1995, pp.60-4.
9. 'Parliamentary Representation', p.273.
10. Staffordshire Records Office D1287/10/4a.
11. Barbara Coulton, *A Shropshire Squire*; 'Parliamentary Representation', pp.273, 319.
12. Messenger, *Coalport*, pp.195, 196, 197.
13. Excerpts published in TSAS 'Loton Park Diaries, Sir Baldwin Leighton'.
14. Speech quoted in the *Shrewsbury Chronicle* of 1 April 1895.
15. 'Loton Park Diaries'.
16. Sir Clement's obituary in the *Shrewsbury Chronicle*, 11 April 1913.
17. Sir Clement's victories were also commemorated—see Messenger, *Coalport*, p.341 for the plainer example.

Chapter 8: Hawkstone Hall · The Park · The Citadel

1. *Correspondence of Richard Hill* and his Papers in the Attingham Collection in Shropshire Record Office, boxes in Series 112.
2. TSAS vol.XV, 1954-6, article by Miss E. Jancey on the purchases of Richard Hill, and correspondence in E. Bygott Collection in SRO.
3. Attingham Collection, Series 112.
4. The Prince of Wales referred thus to Sir John Hill regarding sons Rowland, Robert, Clement, Thomas Noel and youngest son of all, Edward. With the exception of Edward, who was present at Waterloo, all fought through the Peninsular Campaign and at Waterloo.
5. These forecourts cannot have lasted long because they do not appear in any known paintings, with the exception of an aquatint by Williams that shows a courtyard to the north and certainly not outside the main entrance.
6. Letter in *Correspondence of Richard Hill*, Series 112 in SRO, dated 16 November 1726.
7. See Department of the Environment's Listed Buildings and Register of Parks and Gardens for detailed descriptions of the architectural construction of the House, ref. SJ5829-5929, Park SJ5729.
8. These paintings were left after the sale of the rest of the contents. They are all badly in need of cleaning. Other very similar portraits of the Great Hill exist at Attingham Park, Tatton Park and the Shrewsbury Museum. The last named was purchased through the efforts of the Rev. Richard Hayes at a sale at Sothebys in 2002. It had been put up for sale by a museum in the United States.
9. DOE's Listed Buildings ref. SJ 5829-5929.
10. Quoted in *History of Garden Design—the Western Tradition*, ed. Monique Mosser and Georges Teyssot (Thames and Hudson).
11. See *Follies and Grottoes* by Barbara Jones for a description of black, white and golden rabbits running about.
12. This Tower is now red, the bricks having lost their white coating.

Chapter 9: The Noel-Hills (Berwicks) of Attingham Park

1. TSAS, 'Shrewsbury MPs' Memoirs', p.18; *VCH*, 'Parliamentary Representation', p.262. He was MP for the Borough from 1768-74 and for the County from 1774 to 1784 when he was made Lord Berwick, Berwick being a site on the Attingham Estate.
2. Michael Rix, 'Attingham Hall', *Country Life*, 21 October 1954, pp.1350-3.
3. Barbara Coulton, *A Shropshire Squire*, pp.58-65.
4. H. Avray Tipping, 'Attingham, Shropshire. The Seat of Lord Berwick', *Country Life*, 5 February 1921, part 1.
5. *Idem*, part 2, 12 February 1921.
6. Belinda Cousens, *Attingham Park*, p.18; Tipping, *Country Life*, 12 February 1921.
7. Lesley Blanche (ed.), *Harriette Wilson's Memoirs*.
8. For Richard, 4th Baron Berwick's capacity for wine, see *Attingham*, the National Trust's Guide to the Park, p.49; 'Loton Park Diaries of Sir Baldwin Leighton'.
9. Geoffrey Tyack, 'Cronkhill', *Country Life*, 19 February 2004, pp.62-7.

Bibliography

General Sources and Collections

Dictionary of National Biography entries for:
    Sir Rowland Hill, 1492-1561
    The Hon and Rev. Richard Hill, 1654-1727
    Sir Richard Hill, 2nd Bt, 1733-1809
    The Rev. Rowland Hill, 1744-1833
    Rowland, 1st Viscount Hill, 1772-1842
    Sir Thomas Noel Hill, 1784-1832

Collections in the Shropshire Records Office (SRO):
    Edward Bygott series 731
    The Rev. J.C. Hill, 549, 592, 811
    The Attingham Collection series 112

Aldington, Richard, *Wellington* (Heinemann, 1946)
Apperley, C.J. (Nimrod), *Life and Memoirs of John Mytton* (1837)
Biographie Nouvelle des Contemporains, *Hommes Illustres* (Paris, 1823)
Bindoff, S., *History of the House of Commons 1509-1558*
Blackley, The Rev. (ed.), *Correspondence of the Rt Hon. Richard Hill* (Murray, 1845, 2 vols.)
Blanche, Lesley (ed.), *Harriette Wilson's Memoirs* (Phoenix, 2003)
Bryant, Arthur, *Years of Victory, 1802-1812* (Collins, 1944)
Casseys, *Parishes of Shropshire* (Hodnet) 1874
Chandler, David, *Dictionary of the Napoleonic Wars* (Wordsworth Military Library, 1993)
Charlesworth, The Rev. V., *The Reverend Rowland Hill* (Hodder, 1877)
Coulton, Barbara, *A Shropshire Squire* (Swan Hill Press, 1989)
Country Life, 27.3.1958, 3.4.58, 3.7.58, 10.7.58, 2.8.58
Coupland, Reginald, *Wilberforce* (Collins, 1945)
Cousens, Belinda, *Attingham* (The National Trust, 2000)
Creevy Papers (ed. Herbert Maxwell, John Murray, 1903, 2 vols)
English Heritage, Register of Parks and Gardens, Shropshire, November 1998
Esdaile, Charles, *Peninsular War* (Penguin, 2002)
Fletcher, Ian, *Galloping at Everything* (Spellmount, 1999)
Forrester H., 'Some Old Shropshire Houses and Their Owners', TSAS, 1924
Griffiths, Major Arthur, *The Wellington Memorial* (George Allen, 1892)
Haythornthwaite, Philip, *Who's Who in the Napoleonic Wars* (Arms and Armour, 1995)
Hayton, D.W, *The House of Commons 1690-1715*
Hibbert, Christopher (ed.), *Recollections of Rifleman Harris* (Windrush Press, 1970)

Hibbert, Christopher, *Wellington: a Personal History* (Harper Collins, 1997)
Howarth, David, *A Near Run Thing* (Collins, 1968)
Hussey, Christopher, 'Mid Georgian', *Country Life*, 1956
Jancey, E.M., 'The Hon. and Rev. Richard Hill', TSAS, vol. XV (1954-6)
Jones, Barbara, *Follies and Grottos* (Constable, 1974)
L'Anson, 'The Noble Collection of Ephemera', Museum Library, City of London
Leighton, Sir Baldwin, 'Loton Park Manuscript', Diaries of Sir Baldwin Leighton, Bt, TSAS, vol.LIX (1971-2), pp.143, 146-8
Lewis, John E. (ed.), *Soldiers at War* (Robinson, 2001)
Longford, Elizabeth, *Wellington; Years of the Sword* (London 1969)
Machyn, 'Diaries' (Camden Society)
McBride, Father Denis, *A History of Hawkstone* (1993)
McLynn, Frank, *Napoleon* (Cape, 1997)
McQuick, Julian, *Sir Richard Hill*, TSAS, vol. LVIII
Messenger, Michael, *Coalport* (The Antique Collectors' Club, 1995)
Morris, George, *Shropshire Genealogies*
Namier and Brooke, *History of the House of Commons 1754-1790*, vol.2 (HMSO, 1986)
Napier, Sir William, *History of War in the Pensinula* (London, 1851)
Nightingale, *Shropshire, Beauties of England and Wales* (1813)
Oldfield, T.H.B., *Representative History of Great Britain and Ireland* (London, 1816)
Oman, C., *Wellington's Army, 1809-1814* (Oxford, 1912)
Owen and Blakeway, *Sheriffs of Shropshire* (1831)
Parkinson, Roger, *The Peninsular War* (Hart Davis, 1973)
Rix, Michael, 'Attingham Hall', *Country Life*, 21.10.54
Roberts, Andrew, *Napoleon and Wellington* (Weidenfeld and Nicholson, 2001)
Robertson, Ian, *Wellington at War in the Peninsula, 1808-1814* (Pen and Sword Books, 1988)
Rodenhurst, T., *A Description of Hawkstone* (9th edition, 1807)
Romney and Sedgewick, *History of the House of Commons, 1715-1754*
Sherer, Colonel Moyle, *Recollections of the Peninsula* (1827)
Sidney, The Rev. Edwin, *Sir Richard Hill Bt* (Seeley, 1839)
Sidney, The Rev. Edwin, *The Life of Lord Hill* (John Murray, 1845)
Sotheby, Wilkinson & Hodge, 'Catalogue of the British and Foreign Orders, Decorations, Medals etc. granted to General Viscount Hill, GCB', 19 April 1910
Stocqueler, J.H., *A Personal History of the Horse Guards* (Hurst and Blackett, 1873)
Thomas, Donald, *Cardigan* (Routledge & Kegan Paul, 1974)
Thorne, R.G., *History of the House of Commons 1790-1820* (Secker & Warburg, 1986)
Tipping, H. Avray, 'Attingham, Shropshire. The Seat of Lord Berwick', *Country Life*, 5.2.1921, 12.2.21
Uffindell, Andrew, *Great Generals of the Napoleonic Wars and Their Battles, 1805-1815* (Spellmount, 2003)
Urban, Mark, *The Man who Broke Napoleon's Codes* (Faber and Faber, 2001)
Victoria County History (Shropshire) vols.2 and 3
Woodham Smith, C., *The Reason Why* (Constable, 1953)
Wriothesley's Chronicles (Camden Society)

Index

compiled by Ann Hudson

Abbé, General le Baron, 88
Abercromby, Sir Ralph, 68, 69
Aberdeen, Earl of *see* Gordon, George Hamilton
Aboukir, Battle of (1802), 69, 187
Acton Burnell (Salop.), 131, 132
Adam, Robert, 167, 168
Adams, Dr, 47
Adderley (lawyer), 5
Adelaide, Queen, 105, 106, 185
Africa, 124–9; *see also* Egypt
Aglionby, William, 22
Ailesbury, Marquess of *see* Bruce
Albert Victor, Duke of Clarence (Prince Eddy), 123–4
Alcaston (Salop.), 2
Allgood, Mrs, 181
Almaraz, Battle of (1812), 82–3, 111
Amcotes, Sir Henry, 6
American War of Independence, 47–8, 170
Amiens, Peace of (1802), 69–70
Amsterdam, 14
Anne, Queen, 16, 18, 21–35, 185
Anthoine, Colonel, 86
Antibes, 26, 28
Archer, Giles, 45
Aremberg, Prince d', 81, 96
Arnaud, Monsieur, 23
Ashton family, 9
Atcham (Salop.): bridge over Severn, 6; *see also* Attingham
Atcherley, Richard, 37
Attingham estate (Salop.) (originally Tern estate), 36, 134; *see also* Cronkhill
Attingham Park (Salop.), 133, 163–77, **169**, 189; as Tern Hall 36, 37, 163–4, 165, 167–8
Austerlitz, Battle of (1805), 71
Australia, 125, 129
Aversberg, Count d', 21

Bacchante, HMS, 123–5, **124**
Badajoz, capture of (1812), 82
Bangalore, monument to Clement Hill, 118–19
Barbour, Samuel, 36
Barclay, Sir David and Sir Frederick, 151

Barker, Alice, m. Sir Thomas Leigh, 8
Barker, James, 5, 8
Bavaria, Elector of, 14, 15, 20, 21, 23, 25
Bayreuth, 113
Belgium *see* Brussels; Namur
Bennett, Hon. Henry, 85, 136
Beresford, William, Viscount, 76, 78, 79, 86, 93
Berridge, John, 56, 58–9
Berrington (Salop.), 176
Berwick, Lords *see* Hill; Noel-Hill
Betton (Salop.), 5
Birde, Agnes, m. Humphrey Hill, 1
Blatch, ___, 47
Blenheim, Battle of (1704), 17, 25, 26
Bletchley (Salop.), 1, 9
Blücher, Prince, 93, 96, 97, 98
Bolas (Salop.), 42, 161
Bridgeman family, 131
Bridgeman, Orlando, 98–9
Bridgnorth (Salop.), 46, 131
British and Foreign Bible Society, 59, 96
Broughton, Jane, m. Sir Rowland Hill, 1st Baronet, 153
Bruce, Charles, Marquess of Ailesbury, 172
Brudenell, James, later 7th Earl of Cardigan, 64, 81, 104–5, 106–7
Brussels, 15, 61, 95–6, 97
Buntingsdale (Salop.), 1, 3
Busaco, Battle of (1810), 78–9, 112
Bygott, Edward, 181
Byron, Lord *see* Gordon

Cambridge: Jesus College, 8, 174; St John's College, 12, 36, 43, 56–8, 165–6
Campbell, Muriel, m. Sir Clement Lloyd Hill, 127
Canada, 108, 112, 182
Cardigan, Earl of *see* Brudenell
Carline, John, 94, 102
Caughley (Salop.), 136

Cavallier, Major-General Jean, 29
Cavendish, William, 8
Chambré family, 43, 144
Chambré, Francis, 64, 144, 146
Chambré, Mary, d. of John, m. Sir John Hill, 3rd Baronet, 62, 64, 65, 71, 144
Charles II, King of Spain, 19, 20
Charles, Archduke, later Charles VI, Holy Roman Emperor, 17, 20, 22, 24, 25
Charles Albert, King of Sardinia, 17
Chartist riots, 64, 107–8
Chester, school at, 65
Chetwynd, John, later 2nd Viscount, 16, 31, 33
Childs Ercall (Salop.), 8
Churchill, Colonel C.H., 86, 99
Churchill, John, later 1st Duke of Marlborough, 13, 14, 21, 27, 31, 34; and Battles of Blenheim and Ramillies, 17, 25, 26
Citadel, The (Hawkstone estate, Salop.), 54, 110, 122, 160–1, **161**, 176, 181, 182; sale after bankruptcy, 123, 180, 184
Ciudad Rodrigo, capture of (1812), 77, 81–2, 112
Civil War (England), 2, 11, 142–3
Clarence, Duke of *see* Albert Victor
Clarke, Edward, 171–2
Clee Hill (Salop.), 2, 3
Clegg, Anne, d. of Joseph, m. Rowland Hill, 4th Baronet and 2nd Viscount, 120, 140, 183
Clegg, Arthur, 120
Clegg Hill, Caroline *see* Corbett, Caroline
Clegg Hill, Charles Rowland, 6th Viscount Hill, 188
Clegg Hill, Francis William, 7th Baronet and 5th Viscount Hill, 182, 183, 187–8
Clegg Hill, Sir Rowland, 5th Baronet and 3rd Viscount Hill, 121–2, 140–1, 146, 178–82,

184, 185
Clegg-Hill, Rowland Richard, 4th Viscount Hill, 121, 182, 183–4, 188
Clement XI, Pope, 26
Clive family, 131, 138, 140, 166
Coade and Sealy, firm of, 94
Coalport (Salop.), 136
Combermere Abbey (Cheshire), 5
Congress of Vienna (1814–15), 95, 113
Copenhagen, 113
Corbet family, 8, 9, 45–6, 131, 132, 154
Corbet, Elizabeth, d. of Sir Richard, m. Thomas Hill, 9
Corbett, Alice, w. of Sir Reginald, 8
Corbett, Caroline, m. Francis Clegg-Hill, 7th Baronet and 5th Viscount Hill, 188
Cornish, Elizabeth, m. Colonel John Hill, 50, 110, 161, 183
Corunna, retreat to (1809), 55, 73–4
Cotes family, 137, 138
Court of Hill (Court of Hull), 1, 2–3
Cromwell, Thomas, 4
Cronkhill (Salop.), 172, 176, **177**, 189
Currie, Captain (later Colonel) Edward, 70, 75, 76, 78, 79, 81, 83; killed at Waterloo, 98, 99, 101
Cust, Captain H., 118

Darnell Grange (Salop.), 8
Dartmouth, Earl of *see* Legge
Davies, Sergeant ____, 94
Davies, Robert, 145
Delabriere, Louis André, 168
Denmark *see* Copenhagen
Deval, John, 171
Dicken, John, 144, 146
Dixon, Dr, 46
Dod family, 140, 178
Dodington (Salop.), 102
Dolman, Captain, 25, 28
Downward, George, 54, 160
Drake, Francis, 66, 67–8, 113
Drayton (Salop.), 8
Dubouchet, Sophie, m. Thomas Noel Hill, 2nd Lord Berwick, 173–4

Eddy, Prince *see* Albert Victor
Edward VI, King, 4, 6, 7, 9
Edward, Prince of Wales, later King Edward VII, **124**, 127
Egerton, Colonel John, 84, 94, 101, 108

Egypt, 69, 70, 113–16
Elbeuf, Prince d', 34
Elizabeth I, Queen, 4, 9
Emes, William, 154, 155, 167
Eton College (Bucks.), 12, 27, 35, 36, 42, 56, 121, 164
Eugene, Prince of Savoy, 17, 25, 31, 32, 34
Eyton, Thomas, 100, 136

Felhampton (Salop.), 123
Ferris (MP), 7
Finch, Daniel, 2nd Earl of Nottingham, 22–3, 24, 25
Fisher, Captain, 28
Fitzgerald, Lieutenant Colonel John, 88
Fletcher, John William (Jean Guillaume de la Fléchère), 43–4, 45, 58, 165
Flitcroft, Henry, 148
Floquerel, Captain, 88
Flotard, David, 29–30
Fox, Charles James, 48, 55, 166
France: under Louis XIV, 12, 13–34, 149; French Revolution, 50, 66, 171; Revolutionary and Napoleonic Wars, 54, 66–100, 172; Protestants, 13, 18, 23, 28–30, *see also* Vaudois; places in *see* Antibes; Lyons; Nice; Paris; Strasbourg; Toulon; Toulouse; Versailles; Villefranche
Frederick Augustus, Duke of York, 66–7, 71, 81, 98, 99, 105, 187
French Revolution, 50, 66, 171

Geneva, 28, 29
Genoa, 22, 25, 27, 30, 32–3
George III, King, 47, 48
George, Prince Regent, later King George IV, 81, 91, 99, 101, 104, 168, 185
George, Prince, later King George V, 123–5, **124**
Germany *see* Bayreuth; Munich
Gibraltar, 26, 27, 68, 69
Gilpin, William Sawrey, 150
Godolphin, Sidney, 1st Earl of Godolphin, 17, 23, 26, 30
Gordon, George, Lord Byron, 174
Gordon, George Hamilton, 4th Earl of Aberdeen, 17
Graham, General Thomas, later Lord Lynedoch, 67, 88–9, 90
Grey, William, 188
Grinshill stone, 39, 146, 168, 189
Grosvenor, Richard, 167, 170
Grove, ____, 47
Guillet, Captain, 88

Hadnall, 5, 144; church, 109–10, 118; *see also* Hardwick Grange
Hague, the, 15, 18, 20, 21–4, 29, 35
Hallward, John, 46
Halston (Salop.), 131, 137
Hamilton, Emma, Lady, 52, 171
Hamilton, Sir William, 52, 171
Hanover Expedition (1805–6), 71, 72
Hardwick Grange (Salop.), 5, 144, 178, 181; General Rowland, 1st Viscount Hill and, 55, 74, 94, 102, 144, 160
Harley, Robert, 1st Earl of Oxford, 17, 25
Harman, Captain, 88
Harrison, Thomas, 102, 160
Harvard University, Hawkstone bird collection, 121
Harwood, Anne, m. John Kynaston, 164
Harwood, Rowland, 164
Harwood, Thomas (1661–1738), 36, 37, 163
Harwood, Thomas (1693–1782) *see* Hill, Thomas (Harwood)
Haste, Edward, 179, 180
Hastings, Selina, Countess of Huntingdon, 44, 45
Haughmond Abbey (Salop.), 5, 8; *see also* Hadnall
Hawkstone estate (Salop.), 1, 8, 9, 11, 36, 64, 120–1; purchased by Sir Rowland Hill (1556), 3, 5, 142; bankruptcy, dispersal sales and lawsuits, 178–88; Industry Hall, 50–1; *see also* Citadel, The
Hawkstone Hall and gardens (Salop.), 36, 120, 142–50, **144–5**, **147**, **157**, 189; bankruptcy and dispersal sales, 180, 183–8; bird collection, 121, 155, 183–4
Hawkstone Inn (later *Hawkstone Park Hotel*), 51, 55, 64, 152
Hawkstone Otter Hounds, 111, 120, **143**
Hawkstone Park (Salop.), 50, 51, 70, 129, **147**, 151–60, **156–9**; golf course, 142, 151, 152; Grotto, 151, **151**, 155–9, **158**; Grotto Hill, 121, 146, 153, **154**; Hawk Lake, 51, 55, 154; 'Obelisk', 159–60, **159**; 'Rangers Lodge', 176; Red Castle, 2, 11, 142, 148, 153, **157**, 159, 184
Heber, Bishop Reginald, 51, 153
Heber-Percy family, 51
Hedges, Sir Charles, 17, 21, 22, 26, 27, 29, 30, 31, 32, 33
Heinsius, Anthony, 18

INDEX

Henry VIII, King, 4, 5, 7, 8, 9
Higson, ___, 46
Hill family: Alcaston branch, 2; Court of Hill branch, 2–3; early history, 1–2, 131; family trees, 162, 191–9; Soulton branch, 9; *see also* Clegg-Hill
Hill, Agnes *see* Birde
Hill, Colonel Alfred, 103–4, 111
Hill, Algernon, 130
Hill, Amelia, 172
Hill, Andrew, 2, 3
Hill, Anna Maria, m. W. Trevenon, 181
Hill, Hon. Anna Maria, née Shore *see* Shore
Hill, Anne (1772–1837), d. of 1st Lord Berwick, 172
Hill, Anne, née Clegg *see* Clegg
Hill, Anne, née Powys *see* Powys
Hill, Anne, née Vernon *see* Vernon
Hill, Annette Catherine, m. Vere Somerset, 179, 181
Hill, Arthur, 187
Hill, Arthur William, 185
Hill, Brian (1847–93), 161
Hill, Rev. Brian (1756–1831), 42, 50, 51–4, 66, 153
Hill, General Charles, 181
Hill, Charlotte *see* Kenyon
Hill, Clement (son of Sir Clement Lloyd), 127
Hill, Clement Delves (1808–83), 129
Hill, Major General Clement Delves (1781–1845), 93–4, 95, 99, 105, 113, **118**, 137, 185, 187; in Peninsular War, 63–4, 75–7, 79, 81, 89, 91, 92, 93, 113, 188; and Waterloo campaign, 98, 101; journey to and death in India, 113–19, 188
Hill, Sir Clement Lloyd, 125–9, **126**, **128**, 141, 161
Hill, Edward, 119
Hill, Elizabeth, m. Samuel Barbour, 36
Hill, Elizabeth, m. Francis Chambré, 64, 144
Hill, Elizabeth, m. Clement Tudway, 41
Hill, Elizabeth, née Corbet *see* Corbet
Hill, Elizabeth, née Cornish *see* Cornish
Hill, Lady Elizabeth, née Stanhope *see* Stanhope
Hill, Emily *see* Powys
Hill, Emma, 95, 101, 110
Hill, Hon. Francis, later 5th Viscount, 110
Hill, Sir Francis Brian, 96, 113, 185

Hill, Rev. Francis Jean, 109, 113
Hill, Lieutenant Colonel George Staveley, 101
Hill, Vice Admiral George William, 123–5, **124**, **143**, 161
Hill, Godfrey, 129
Hill, Griffith (de Hille), 1
Hill, Harriet, née Mytton *see* Mytton, Harriet
Hill, Henrietta (Harriet), m. Charles Bruce, Marquess of Ailesbury, 172
Hill, Humphrey (d. 1486), 1, 3, 144
Hill, Humphrey (16th cent.), 1, 8, 11, 142
Hill, Isabella *see* Wynn
Hill, Jane (1738–96), 44, 45, 56, 58, 101, 153, 161, 183; visit to France and Belgium, 60–2
Hill, Jane, née Broughton *see* Broughton
Hill, John (d. 1713), 36, 144, 146
Hill, John (1840–1928), 122–3, 161, 187
Hill, Colonel John (1769–1814), 50, 65, 67, 80, 92, 136
Hill, Rev. John (1802–91), 93, 109, 122, 161
Hill, Sir John, 3rd Baronet, 42, 62, 64, 74, 102, 120, 144, 154; and education and career of General Rowland Hill, 64, 66, 85, 137; and Eyton case, 100; as MP, 40, 62, 131, 133–6, 185
Hill, Leonard, 2
Hill, Margaret, m. 1. Richard Atcherley, 2. Thomas Harwood, 36, 37, 163
Hill, Margaret, née Warren *see* Warren
Hill, Margaret, née Whitehall *see* Whitehall
Hill, Mary (Maria), d. of Sir John Hill, 75, 80, 92, 93, 98, 100, 110
Hill, Mary, m. ___ Chambré, 144
Hill, Mary, née Chambré *see* Chambré
Hill, Mary, née Madax *see* Madax
Hill, Mary, née Tudway *see* Tudway, Mary
Hill, Mary, née Wilbraham *see* Wilbraham
Hill, Muriel *see* Campbell
Hill, Noel, later 1st Lord Berwick, 37, 43, 48, 100, 112, 163, 165–70; as MP, 132, 165, 166, 170; raised to peerage (1784), 49, 55, 132–3

Hill, Lieutenant General Percy, 111
Hill, Ralph, 1, 142
Hill, Richard ('the Great Hill'), 2, **10**, 11–13, 35–9, 132, 143–4, 163; diplomatic career, 13–35; and Hawkstone, 35, 36, 143–6, 148, 150, 187
Hill, Sir Richard, 2nd Baronet, 37–8, 40–56, 65, 67, 136, 160, 161; and Eyton case, 100; family diamonds, 183; and Hardwick estate, 55, 74, 144; and Hawkstone Hall, 148, 150, 187; and Hawkstone Park, 2, 11, 50–1, 70, 143, 146, 153, 154–9; as Iason, 94; as MP, 47–9, 132–3, 134; religious activities, 40–1, 42–7, 55, 58, 59, 96; tour of Italy and Sicily, 50, 51–4, 66
Hill, Colonel Richard Frederick, 179, 181
Hill, Rev. Robert, 42–3
Hill, Colonel Sir Robert Chambré, 64, 93–4, 111, **112**, 120, **186**; in Peninsular War, 85, 89, 93, 111, 187; and Waterloo campaign, 95, 98, 99, 111
Hill, Rowland (d. 1619), 1, 8, 11, 12, 142, 143
Hill, Rowland (1594–1644), 2, 11, 12, 142, 143
Hill, Rowland (1624–1700), 11, 12, 13, 142, 143
Hill, Rowland (17th cent., brother of 'Great Hill'), 11, 12, 143
Hill, General Rowland, 1st Viscount, 54, 63–111, **72**, **87**, 122, 138, 140, 181, 185; and Peninsular War, 63–4, 72–93, 104, 110–11; and Waterloo campaign, 95–9, 101; General Commanding in Chief, 103–8; and Hardwick Grange, 5, 55, 74, 94, 102, 144, 160; helmet worn at Battle of Aboukir, 69, 187; as MP, 85, 136–7; sale of orders, decorations and medals, 110, 187–8
Hill, Rev. Rowland (d. 1733), 37–8
Hill, Rev. Rowland (1744–1833), 40–2, 45, 46, 49, 55, 56–60, **57**, 93
Hill, Sir Rowland (1492–1561, Lord Mayor of London), 1, 2, 3–9, 11, 131–2, 142, 159, *frontispiece*
Hill, Sir Rowland, 1st Baronet, 2, 37–8, 40, 58, 132; and Hawkstone, 36, 40, 146–8, 152, 153, 155

Hill, Sir Rowland, 4th Baronet and 2nd Viscount, 62, 80, 92, 100, **109**, 110, 113, 118, 120, **122**, 140-1; bird collection, 117, 121, 155, 183-4; extravagance leads to loss of Hawkstone estate, 101-2, 120, 160-1, 181, 182; and Hawkstone Hall and Park, 120-1, 146, 148, 149, 150, 160; as MP for Shropshire and later Shrewsbury, 101, 137-8
Hill, Sir Rowland Clegg *see* Clegg-Hill
Hill, Samuel, 37, 43, 165-6
Hill, Samuel Barbour, 2, 36-7, **37**, 132, 165
Hill, Sarah *see* Stubbs
Hill, Sophie *see* Dubouchet
Hill, Susannah Maria *see* Noel
Hill, Rev. T. Leonard, 2
Hill, Thomas (15th cent., of Malpas and Hodnet), 1, 3, 142
Hill, Thomas (16th cent., of Alcaston), 2
Hill, Thomas (d. 1711, builder of Soulton Hall), 9
Hill, Thomas (fl. 1771, MP for Leominster), 3
Hill, Thomas (18th cent., son of Thomas d. 1711), 9
Hill, Thomas (Harwood), 2, 37, 43, 132, 144, 163-7, 174
Hill, Thomas Noel, 2nd Lord Berwick, 133, 136, 168, 171-4
Hill, Sir Thomas Noel, 44, 50, 55, 64, 93-4, 111-12, 149; in Peninsular War, 71, 76, 78-9, 81, 86, 89, 90, 93, 112; and Waterloo campaign, 98, 99, 112
Hill, William (15th cent.), 1
Hill, William (16th cent, 'of Bletchley', Rector of Stoke upon Tern), 1, 5, 7, 8
Hill, William, 3rd Lord Berwick *see* Noel-Hill, William
Hill-Lowe, A.N.V., 3
Hilton Park (Staffs.), 166, 170
Hodnet (Salop.), Hill estates, 142
Hodnet church (Salop.), 3, 7, 44, 46, 92; monument to 'Great Hill', 38-9; monument to Sir Richard Hill, 55-6; rectors, 37-8, 51, 153
Holcroft, Joseph, 146
Holding, John, 98, 101
Holland *see* Netherlands
Hough (Cheshire), 42-3
Hugetan, ___, 24-5
Hull (Salop.) *see* Court of Hill
Hull(e), de la, family, 1
Hulle, William de la (14th cent.), 1, 131

Hulton, Teresa, m. Thomas Henry Noel-Hill, 8th Lord Berwick, 176-7
Huntingdon, Countess of *see* Hastings
Hyll *see* Hill

Ightfield (Salop.), 65
India, 110, 113-19, 187, 188
Innsbruck, 34
Ireland, 70-1
Italy, 171-2, 175-6; *see also* Genoa; Livorno; Loreto; Milan; Naples; Rome; Savoy; Sicily; Turin; Venice

Jamaica, 50
James II, King, 15, 16
James Stuart (the Old Pretender), 164
Jay, Rev. William, 60
Jenner, Edward, 59
Johnson, Dr Samuel, 152-3
Johnstone, William *see* Pulteney
Jones family, **151**, 159
Jones, ___, 47
Jones, Richard, 1st Earl of Ranelagh, 12-13, 14
Jones, Thomas, 136
Joseph Bonaparte, King of Naples and Spain, 71, 72, 83, 86, 89, 100
Junot, General Andoche, 72

Kauffmann, Angelica, 171
Kay, ___, 47
Keeling (painter), 185
Kenyon family, 93, 123, 125, 131, 140
Kenyon, Charlotte, d. of Thomas, m. Rev. John Hill, 93, 122, 161
Kitson (Kytson), Thomas, 4
Kynaston family, 131, 164

la Feuillade, Duc de, 26, 27, 30-1, 32, 34
la Tour, Count de, 22, 35
Langaterie, Marquis de, 34
Lausanne, 24, 28, 29
Leeke, Lady Hester, 171
Legett, Thomas, 167
Legge, William, 2nd Earl of Dartmouth, 44
Leghorn *see* Livorno
Leigh family, 8
Leigh, Sir Thomas, 8
Leighton family, 131, 132
Leighton, Sir Baldwin, 129-30, 140-1, 178
Leominster (Herefs.), MPs, 3
Leopold I, Holy Roman Emperor, 16, 20, 21, 22, 23, 27, 31, 32

Lichfield (Staffs.), MPs, 36, 40, 132
Lighteach (Salop.), 36
Lilleshall (Salop.), 5
Lisbon, 25, 74, 79
Littleton, Sir Edward, 5
Livorno (Leghorn), 25, 28, 32, 33
Lloyd family, 137, 140
London: Christchurch, Westminster Bridge Road, 60; Cleveland Court, St James, house of 'Great Hill', 15, 36, 38, 55, 164, 167; Imperial War Museum, 188; Inner Temple, 166; Inns of Court, 8; Mercers' Company, 4, 6, 8; Middle Temple, 36; Portman Square, house in, 167; Sackville Street, house in, 167; St Stephen Walbrook, 4, 8, 9; Sir Rowland Hill as merchant and Lord Mayor, 4-5, 6-7, 8-9; Surrey Chapel, Blackfriars Road, 42, 59, 60; Victoria and Albert Museum, 187; Westbourne House, 103; Westminster School, 43
London Missionary Society, 59
Longslow (Wlonkeslowe) (Salop.), 1, 3
Loreto, 51-2
Louis XIV, King of France, 12, 13-34, 149
Louis XVI, King of France, 61
Louis XVIII, King of France, 95, 99-100
Lowe, Thomas, 3
Ludlow (Salop.), 46
Lynedoch, Lord *see* Graham
Lyons, 18

Madax, Mary, m. Rowland Clegg Hill, 5th Baronet and 3rd Viscount, 121, 182
Madeley (Salop.), 43, 44
Maffei, Count, 33
Malpas (Cheshire), 1, 3
Malta, 68, 69
Marchamley, Lord *see* Whitely
Marchamley (Salop.), 146
Marie Antoinette, Queen of France, 61
Market Drayton (Salop.), school, 7
Marlborough, Duke of *see* Churchill, John
Marlborough College (Wilts.), 125, 129
Mary I, Queen, 4, 6, 7, 9
Mary II, Queen, 15, 18
Masonic Order, Salopian Lodge, 94

INDEX

Masséna, Marshal André, 78, 79
Mathews, ___, 47
members of parliament, Shrewsbury, 62, 129, 131, 132, 134, 136, 138, 166, 172; 1749-68, Thomas (Harwood) Hill, 37, 132, 165; 1796 election, 131, 133-6; 1812 election, 84-5, 136-7; election jugs, 134-6, **135**, 138-40, **139**, 185
members of parliament, Shropshire, 47-9, 101, 132, 134, 137-41, 166, 170
Mercers' Company, 4, 6, 8
Methodism, 43, 44, 46-7, 57, 58
Meyrick, Thomas, 178-9
Middleton, ___, 47
Milan, 19
Minorca, 68
Monaco, 26, 28
Monmouth, The Hendre, 129
Moore, Sir John, 68, 73-4
Mordaunt, Charles, 3rd Earl of Peterborough, 31, 32
Mostyn-Owen, Frances, m. Rev. Richard Noel-Hill, 4th Lord Berwick, 176
Munich, 113
Mylne, Robert, 167
Mytton family, 131, 137
Mytton, Harriet, m. Clement Delves Hill, 129, 137
Mytton, Jack, 102, 129, 137-8, 182

Namur, Siege of (1695), 14, 148
Naples, 52, 53, 171-2, 174, 175-6
Napoleon Bonaparte, later Emperor Napoleon I, 66-100, 175
Napoleonic Wars *see* Revolutionary and Napoleonic Wars
Nash, John, 172, 173, 176, **177**
National Trust, 163, 177, 189
Nelson, John, 159
Netherlands: wars, 17th-18th cent., 12, 13-15, 19, 20, 21, 22-4, 28, 67; *see also* Amsterdam; Hague, The
Netherstoke (Salop.), 5
Newborough, Lord *see* Wynn, Spencer
Newport (Salop.), 131, 150, 151
Newton, John, 44-5
Ney, Marshal Michel, 77, 78, 95, 96, 100
Nice, 25, 27-8, 30, 31, 49
Noel, Susannah Maria, d. of Sir William, m. Thomas (Harwood) Hill, 37, 164-5
Noel-Hill family, Barons Berwick, 37, **162**, 163-77
Noel-Hill, Charles, 9th Lord Berwick, 177
Noel-Hill, Ellen *see* Nystrom
Noel-Hill, Frances *see* Mostyn-Owen
Noel-Hill, Mary Selina, 176
Noel-Hill, Rev. Richard, 4th Lord Berwick, 171, 174, 175, 176
Noel-Hill, Richard, 5th Lord Berwick, 176
Noel-Hill, Richard Henry, 7th Lord Berwick, 129-30, 176
Noel-Hill, Teresa *see* Hulton
Noel-Hill, Thomas Henry, 8th Lord Berwick, 163, 171, 176-7
Noel-Hill, William, 3rd Lord Berwick, 40, 52, 130, 171, 172-3, 174; and Attingham Park, 168, 174; diplomatic career, 174-6; as MP, 84-5, 133-6, 137, 172-3, 174
Noel-Hill, William, 6th Lord Berwick, 176
North, Frederick, Lord North, 48
Nottingham, Earl of *see* Finch
Nystrom, Ellen, m. Richard Henry Noel-Hill, 7th Lord Berwick, 130, 176

O'Hara, General Charles, 66, 68, 69
Okeley, Trooper George, 94
Old Pretender (James Stuart), 164
Oswestry (Salop.), 81
Oxford, Earl of *see* Harley
Oxford: Magdalen College, 43; Methodism, 46-7, 58

Palermo, 52-3
Panzetta (sculptor), 94
Paoli, General Pascal, 153
Paris, 61-2, 99-100, 176
Patiala (India), Sheesh Mahal Museum, 110, 187
Peace of Amiens (1802), 69-70
Peacocke, Sir Nathaniel, 90-1
Peninsular War, 63-4, 71-93, 104, 110-11, 112, 113
Peplow (Salop.), 120, 121, 123, 178, 184
Peterborough, Earl of *see* Mordaunt
Petton (Salop.), 62, 64, 144
Philip V, King of Spain, 17, 20
Pitt, William, the younger, 48-9, 50, 70, 72, 132, 133, 166, 174; and Revolutionary and Napoleonic Wars, 54, 55, 71
Plantagenet, Hamlet, 1
Plymouth (Devon), 74, 103, 185, **186**
Portelli, Guy, 159

Portugal *see* Lisbon; Peninsular War
Powell, Sir John, 100
Powys family, 44, 165
Powys, Anne, d. of Richard, m. Thomas (Harwood) Hill, 37, 164
Powys, Emily, m. Sir Francis Brian Hill, 113, 185
Powys, Mrs Lybbe, 3
Pradoe (Salop.), 122, 131
Prees (Salop.): church, 62; Prees Hall (Prees Manor), 42, 62, 64, 111, 180
Price, William, 38, 146
Pritchard, Thomas, 165
Pulteney, Sir William (formerly Johnstone), 132, 133, 134, 166

Ramillies, Battle of (1706), 17, 34
Ranelagh, Earl of *see* Jones, Richard
Red Castle *see* Hawkstone Park
Redemptorist Order, 142, 150, 188, 189
Reform Bill (1831-2), 64, 105, 137
Religious Tract Society, 59
Repton, Humphry, 167, 172, 173
Revolutionary and Napoleonic Wars, 54, 66-100, 172; *see also* Peninsular War
Reynier, General, 78
Reynolds, Sir Joshua, 153
Richmond, Old Palace Yard, Trumpeting (Trumpeter's) House, 15, 36, 38
Roland, 'Chief', 30
Romaine, William, 47
Rome, 16, 52, 54, 171
Rooke, Sir George, 16, 17, 20, 24, 25, 26
Rugby School (Warwicks.), 113, 171, 174
Rundell and Bridge (silversmiths), 175
Ryswick, Treaty of (1697), 15, 18

St Thomas, Marquis de, 29
Salliens, Jean, and family, 28-9, 33
Sampson (painter), 6, *frontispiece*
Sardinia, 17, 174-5
Savoy, 17-19, 21-35, 130, 175; *see also* Nice; Turin; Victor Amadeus, Duke of Savoy; Villefranche
Sellon, William, 45
Shawbury (Salop.), 45-6, 166
Shenstone Park (Staffs.), 2, 36, 132, 165
Shipman, ___, 47
Shore, Hon. Anna Maria, m. Sir Thomas Noel Hill, 44, 50, 96, 100, 112

Shore, Charles, 2nd Lord Teignmouth, 96
Shore, John, 1st Lord Teignmouth, 44, 50, 100, 112
Shovel, Sir Cloudesley, 16, 24, 26, 31
Shrewsbury, Earl (later Duke) of *see* Talbot
Shrewsbury (Salop.): abbey, 5, 129; execution of Jacobites, 164; and General Rowland, 1st Viscount Hill, 93–4, 185, **186**; Hawkstone dispersal sales, 185; 'the Quarry', 94; race meetings, 46; St Chad's Church, 47, 109, 167–8; Shrewsbury School, 12, 62; Thomas Harwood of, 36, 37, 163; *see also* members of parliament
Shropshire, members of parliament *see* members of parliament
Shropshire Militia, 48, 65, 136, 166, 170
Sicily, 50, 52–3
Sidney, Edwin, 63, 114, 120
Slade, General John, 85
Somerset, Lord Fitzroy, 86, 107
Somerset, Granville, 178–9
Somerset, Vere, 178–80, 181
Soult, Marshal Nicolas, 73–5, 82, 83, 88, 89–90, 92
Soulton (Salop.), 1, 5, 8, 9
Spain *see* Peninsular War
Spanish Succession, War of (1701–13), 14, 15, 19, 20–34
Squire, Major, 81
Stanhope, Lady Elizabeth, m. Samuel Barbour Hill, 36–7
Stanhope, Lady Hester, 174
Stanier family, 121, 123, 161, 178, 184
Stepney, George, 16, 21, 22
Steuart, George, 167–8
Stewart, Sir William, 88, 90
Stockholm, 113
Stoke upon Tern (Salop.), 5, 7, 8
Stoneleigh Abbey (Warwicks.), 8
Stoney Stretton Hall (Salop.), 125
Strafford, Earl of *see* Wentworth
Straphen, John, 94
Strasbourg, 54, 66
Stubbs, Sarah, m. John Hill, 36, 146
Suckley, Henry, 7
Sussex, HMS, wreck of, 14
Sweden *see* Stockholm

Switzerland, 22, 28–9; *see also* Geneva; Lausanne

Talavera, Battle of (1809), 75–6
Talbot, Charles, 12th Earl, later 1st Duke, of Shrewsbury, 15–16, 17
Talleyrand-Périgord, Charles de, Prince of Benevento, 72, 95
Teignmouth, Lords *see* Shore
Tern (Salop.) *see* Attingham estate; Attingham Park
Thrale, Mrs Hester, 153
Toplady, Augustus, 58
Torn, Count, 27
Toulon, 23, 25, 29, 30, 33, 66–7
Toulouse, Battle of (1814), 92, 111
Trevenon, Mrs, 181
Tudway, Clement, 41, 58
Tudway, Mary, m. Rev. Rowland Hill, 41, 58
Turin: 'Great Hill' at, 16, 18, 19, 21, 24–33, 34–5; Thomas Noel Hill at, 171, 175

Uganda, 128–9, **128**

Vale Royal Abbey (Cheshire), 5
Vaudemont, Prince de, 19, 33
Vaudois, 12, 17, 34, 175; 'Great Hill' and, 17, 18, 19, 20, 22, 23, 28, 35
Vendôme, Duc de, 26, 27
Venice, 22, 26, 33, 172
Vernon, Anne, m. Noel Hill, 1st Lord Berwick, 48, 166–7, 170, 171–2
Vernon, Henrietta (Harriet), m. Richard Grosvenor, 167
Vernon, Henry, 170
Vernon, James, 15
Verrue, siege of (1704-5), 26, 27
Versailles, 60, 61
Victor Amadeus, Duke of Savoy, later King of Sardinia, 14, 16, 17, 18–20, 21–35
Victor Emanuel I, King of Sardinia, 175
Victoria, Queen, 107, 108, 110, 123, 127, 185
Vienna, 21, 27, 31, 32, 33; Congress of (1814–15), 95, 113
Villefranche (Villa Franca), 20, 23, 25, 26, 27–8, 30
Vimiero, Battle of (1806), 73
Vittoria, Battle of (1813), 88–9, 111, 112

Walcot (Salop.), 8

Walding Associates, 150, 151
Walford, Francis, 172
Warren, Margaret, m. Griffith de Hille, 1
Waterloo campaign (1815), 95–9, 101, 111, 112, 119, 160, 187
Wathen, Captain, 106
Weller, David and Monica, 150
Wellesley, Sir Arthur, later 1st Duke of Wellington, 64, 68, 71, 95, 100, 101, 103, 173; and Peninsular War, 72–3, 74–93, 111; and Waterloo campaign, 95–9; as Prime Minister, 103, 105, 106, 107, 108, 110, 111, 137
Wem (Salop.), 36, 44, 142, 181; *see also* Soulton
Wentworth, William, 4th Earl of Strafford, 170, 174
Wesley, John, 41, 44, 57, 58
Weston under Redcastle (Salop.), 3, 51, 121, 122, 146, 161
Whitchurch (Salop.), 129
Whitefield, George, 44, 56–8
Whitehall, Margaret, m. Rowland Hill, 11, 12
Whitely, George, 1st Lord Marchamley, 149, 150, 188
Wilberforce, William, 41, 45, 48, 49–50, 54, 101
Wilbraham, Mary, d. of John, m. Rev. Robert Hill, 42
Willaume, David, 38, 187
William III, King, 13, 14–21
William IV, King, 103, 105, 106, 107, 185
Williamson, Sir Joseph, 18, 20
Wilson, Harriette, 173
Winter, Rev. Cornelius, 58
Wlonkeslow (Longslow), Hugh de, 1
Wlonkeslowe (Longslow) (Salop.), 1, 3
Wombridge (Salop.), 5
Wotton-under-Edge (Glos.), 59
Wyatt, Lewis, 120, 148–9, 185
Wynn, Isabella, d. of Lord Newborough, m. Rowland Clegg-Hill, 5th Baronet and 3rd Viscount, 121, 161, 181, 182, 183
Wynn, Spencer, 3rd Lord Newborough, 121

York, Duke of *see* Frederick Augustus

Zanzibar, 125–7